THE
BINARY
REVOLUTION

THE
BINARY
REVOLUTION

The development
of the computer

Neil Barrett

W&N

As always, for my family

First published in Great Britain in 2006
by Weidenfeld & Nicolson

10 9 8 7 6 5 4 3 2 1

© Neil Barrett 2006

A CIP catalogue record for this book is available from the British Library

ISBN 0 297 84738 4

Design by www.carrstudio.co.uk
Printed in Great Britain by Clays Ltd, St Ives plc

Weidenfeld & Nicolson
The Orion Publishing Group Ltd
Orion House
5 Upper Saint Martin's Lane
London, WC2H 9EA
www.orionbooks.co.uk

Contents

Acknowledgements

I should like to thank a number of people, without whom this book wouldn't have been written. Most obviously, my family for giving me the time and opportunity to research and write the book; and my father for asking me the questions that inspired it.

For help in making sure that this book was written and published, I would like to thank my agent, Patrick Walsh, and all at Orion who have brought the book to its current state. And for teaching me the subject, giving me the chance to work in the discipline, and for listening to my daft ideas, I would like to thank David Brailsford, Ian Wand, Jim Austin and Gary Morgan. Of course, if I've got anything wrong, it's my fault, not theirs!

Preface

'So, why shouldn't I want to buy a computer? I mean, you have one; your brother has one... your mother uses one at work... even the kids next door have one! Now I'm retired I'm going to have time to play and learn about the thing. And you're always telling me how wonderful they are. So, why shouldn't I spend my money on one, huh?'

'No reason, Dad... In fact, I think it's a great idea!'

My father, some 35 years ago, introduced me to science fiction and a world of robots, aliens and monstrously intelligent computers. For some reason it was the computers that stayed with me – Arthur C. Clarke's HAL and Isaac Asimov's MULTIVAC are two that most stick in my memory, even though when I read them I was too young to understand the joke behind either name.[1] I devoured the scruffy paperbacks that my father put in front of me and then hunted out more. In time, I decided that I wanted to learn as much as I could about the science on which that fiction was built. How possible was it? What things were true? Perhaps most importantly, what things might *become* true?

So I studied physics, mathematics and computer science, not simply because I wanted a job with computers but because I wanted to know more about the science-fiction world my father had presented to me. Now, in my turn, I can present to my father the reality of *this* world of today, the future that evolved from the imagination of my childhood. It is a world that really does feature intelligent computers, robots and space travel as a matter of routine – perhaps not in exactly the way that Asimov et al anticipated, but still they are there.

Computers have been programmed to play chess better than all but a handful of the most expert grandmasters; they can hold apparently meaningful conversations; they can appear to understand what has been said to them; and they can even carry out complex tasks, such as flying aeroplanes. The computers themselves have shrunk to the size of a single character on this page and have been built into everything from cars to cookers, mobile phones to shopping trolleys. Computers have moved from being the stuff of science fiction to the stuff of everyday life, and we use computers as a routine part of our work and our social life. However, whilst we can all (with greater or lesser degrees of confidence) work the computers that are presented to us in the guise of bank cash machines, pub slot machines, game consoles or the like, very few of us *really* know what the computer elements are or how they actually work.

This book addresses the 'What they are and how they work' question. I assume that the reader, like my father, has the necessary wit to operate a computer; that the reader can use a mouse and a keyboard; and that they can make simple applications or computer games do more or less the things that they want. So I have not written a book about how to work a computer but rather about how a computer works, how it came to work that way, and who the people were who created it.

I want the reader to be able to grasp the underlying elements – the foundations and principles – of just what a computer is doing when, for example, it opens a new file and lets you type characters into a document and then print it out. I want to show the mathematics, the physics and the sheer, impossible clever-stupidity of operation of these frustrating but fascinating machines; and to tell the equally fascinating stories about the accidents and characters that contributed to their invention and development.

⌐

Time was, not so long ago, when we could safely ignore computers. They were immense, mysterious, infinitely complex devices that somehow made any number of large companies work; and which somehow also produced any number of meaningless excuses for those companies to explain away their mistakes. Your bill must be correct, because the computer worked it out; I'm sorry, I can't find that information because the computer is down; it's not my fault, it's the computer, etc. The computer was the omnipotent central power whose authority and sway went unquestioned. What the computer *did* and how it did it, though, was a complete unknown. The computer was a voracious consumer of data, time and electricity, transforming stacks of cards and reels of tape into miles of folded paper printout. It needed endless care and attention from white-coated suppli- cants who jealously guarded their access and their expertise, whose ranks you could join only with a high IQ and a math- ematics PhD. What is more, the tasks for which the computers were used were serious, grown-up things like working out electricity bills, forecasting the weather or calculating rocket trajectories. In day-to-day life, though, the computer was an invisible, backroom machine. It was a cumbersome steam engine of information, which drove the companies and their operation but which was beyond most people's experience or under- standing.

Now, computers are everywhere. Schools have whole rooms full of them; every desk in every office throughout the world seems now to hold a humming computer and a flickering screen; every other home has one, as does every shop and every reception desk. The modern computer is small, inexpensive and almost unimaginably powerful, and used for a wealth of tasks. It provides a diary and scheduler, a notebook and a calculator; it serves as word processor or database, or merely to divert with games of near-infinite imagination. We have connections between computers that span the world with electronic mail or give access to a vast pool of information. As simple processing units, computers control our cars and planes; our trains and our telephones; our medical devices and our microwaves. If an electronic plague were to attack the silicon chip, then the modern, connected, switched-on world would grind to a clumsy and no doubt painful halt.

The computer took us over by stealth in an 'overnight success' that took decades (or rather, in truth, *centuries*) of groundwork before it seemed to blossom fully formed on our desks only a few years ago. I remember as a child in my mid-teens sitting through a Physics O level lesson in 1977 when the teacher handed round one of the earliest microprocessor-based computers, the Apple 1. It was a clumsy thing, wired onto a thick circuit board the size of an A3 pad. Just two years later my school bought a small Research Machines computer for the Mathematics department, and I had the chance to play. Now, 25 years later, both my children have their own computers, I have a third computer in the study and a laptop in my briefcase. And that is by no means unusual.

From the stuff of fiction to the fabric of everyday life in such a short time. *No* other technology or development has been that rapid.

What is more, computers *have* embedded themselves in our everyday lives, not just in the workplace. Our very language is now redolent with words and phrases that I remember first hearing and using when I studied how computers worked. We complain of how we are so busy that we have to 'multitask' or take a particular job 'offline'; we say of a difficult activity that we can 'hack it'. Our language is enriched by the phrases of modern computer operations. We 'boot up', 'point and click', and think of 'icons' and 'backups' as though they were all a long-standing part of our lives, rather than something familiar only from the last few years of intense computer exposure.

For all that exposure and for all that familiarity, a computer *is* still a strange device, its details of operation every bit as mysterious as those of a television, a telephone or a microwave. We know the basic mechanics of the way that computers are used but almost nothing about how they work. Even with practice and confidence, there is still that sense of some unknown element. Why *did* it do that? What *was* it thinking of? Why won't it do what I *tell* it?

For all the frustration of handling a recalcitrant computer, the skills of computer use are now embedded in our society. The ability to use a computer dictates employment opportunities. The accountant must be able to handle a spreadsheet package; and the secretary, a word processor. Administrators must be able to handle database applications; and professors must know how to drive slideshow presentations from their laptop. Computer literacy is the new social and employment skill. Just as employment opportunities in the 19th and 20th centuries were dictated by the ability to read and write, those in the 21st century are surely determined by the ease and skill with which computers are handled.

None of us can afford to ignore computers any more. We should all grab at the opportunity to enrich our lives – or add to our frustrations – through these wonderful, intricate and puzzling machines.

1

What is a computer?

'Hey, it's me... So listen, I want to get that computer I was telling you about. But honest to God, I hadn't realized that there were so many things to choose! The guy in the shop is asking me awkward questions: whether I wanted a tower or a laptop? A VGA or a flat screen? A Mac or a PC? Windows, Linux, Apple...? I kept on expecting him to ask me about woofers and tweeters and a paper bag on my head! What do they all do? I thought a computer was a computer was a computer? Where do I start?'

What *is* a computer? Depending on your interest and your profession, this question is going to have dramatically different answers. At the simplest level, most people probably think of a computer as little more than a television with a typewriter attached, perhaps connected to a cabinet with flashing lights and spinning tapes.

For those with a little more experience, a computer is a keyboard and a screen connected to a box containing the processor, disk drive and memory. They might also think of it as having a printer and perhaps even a scanner attached to it, and almost certainly a mouse or something similar. They will probably know that programs and files get stored on the disk drive, arranged in an organization of folders and named files; and that the file contents get copied into the computer memory to be used or changed and are displayed on the screen. The mouse can be used to point and click, the keyboard to type in characters or to enter commands.

Most users know, of course, that a computer can come in slightly different shapes and forms, from a laptop about the size of an ordinary ring-binder, to a desk-side tower system; from a pocket-sized Personal Digital Assistant (PDA) to a fridge-sized mainframe. The components might be separate, as in a classic PC, or integrated into one unit, as with the new Apple iMacs. Others might define a computer more in terms of the tasks that it is designed to perform, as a device to perform calculations; a 'number cruncher'; a machine used to work out complicated formulae. Certainly this is the origin of computers, but of course they are equally commonly used for purposes well beyond those simple tasks – for controlling real-time processes; for displaying and manipulating pictures; and of course, for word processing.

To a computer scientist, a computer is all of these things but also something altogether different and more subtle. A computer is a device that stores and executes general program instructions to act upon input data. To appreciate the distinction, it is important first to understand how computers came to be developed.

The first 'computers'

Devices to help us calculate are no new thing; in fact calculators are millennia old. The word 'calculate' comes from the Greek for 'pebble', which hints at the earliest form of computation – piles of pebbles arranged so as to allow the user to reckon sums and differences. Of course, these pebbles can then be strung on wires in a framework to give the very oldest recognizable calculating device, the abacus. This is believed to have been invented sometime between 1000 and 500 BC and is known to have been used not only in China but also around the Mediterranean.

For some 2000 years, the abacus was the only reliable means of counting and calculating. As with so many things, though, the Renaissance in Europe accelerated the development of more sophisticated mechanisms. As ever, it was Leonardo da Vinci who put down the first tantalizing hint of the future. Discovered in 1967 in Madrid, one of his notebooks from the early 1500s showed that da Vinci's interests in mechanical devices had progressed from the invention of the first pendulum clock to a sketch of the first calculating machine. Most intriguingly of all, this was at a period when much of his other work was focused on studies of human anatomy and capability. Perhaps da Vinci was anticipating the idea of improving at least some aspects of human thought, just as, with his work on telescopes, he would later improve on human vision?

For his calculating machine, da Vinci devised and drew a framework holding 13 cogged wheels, powered by a handle at one end. The first wheel represented the units, the second the 10s, the third the 100s, and so on. A complete turn of the handle would move the unit wheel from 0 to 1, and 10 turns would make the first wheel go through a full revolution and knock the second wheel from 0 to 1. When that second wheel had gone all the way around, it would in turn knock the third wheel from 0 to 1, counting the hundreds. It worked, in other words, exactly like a car odometer. Each wheel could be individually rotated, so that simple sums could be calculated by setting the relevant wheel to the required value and then stepping it forward as appropriate. It was just like an abacus, but it relied on mechanical procession rather than a user shuffling beads along wires.

Like much of da Vinci's other work, this calculator was an idealized machine that could not have been constructed with the technology of the day. Thirteen wheels each linked by several teeth to the next would have generated so much friction that the handle could not have been turned. Nonetheless, it is the earliest known way in which mechanical devices were proposed to extend mental rather than simply physical capabilities.

It took over a century for these first hints of calculating 'engines' to be developed further. In the 17th century, a variety of mathematicians developed simple calculating devices. Perhaps the most famous is that devised by the young Blaise Pascal in 1642 to help his father, a tax collector, with his sums. In the principles of its operation, Pascal's device was essentially identical to the machine sketched by da Vinci. The progress was in implementation, in that Pascal's calculator was in fact constructed by him and used by his father. Copies were even advertised for sale in Paris by the enterprising young mathematician.

Pascal's device automated the process of addition – and by implication, of subtraction – but could manage multiplication only by a process of repeated addition of a number to itself. The next important step in automated calculation came in an even cleverer machine devised and built by Gottfried Leibniz in 1671. With a wonderfully sophisticated gearing mechanism, Leibniz found a way to automate multiplication directly, rather than through time-consuming repetitions. So sophisticated was the Leibniz device that it continued to be the basis of mechanical calculators until they were replaced by electronic devices in the 20th century. In fact, when the first commercially manufactured calculating machines were produced in Germany in 1810, they featured the Pascal–Leibniz model of linked and geared cogwheels.

In machines able to automate the simple arithmetic processes of addition and multiplication, the foundations of the Age of Computers were, if not actually begun, then at least marked out. The true start of the computer revolution, however, was to come in the 19th century, at the hands of two people who can justifiably be called the grandparents of information technology – Charles Babbage and Ada, Countess Lovelace.

Babbage's engines

Charles Babbage was the Lucasian Professor of Mathematics at Cambridge University, the post held by Isaac Newton in the 17th century and by Stephen Hawking today. An unquestioned genius, Babbage was fascinated by many things. He was an active participant in the activities of the Royal Society, again just as Newton had been before him. Just like Newton, Babbage was closely involved with the Greenwich Observatory and with reviewing and revolutionizing mathematics teaching at Cambridge. Beyond this, however, Babbage was also fascinated by mechanical devices and by the operation of manufacturing companies. He closely studied, for example, the economics of the pin industry and of the printing trade, examining and improving the way in which work was propagated throughout a factory. In many ways, had he not become famous for the foundation work in computation, it is likely that he would have become famous for no less fascinating foundation work in a discipline now called 'operational research'.

Babbage's involvement with automatic computation began in 1821, when he was studying an error-ridden table of logarithmic values. He found himself constantly repeating a sequence of simple calculations involving the differences between the values laid out in the tables. He began to wonder whether those difference calculations could not in some way be automated so as to produce tables quickly and accurately. Already familiar with the operation of calculating machines based on Leibniz and Pascal's work, Babbage realized that more complex calculations could be managed by more sophisticated combinations of those geared cogwheels. With his knowledge of machinery, Babbage also believed that it was within his capabilities to design and build such a device. The result was an idea for what became known as the Difference Engine.

The first version of the Difference Engine was a small machine that in modern terms was a proof-of-concept implementation – a simple device which proved that a more ambitious machine was possible. This first engine was sufficiently powerful to calculate some mathematical operations, quadratic functions to eight decimal places: simple, but nonetheless impressive for the time. In 1822 it was demonstrated to the Royal Society to great acclaim, securing Babbage further funding from the Society and from the British government. This funding, Babbage promised, would produce a calculating engine capable of computing functions three times more complex to an accuracy of a full 20 decimal places. In a time of hand-produced and error-ridden mathematical tables, this was unheard of. It meant that, for the Royal Society, astronomical and logarithmic tables would be improved immeasurably; and for the government, the tables relied upon by their artillery officers would become the most accurate in the world.

At least initially, Charles Babbage worked enthusiastically on the impressive plans for the Difference Engine, producing detailed drawings and even engineering some of the core components of the machine. Gradually, however, his attention began to be diverted to an even more ambitious vision that he called the Analytical Engine. Where the Difference Engine automated the calculation of one specific type of function, the Analytical Engine would be able to automate the calculation of *any* specified function.

In the Analytical Engine we encounter a purely mechanical device that could be considered the world's first stored-program computer. It was a universal or general-purpose computing device, able to follow a series of instructions given to it in the form of a program. The Analytical Engine had a form of memory, input and output devices, a processor and a control unit, all essential components for a general-purpose, programmable computer. Although Babbage proposed to implement his invention with wheels and cogs, relying on muscle or steam power for its operation, it is recognizably an early ancestor of the modern computer – though only in the same sense that the Wright brothers' first plane is recognizably an ancestor of the Space Shuttle.

In 1832 Babbage began to make detailed notes of his plans for this more ambitious machine. By 1840 he had all but abandoned his work on the Difference Engine, to the annoyance of the British government which had by that time spent some 17,000 pounds (a fortune in those days) on the apparently already outdated concept: an early example, perhaps, of the habit in today's computer industry of accelerating the pace of development in order to make older models rapidly obsolete.

Babbage was to continue work on this first computer up to his death in 1871, but it was destined never to be completed. The government withdrew funding and Babbage's own resources were not sufficient. Nonetheless, he continued to make his plans and detailed drawings, and even to construct what components he could. In truth, though, his designs for both the Difference and the Analytical Engines required a degree of engineering accuracy well beyond the 19th-century's technology. Not until the end of the 20th century would a working engine be constructed, by the Science Museum in London, following Babbage's own drawings for components of the Difference Engine.

Despite this, some of the details of Babbage's design are startlingly prescient. Most importantly, he envisaged not simply entering data and instructions into his engine but doing so by means of punched cards, just as was to become common practice in modern computers of 1960s and 1970s vintage. Babbage had encountered punched-card controls in his studies of manufacturing companies, where he had learned about the Jacquard loom. Constructed by Joseph Jacquard in Lyon in the early 19th century,[1] this was a system of linked cards that were passed through a loom control unit and used to direct the weaving of different-coloured threads in a final design. Babbage even had a woven portrait of Jacquard himself hanging on his study wall, acknowledgement of the debt of inspiration owed to this clever invention.

Jacquard cards were used not simply to control looms but also to control the notes played by steam-driven organs. Ironically, Charles Babbage had a lifelong hatred of street organ grinders and had campaigned fervently for them to be banned. So famous was he in his day for this campaign that organ grinders would deliberately serenade him outside his London rooms when he was in town. He would perhaps think it fitting that punched cards would come to be more associated with the descendants of his invention and that steam-driven organs would become rare curiosities and museum pieces.

The cards themselves Babbage called 'operation cards' and 'cards of the variables', just as modern computers have both program instructions and data variables that were, until relatively recently, input on punched cards. He called the engine's wheels holding the data variables the 'store', and the calculating and decision-making unit was called the 'mill', since that was what it most closely resembled. Interestingly, until recently these two terms were in widespread use in the USA for modern computers' memory and arithmetic processing components.

The single most important advance that Babbage made, however, was not in relation to these design ideas but rather to something much more fundamental. Babbage conceived of the instructions to drive the engine's operation as being a distinct element that could be manipulated. He invented the idea of a computer *program* and so paved the way for the world's first programmer, Ada, Countess Lovelace.

In 1840 Babbage delivered a series of lectures in Turin describing the principles of the Analytical Engine. Notes from these lectures were published in Geneva in 1842 and translated into English in 1843 by Lady Lovelace, a gifted mathematician in her own right. The only child of Lord Byron, Lady Lovelace dramatically extended the original notes from Babbage's lectures into a long and detailed presentation on what we would now recognize as programming. She praised the concept of the Analytical Engine as a device which 'weaves algebraic patterns just as the Jacquard loom weaves flowers and leaves': high-flown and poetic descriptions, as would be expected from Byron's daughter, but then she proceeded to give the most detailed and well-considered presentation of the central concepts of programming computers. This was a startlingly impressive intellectual feat, given that the ideas themselves would then lie undisturbed for well over a century until the modern trade of software design and programming rediscovered them.

Lady Lovelace wrote of solving complicated problems by dividing them into a series of simpler and ever simpler problems that could be easily solved and then combined. We now think of this as the design principle of 'functional decomposition'. She wrote of the Analytical Engine making decisions based on which of 'two or more possible contingencies has occurred'. These we now know as conditional operations such as 'if-then-else' constructions. She wrote of whole sections of operation cards being repeated a specific number of times – program loops, to the modern programmer. Almost every fundamental aspect of operation for modern computers was anticipated by Lady Lovelace, who even wrote of what we would now recognize as artificial intelligence in the activity of the engine. More impressive still, she was able to give concrete examples of instruction sequences to solve a variety of knotty mathematical problems.

Charles Babbage and Lady Lovelace corresponded closely on the principles and the operation of the Analytical Engine. Between them the pair anticipated and illustrated the direction that would be taken a century later in the development of what we would now recognize as *real* computers. Just as da Vinci before them, however, they were unfortunate enough to do so at a time when the technology and engineering practices of the day simply were not able to realize their dreams. In truth, the construction of an 'artificial brain' from cogwheels and clattering cards was always doomed to failure, even if they did manage to make some dramatic developments. In their day, Babbage and Lady Lovelace were essentially dismissed – Babbage as a wastrel and a dreamer more interested in complaining about street noise; and Ada as an admittedly gifted amateur, more famous for being her father's daughter than for her own accomplishments.

In the years that followed, work on automatic computation essentially faltered. True, in the USA a statistician in the Census Bureau, Herman Hollerith, used Jacquard cards to automate analysis of census returns in 1890. In 1896, in order to exploit his tabulating machine, he founded a company, which in 1924 would come to be called IBM. Other than that, however, 'computer science' came to a halt, and much of the impetus provided by its early enthusiasts was lost. What was missing were two vitally important elements: reliable technology from which the devices could be made; and an understanding of the underlying mathematical basis (the 'computational model') for the activity of programming.

These two things were created in the 1930s and 1940s by the two true founding fathers of computer science, Alan Turing and John von Neumann.

Turing and von Neumann machines

At the end of the 19th century, science in general, and mathematics in particular, were in a confident state. There remained, as far as most Victorian gentlemen of science were concerned, little or nothing left to be discovered. It was considered merely to be a case of 'mopping up' what few stray elements remained. The same was true of technology, according to the director of the US Patent Office, Charles Duell. In 1899 he confidently claimed that 'everything that can be invented has been invented'.

The gods do not leave such hubris unpunished. Within a few short years of the start of the 20th century, Einstein's theory of relativity had shown that the universe was immeasurably more complicated than had been thought and quantum theory had shown that even empty space was an angry cauldron of mysterious energy and strange events. From the well-behaved, mechanistic universe of the 19th century, scientists suddenly had to contend with a world in which random chance seemed to be the driving force; a universe in which supposedly indivisible atoms could be split into yet smaller fundamental particles; a universe featuring gravitational black holes, undetectable 'dark matter' and a host of other, even less comprehensible things. Far from being nearly finished, scientists were forced to realize that they had in fact barely taken their first few tottering steps.

If physicists had to change their world-view, then mathematics suffered a far worse fate. While science had to re-examine some of its most fundamental and long-held beliefs about the behaviour of the universe, mathematics by contrast had to reinvent itself completely. The very foundations of mathematics were shown to be flawed and crumbling. The problem was to do with one of the most fundamental aspect of mathematics: the idea of a 'set'. A set is a precisely defined collection of items that satisfy some specific criteria, such as, for example, the set of all positive numbers divisible only by themselves and by 1. Mathematics is a process of deduction of further properties about the items contained in particular sets or in groupings of sets. Almost all mathematical proofs begin with the time-honoured phrase 'Consider the set of all …'. Unfortunately for mathematics, early in the 20th century a paradox emerged that showed that the basic handling of sets in mathematics was incorrect and that therefore *all* of pure mathematics (logic, analysis, number, etc.) could no longer be considered correct. It was not necessarily *false* but it could no longer be taken as *proven true*.

The paradox itself was even distressingly simple, the mathematical equivalent of the well-known Barber Paradox. The village barber shaves all those villagers who do not shave themselves, so who shaves the barber?

In mathematical terms, the existence of such paradoxes in set theory meant that it was possible for there to be well-defined, well-behaved, perfectly well-specified sets (such as the set of all villagers shaved by the barber) and for there to be valid elements (such as the barber himself, who is a villager) that could be neither included nor excluded from that set. The status of these elements had to remain undecided, a fatal anathema for mathematics.

Holed disastrously by what was on the face of it a trivial problem, mathematicians began the 20th century bailing frantically and searching for a resolution. The answer was provided by a philosopher mathematician, Bertrand Russell. Discarding set theory as insufficiently well defined, Russell began with a substantially more rigorous specification for collections of elements and then proceeded to rebuild the entire foundations of mathematics. His work, the *Principia Mathematica*, stands as one of the most impressive monuments of 20th-century mathematics.

The reinvention of mathematics was successful. It produced, however, a particularly interesting concept: the realization that mathematics could be applied *to itself* and that mathematical statements and deductions could be applied to mathematical statements and deductions. The most important of these statements in the 1930s was the Decidability Problem, set by the British mathematician David Hilbert.

Mathematics begins with a group of elements such as numbers, for example, and a variety of initial assumptions, called 'axioms', which are declared to be true. Analysis of real numbers, for instance, takes as axiomatic the assumption of 'continuity' – that between any two numbers, no matter how close in value, there is always a third number that lies between the pair. That is, we have an axiom that the number line can be split as finely as we choose. From these elements and axioms, mathematicians proceed to make a number of claims, expressed as 'statements', which they then try to prove by applying logical deductions to the axioms. For example, continuity implies that if a function has a negative result for one value and a positive result for a second, then there is a third value between those two for which the result is zero.

Some mathematical statements can be shown to be true, others are shown to be false. The Decidability Problem asks the question whether *every* validly expressed mathematical statement can be shown to be either true or false. That is, are there any valid mathematical statements whose status cannot be decided? By analogy with the Barber Paradox, mathematicians' instincts were that there would indeed be valid mathematical statements that would not be decidable. Proving this, though, was another thing. An entirely new branch of mathematics had to be invented, in which the 'Consider the set of...' statements referred to mathematical deductions themselves.

Two men solved the Decidability Problem in the 1930s, approaching it in wildly different ways. One was a logician, Alonzo Church at Princeton University, who developed a novel branch of mathematics called 'lambda calculus'. In this, lambda is a 'function of functions', used as a way of representing mathematically the idea of *performing* a defined series of mathematical operations. Church articulated and reasoned with these lambda functions, building a complex series of statements about statements and proofs about proofs, and finally showing that there were indeed statements that could not be decided. It was a wonderful achievement. However, until relatively recently in computer science, it was an achievement overshadowed by the approach taken independently by the second mathematician, Alan Turing.

Turing invented the mathematical foundations of computation. A Fellow at Cambridge University, he was a gifted mathematician with a penchant for chess, puzzles and music. In 1935 he attended a lecture where the Decidability Problem was explained and, for whatever reason, the young Turing became fascinated by the question. What was more, in 1936 he was able to find an entirely novel way of addressing the issue. He approached the Decidability Problem by considering the processes performed by mathematicians as they formulate and derive proofs, thinking of each one of these as a 'method'. Turing considered an idealized machine that would step through the procedure of applying these methods to different mathematical expressions, reflecting the changing 'state of mind' of the mathematician as his work progresses.

Turing realized that he needed a way of representing the *expression* to his machine and that he also needed a way of representing the *method*. Turing's first great achievement was in appreciating that the methods could be divided into much smaller and simpler steps, and that those simpler steps could be recombined in different ways so as to create different methods. He had discovered 'instructions'. His second achievement was in realizing that the same 'alphabet' could be used to represent both the instructions for the method and the detail of the proof to be addressed – the 'data'.

The idealized machine that Turing imagined had two elements. The first was an infinitely long tape divided into distinct cells, in each of which was written one of his alphabet characters, representing instructions or data. The second element was a read/write head connected to a decision and control unit. The head is free to read characters from the tape. Some of these characters tell the control unit to move the head to the left or to the right a certain number of cells; some tell the head to write another, specific character at a given point; and some tell the head to read a character from a specific place.

Turing's genius was in appreciating that the simple atomic instructions represented in the characters on the tape were sufficient to construct *every* possible mathematical method for manipulating the characters that represented mathematical statements.

Each one of these 'Turing machines' that he imagined being built and 'programmed' (with the instructions representing a method and the data representing a statement) could then be run. The head would step through the instructions, sequentially and gradually altering the state of the data character by character until, in time, an answer was produced.

Beyond this, however, he also realized that the Turing machine was *itself* a method. The Turing machine programmed with specific instructions and specific data could be thought of as a mathematical proof. This meant that the Turing machine could be written out in the language of his 'method alphabet' and itself executed by another Turing machine, a *universal* Turing machine. In a universal Turing machine, we see a mathematical expression of an idealized device that can be programmed with instructions and data to solve any problem that can be solved. The universal Turing machine is the theoretical expression of a 'stored-program, general-purpose computer', the computational model missing from Babbage and Lady Lovelace's earlier work.

Turing worked wholly independently of Alonzo Church in Princeton but yet derived exactly the same result. He found that there were mathematical expressions that could not be decided. Turing thought of them as being 'non-computable numbers', represented by specific types of Turing machine with properties he could grasp. Where Church represented a general 'function of functions' as an operator called 'lambda', Turing represented it as an idealized general-purpose computer. Church's work was more rigorous and 'mathematical', Turing's more accessible and more easily appreciated and applied. Unfortunately, Church published before Turing, and as a result Turing's short paper ('On Computable Number with an application to the Decidability Problem', written in April 1936) had to be rewritten so as to credit Church for his prior result. It was eventually finished in August 1936 and published at the end of that year.

Turing was also at Princeton University by that time, enrolled in September 1936 as a graduate student at the famous Institute for Advanced Study, home of Albert Einstein. During his stay, three important steps were taken by the young mathematician. First of all, Turing was able to show rigorously that his conception of 'method' as represented in an idealized machine corresponded exactly with Church's more 'mathematical' notion of lambda calculus. This meant that his Turing machines were not only intuitively appealing, they were also shown to be mathematically valid. Second, he met one of Princeton's many resident geniuses, John von Neumann. Third and most prophetically, Turing found a way of applying his idealized machine to the question of analysing ciphers.

Turing stayed on the graduate programme at the Institute for Advanced Study at Princeton for two years, and at the end of that period had impressed von Neumann enough to be offered an extension. War with Germany was looming, however, and even a mathematician as unworldly as Alan Turing (and he *was* as unworldly as any caricature of the ivory-tower genius) realized that his skills at cryptography might well be useful in the coming conflict. He returned to London and began to work covertly for the newly formed Government School for Codes and Ciphers. This work would eventually take him to the now-famous Bletchley Park and give him the chance to apply his genius in the fight against the German Enigma code.

At Princeton, though, Turing had done enough to excite von Neumann's interest in the issue of automatic computation. Along with Albert Einstein, von Neumann was one of the six founders of the Institute for Advanced Study. Science is littered with individuals who are referred to as geniuses, but von Neumann was a genius of an entirely different order, perhaps more so even than

Einstein himself. His intellectual ability was truly staggering, allowing him to make fundamental advances in disciplines as diverse as number theory and quantum mechanics, turbulence and electronics, game theory and ballistics. He was provocative, imaginative and, above all, creative. Beyond this, however, he was also surprisingly practical. Throughout the course of World War II he was a general scientific consultant to the US government, involved in almost every significant scientific project of the period.

Von Neumann quickly grasped the way that Turing's ideas could be practically applied to the mathematical problems faced by all of these projects, perhaps most importantly the Manhattan Project at Los Alamos in New Mexico, where the first atomic bomb was being designed. His position as a senior scientific adviser gave him visibility of many interesting projects, including work at the Moore School of Engineering in Pennsylvania, where a team had designed an electromechanical calculator called ENIAC, the Electronic Numerical Integrator and Computer. First, von Neumann ensured that the ENIAC facility was made available to the workers at Los Alamos, then he applied his intellect to improving the Moore School concept.

At Harvard, Howard Aiken of the US Navy had been funded by IBM to develop a programmable calculator called the 'Automatic Sequence Controlled Calculator', later called 'Harvard Mark 1'. This worked on a sequence of instructions input from a paper tape and relied on electromechanical relays, but it also featured data stored on cogwheels (just as Babbage had designed) and worked in decimals to a precision of 23 places. The Mark 1 was a full five tons in weight and a hefty 51 foot long. It was enormously complicated, but it worked almost continuously at Harvard for 15 years.

Von Neumann was fully familiar with the Aiken design and had already discussed improvements that could be made to the basic scheme. He was also equally familiar with the ENIAC design; and in his game-theory research he had worked closely with Arthur Burkes, a mathematician specializing in sequential automata. Blending these different elements gave von Neumann a wholly novel perspective on what automatic computing could become. The result, published in June 1945, was a design called EDVAC (Electronic Discrete Variable Analytic Computer). It balanced Turing's foundational ideas of stored instructions and sequentially applied changes in state, with the physical requirements of being able to store and execute instructions that manipulate data.

In EDVAC, John von Neumann had produced the first clear articulation of the basic principles of computer architecture. He specified that a computer should have input and output devices; he specified the requirement for a memory to store both instructions and data, which could be accessed randomly rather than sequentially; and he specified that the device should have an arithmetic and logic unit, alongside a control unit. These elements had been *used* before but almost by accident. We now consider that aspects of the Analytical Engine, for example, conform approximately to this model; but it was von Neumann that first articulated this *as* a model. To Babbage the elements were an aspect of a physical implementation, whereas to von Neumann they were the reflection of an underlying principle of operation.

Perhaps von Neumann's greatest contribution to the principles of computer architecture was in the specification of the 'fetch–decode–execute–store' cycle. He devised the idea of a series of timed impulses – an electronic clock or heartbeat – that would drive the device through a series of steps. In the first heartbeat, an instruction would be fetched from memory; in the next, any data required by the instruction would be fetched; in the third, the instruction would be executed, transforming the data into the result; and finally in the fourth, that result would be copied back to memory. This sequence of activities is is so fundamental to computer operation that it is almost impossible to imagine how a computer could work without it. Very nearly all modern computers are at heart von Neumann machines conforming to the computational model devised by Alan Turing. The fetch–execute cycle on a von Neumann architecture operating with a stored program is practically the definition of a modern computer.

⁂

There, the development of the practical computational model has stopped. Between the computers built immediately after World War II and the computers built today there is very little theoretical difference. Today's computers are faster, smaller, cheaper and more powerful, but they are still essentially von Neumann architectures and Turing machine programs. John von Neumann himself worked on alternative, multiprocessor models, called cellular automata, but other than in a few specialized tasks these have not been widely used as a basis for computer design.

Sixty years old, the von Neumann design has proved so popular and so easy to apply that it has been all that we have needed to create the digital world that we live in today. Modern microprocessors, though, have a number of clever ways of making that von Neumann scheme work better. Instead of fetching just one instruction at a time from main memory, the processor might fetch several instructions in anticipation of them being required, storing the instructions in a set of very fast local storage containers called a 'cache'. The microprocessors themselves are now as small as possible, minimizing the distance that instructions and data must travel, limited only by the speed of light. In the most recent Intel Pentium microprocessors, specialized modules for dealing with graphics and with arithmetic operations run several times faster than the rest of the microprocessor. Everything possible is done to make the von Neumann system as fast as possible, given the limitation of the 'von Neumann bottleneck' of having to fetch and execute instructions.

The development path that has led from the implementation of the von Neumann scheme in machines the size of rooms to machines not much bigger than a full stop is an astonishing story of experiment, accident and genius. Like so much of the modern world of technology, it starts with World War II.

2

How did computers develop?

'You know, Dad, if cars had developed in the same way that computers did, they'd all still look pretty much like a Model T Ford. But by now they'd go, like, to Pluto and back on a teaspoon of petrol, would have more power than a hundred space shuttles, would cost about a penny...'

'... And would need to be rebooted every time you wanted to adjust the mirror?'

Modern computers – electronic devices executing stored program instructions – are considered to have begun in 1945 with John von Neumann's description of the EDVAC concept. However, EDVAC was not conceived in isolation. Other projects had developed separately many of the ideas that were brought together in the proposal. Perhaps the most intriguing of these developments, though, was made not by the Allies but by a German aeronautical engineer. Fortunately for the progress of World War II and for the subsequent rapid rise of the British and US computer industries, the work performed in Germany was in fact completely ignored by the German government.

The first computers in Europe

The creation of the very first, electromechanical computers in Europe occurred almost by chance when an engineering student called Konrad Zuse decided (just as Babbage had done over a century before him) that he needed a simple device to calculate numerical tables accurately.

Konrad Zuse was born in Berlin in 1910 and trained before World War II first as a civil engineer and then as an aircraft engineer. From 1936 onwards, Zuse designed and built four computing devices that anticipated many of the developments that would subsequently be 'discovered' by US and British engineers. Zuse worked wholly independently of any other efforts being undertaken anywhere else in the world. Writing of his work after the war, Zuse in fact confessed never even to have read of the work of Charles Babbage or any other developments. The designs and engineering concepts that Zuse invented are a remarkable example of parallel evolution in the field of computing. And there is no evidence to suggest that for their part the US engineers had even heard of Zuse, let alone been influenced by his ideas.

Zuse's first computer, the Z1, was built between 1936 and 1938, when he was an engineering student in Berlin living with his parents.[1] The Z1 was in fact built in his parents' living room. Quite simply, Zuse wanted to have a device that would calculate engineering formulae for him quickly and reliably. Knowing of no such device at the time, he began the task of constructing one for himself. In doing so, he introduced a number of ideas which, at the time, he did not realize were revolutionary; to him, they were simply logical design decisions. Perhaps the most important innovations he made were using binary values and representing large numbers in the 'floating point' style of scientific notation.

Before Zuse and the Z1, mechanical calculators represented numbers by 10 teeth on a cogwheel, so that the numbers were stored and processed in base 10. Zuse, however, elected to represent the numbers as patterns of 1s and 0s, represented by the 'on' or 'off' state of telephone relay switches. He did not call these states 'bits' (the modern term for binary digits) but *Ja-Nein-Werte* ('yes/no words'). These binary values were collected into discrete, fixed-length memory cells, which today we would call 'words'.

Another interesting aspect of the Z1 design was that these words could be individually addressed in a random-access memory, rather than the sequential-access memory of the Babbage design, with the word's location itself specified in a binary value. Finally, the instructions for opening and closing the relays so as to do arithmetic and logical operations were also specified in binary. Independently of Turing's work, Zuse had discovered that instructions and data (and now, even addresses) could be represented in the same 'alphabet'. The Zuse alphabet consisted of fixed-length binary words, just as is the case with all modern computers.

For the floating-point number representation, again just as in modern computers, Zuse divided the binary word values so as to give the number's sign, mantissa and exponent separately within the 22-bit word.[2] This allowed him to calculate using large numbers, but had a corresponding impact on the accuracy of representation of those numbers. For the early trial system this was not important, but it was something that Zuse had to address for later work with his scheme.

The Z1 was completed by Zuse working alone, using purely mechanical telephone relay switches which were bulky but reliable, though (to his parents' consternation) very noisy. By 1938, Zuse had decided that, with a working prototype computer to his credit, he would redesign the machine to use the faster electromechanical telephone relay switches. A working prototype called the Z2 was completed by the end of that year. Confident that his design would work, in 1939 Zuse began to construct the Z3 computer, a Z1 design implemented with electromechanical telephone relay switches.

The Z3 is believed to be the first electronic computer ever built. It had a memory capacity of just 64 words, each 22 bits wide. It had 1800 electromechanical relays to provide the memory and 600 to provide the arithmetic and logic unit. It was able to do simple arithmetic calculations, along with more powerful operations such as square roots. Unfortunately, development was hampered by the war. Lacking both time and materials to dedicate to the project, it was 1942 before Zuse, who had managed to be released from military service so as to work in aircraft design, was able to complete the machine. In 1942, though, Zuse began to work towards an even more ambitious computing machine, unsurprisingly called the Z4. This had 1024 words of memory, each 32 bits wide; its programming functionality included conditional branching, necessary to implement 'if–then–else' processing styles; and it featured punched tape for input and output.

Almost immediately, construction on this latest design was also badly affected by the progress of the war. As with the Z3, the severe shortages of materials, particularly metals, introduced delay upon delay. Then, in 1943, the bombs began to fall on Berlin almost continuously, and Zuse was forced to move again and again, able only to transport and save his precious, part-completed Z4 computer. The Z2 prototype and the Z3 (built from the components of the original Z1) were destroyed in the air raids.

The end of the war saw Konrad Zuse, his pregnant wife and the Z4 in a small village in the Bavarian Alps. Finally free of bombing and able to dedicate his time to the exercise, Zuse managed to scavenge old tin cans and finish the construction of the computer in a former flour store. In 1948 the machine was complete, and the following year, having formed his own computer company, Zuse KG, he was able to make the computer industry's first ever sale – to the Institute of Applied Mathematics in Zurich for 50,000 Deutschmarks. The machine continued to be used for serious computation at the Institute until 1955.

Zuse KG went from strength to strength. Between 1949 and 1969, the company owned by Konrad Zuse and his wife sold over

250 computers with a value of 100 million Deutschmarks. In 1957 Zuse began to produce computers relying on valve technology instead of electromechanical relays, and in 1959 he moved on to transistor-based circuits. In modern terms, Zuse KG was producing mainframe computers (large, high-speed and expensive machines) that were used successfully in the German steel and banking industries. Unfortunately, the decision to move to transistor circuits proved to be the first and biggest mistake in Zuse's involvement with computers. The transistor circuits proved difficult to manufacture efficiently, and from 1962 onwards, with increasing competition from IBM, Zuse KG got deeper and deeper into debt. Finally, in 1967 the company was acquired by Siemens (now the European computing and electronics giant Siemens-Nixdorf).

Though the Z series of mainframe computers is now all but forgotten, eclipsed by IBM systems in popular imagination, Konrad Zuse and his company all but single-handedly created the computing industry on the European mainland. Although developed in isolation and ignored by the Nazi government, the Z4 is now recognized as the earliest true computer and Konrad Zuse himself as one of the most important founding fathers of computing.

The ENIAC machine

With the exception of Zuse in Germany, the computer industry was dominated first by the Americans and the British, then more recently by the Americans alone. In almost every case, the 'family tree' of those early computers can be traced back to one ground-breaking machine, the ENIAC. While Zuse worked alone and the early Z-series machines were hampered by the war, ENIAC benefited from being funded by the US Army as a direct result of the conflict.

The Ballistics Research Laboratory at the Aberdeen Proving Ground in Maryland was the foremost organization for the Army

Ordnance Department in calculating artillery and bomb trajectory tables, essential for accurate gunnery and airborne bombing missions. At the dawn of World War II, in September 1939, the officers running the calculating group quickly realized that the handful of staff using desktop calculators and a primitive analogue trajectory calculator (called a Bush differential analyser) would soon be swamped with work.

The Bush analyser worked by using a varying, continuous electric current to mimic the instantaneous values of some specified function, in this case the ballistic trajectory followed by the bomb or shell. It was a speedy but complicated and decidedly temperamental piece of equipment. The development of the ENIAC machine arose from a simple, happy coincidence – the fact that at the Moore School of Electrical Engineering in the University of Pennsylvania a similar but much more reliable Bush analyser was in regular use. The Army awarded a contract to the Moore School to allow this device to be used by the team at Aberdeen. The result of this small contract was an increasingly close working relationship between the army officers in Aberdeen and the electrical engineers in Pennsylvania. Inevitably, discussions turned to possible improvements that could be made in the calculating of ballistic tables using the Bush analyser.

This series of improvements to the Bush analyser itself and to the operation of the computers[3] led in time to a proposal for a completely new calculating device. This proposal was written by two of the engineers at the Moore School, William Mauchly and J. Presper Eckert. It was for an Electronic Numerical Integrator and Computer (ENIAC) and was submitted to the Aberdeen sponsors in June 1943. The result was an initial outlay of around 60,000 dollars by the US Army Ordnance as funding for the development of the machine to be used in Aberdeen.

Under the impetus of the war, development of ENIAC was rapid. The first components became operational in June 1944 at the Moore School and development continued piecemeal through to 1945. Work on ENIAC was finally completed in 1946, when the total US Army Ordnance funds spent on the project stood at almost half a million dollars. Even before it was fully complete, however, ENIAC had entered service. It was used to perform urgent calculations on behalf of the Manhattan Project, for example, following John von Neumann's involvement and interest.

With these early computers, it is tempting to believe that, as they were superseded by further developments (ENIAC by EDVAC, for example), the older model was simply shelved and forgotten. This was simply never the case in practice. ENIAC continued to have a very long and decidedly useful life, even after von Neumann had taken computing forward in a series of dramatic advances at Princeton.

In July 1946, ENIAC was formally accepted as a completed model by the Aberdeen Proving Ground. It continued to operate at the Moore School on behalf of the Army until the end of that year, and in January 1947 it was dismantled and moved to Aberdeen. It began its full-time operational life in August of that year and continued in service through to 1955, when, at 11.45 pm on 2 October, it was finally turned off.

ENIAC had been one of the most successful computers of the period, working on problems ranging from turbulence to weather forecasting, from ballistics to nuclear research. It averaged 100 hours per week of trouble-free operation – astonishing reliability for the time, given that it required some 200 kilowatts of electricity to run over 19,000 vacuum tubes and 1500 relays. ENIAC itself consisted of some 30 distinct units plus air-conditioning and weighed in at over 30 tons – a monster by today's standards. But it was also a supremely fast monster. Using the algorithms for trajectory calculations, a trained ballistics mathematician could use a desktop calculator to compute a 60-second trajectory in about 20 hours; the Bush analyser could do the same calculations in 15 minutes; but ENIAC could perform the calculation in only 30 seconds. ENIAC, in fact, could compute the trajectory while the projectile was still in flight, an unheard-of achievement before then.

ENIAC was also a monster that inspired an industry as, over the years of its operating life, scientists from Britain and the USA came to understand its promise. In particular, ENIAC begat EDVAC.

The EDVAC machine

John von Neumann's report of June 1945 on the design proposal for the EDVAC computer acted as an encouragement and a spur for Mauchly and Eckert at the Moore School. Once the design of the ENIAC system had been agreed, it had to be more or less fixed if the device itself was to be constructed in any realistic timeframe. This meant, of course, that any further ideas could not be introduced on the ENIAC platform. The EDVAC design provided Mauchly and Eckert with a means of developing their ideas further.

The contract for the development of EDVAC (Electronic Discrete Variable Automatic Calculator) was placed by the US Army Ordnance in April 1946 for an initial value of 100,000 dollars; this contract was extended to a final total value of almost half a million dollars. The work was to be divided between the Moore School of Electrical Engineering, who would undertake the actual construction work, and the Institute for Advanced Study at Princeton, under von Neumann, where the principal design work would continue.

The final design of the EDVAC system incorporated all of von Neumann's ideas for stored programs, randomly accessible memory, and instructions encompassing both arithmetic and logical operations. The machine was completed and delivered to the Aberdeen Proving Ground in August 1949, and after a few installation problems it finally began part-time operation in 1951. By 1952 it was operating for just 20 hours a week; by 1961 its reliability had improved to the point where it was operational for some 145 hours a week.

The machine had a memory of 1024 words, each 44 bits wide, and relied heavily on vacuum-tube or valve technology. Initially, EDVAC used paper tape for input and a teletype machine for output, but in June 1953 a punched-card system was installed. In 1954 a magnetic-drum memory was provided, extending the available memory of 1024 words by an additional 4608 words. Finally, in 1960 a magnetic-tape device was added to the design.

EDVAC was used almost continuously by the Army Ordnance Proving Ground at Aberdeen, though in many ways its importance lies not in the details of its operation but rather in the publication of its design by von Neumann and in the impact the work had on Mauchly and Eckert. Von Neumann's design principles were soon being copied around the world, though the impact on the two engineers was more dramatic.

In March 1946 Mauchly and Eckert were forced to resign from the Moore School of Electrical Engineering following an argument over their patent for the ENIAC work. Determined to continue their work on computers, the pair formed a company in Philadelphia. Initially called the Electronic Controls Company, this became EMCC (Eckert-Mauchly Computer Corporation) in December 1948. Their first task was to produce a computer based on their EDVAC designs which they could offer for sale. Cleverly, they anticipated that the US Census Bureau would require computer facilities for the processing of the 1950 census and were able to persuade them to fund the development of what would become the UNIVAC-1.

UNIVAC-1 did not quite beat the Zuse Z4 to be the first commercially sold computer. Although the sale was completed before Zuse's contract, delivery of the UNIVAC-1 was not until June 1951. Unfortunately for Mauchly and Eckert, though they were superb engineers and researchers, they were not businessmen, and they found the cost of developing a commercial computer beyond them. In February 1950 EMCC was acquired by Remington Rand Corporation, who formed the Univac Division, which ultimately became the modern computer giant Unisys.

UNIVAC-1 was the computer which kick-started the US computing industry, leading eventually to their dominance. In those early years, though, the Americans faced stiff competition from British computer developers.

Computers in the UK

Computing in Britain had got off to a flying start, only to be abruptly halted at the end of World War II. At Bletchley Park near the modern Milton Keynes, efforts to decipher German communications had led the mathematician Alan Turing to propose and construct a series of increasingly complex specialized devices, called the 'Heath-Robinsons' because of their 'knotted string and kitchenware' appearance. Eventually, through the summer of 1943, it was realized that a much more powerful and flexible machine was required – a machine capable of being 'reprogrammed' so as to act on any and all variations of the all-important Enigma cipher.

Built by Tommy Flowers, an electrical engineer employed at the Post Office's Dollis Hill research laboratory in London, the Colossus computer became operational in December 1943. It had 1500 electronic valves, used punched paper tape for input, and was one of the most reliable computing devices constructed during the period. It was also blisteringly fast, able to decipher at a rate of 5000 characters per second. Colossus could truly be said to have been one of the most important reasons why Britain won the Battle of the Atlantic against the German U-Boats and why in turn the Allies were able to defeat the Axis forces.

Unfortunately, at the close of the war orders came that Colossus and all the notes, drawings, plans and discussion documents recording its design and construction had to be completely destroyed. Why this should be so has never been explained, though it may have been so as to encourage the Russians to continue to use ciphers such as the ones on which Enigma was based, by making them believe that the British and Americans were not able to read their codes. For whatever reason, British computing was set back behind the Americans at the close of the war. The result was that the two most influential projects in Britain – at Cambridge under Maurice Wilkes and at Manchester under Fredrick Williams and Tom Kilburn – were based on the ENIAC/EDVAC models and heavily guided in particular by the work of von Neumann.

The Manchester machine was initially called 'Baby' but then renamed the 'Mark 1'. It introduced the then revolutionary idea of storing both the program instructions and the data in the same random-access memory. Although this was a foundational aspect of the original Turing machine ideas, before Baby it had never been attempted in practice. Baby ran its first successful program in July 1948, and by 1949 two more, much larger and more powerful designs had been completed. The Manchester team went from strength to strength, even encouraging a number of the former Bletchley Park stars (including Alan Turing himself) to join them. Perhaps even more importantly, the researchers struck a deal with Ferranti to build and sell computers based on the Mark 1 design. The first of these was installed at Manchester University in February 1951. What followed for the Manchester team was a long and fruitful relationship with Ferranti in researching, developing and selling a variety of increasingly powerful computers. Amongst these was the Atlas machine launched in December 1962, at the time the most powerful supercomputer in the world.

To this day, Manchester University remains one of the foremost computer-science research institutions.

The second important research project in Britain at the time was at Cambridge, where in May 1949 Maurice Wilkes developed a machine called EDSAC along the same lines as the EDVAC design. Although EDSAC introduced a number of innovations (and led to the establishment of the world-class Cambridge Computer Laboratory), it is perhaps best remembered for the influence that it had in its turn on the development of an intriguing computer called LEO.

LEO was designed and built not by a university or military research establishment, but rather by a commercial company whose business was providing elegant high teas and cream cakes in fashionable dining rooms around the country. The Lyons Corner Tea Shop had been a feature of English towns for decades, with attentive waitresses in neat uniforms serving a predominantly middle-class clientele. Behind the scenes, though, an army of clerks was required to process wages, receipts and invoices; to balance books; and to ensure forward orders of bakery goods and tons of tea and coffee. That this could be done with a computer seems all too obvious to us now, but it took a peculiar imagination to appreciate that a tool used to calculate ballistic trajectory tables could as easily be applied to the mundane activity of reconciling business invoices.

J. Lyons & Co. was an unusual company in two particular regards. First of all, although on the surface it appeared to be a traditional, Edwardian-style concern, it had in fact grasped early many of the then modern concepts of business management. In particular, it was a keen advocate of the new practice of 'Organization and Methods' to streamline an efficient system of clerks and paperwork. Second and perhaps more importantly, Lyons had a culture of *total* self-reliance. It sourced all its own supplies, manufactured all its own baked goods, and built and maintained all its own factory equipment; the company even built its own delivery vans. It is hardly surprising, therefore, that when they decided they needed an 'electronic brain' they built it for themselves.

The main driver behind Lyons's computer project was John Simmons, a young mathematician in the Organization and Methods department who had joined the company from Cambridge University shortly after the war. Simmons was an enthusiastic advocate of automatic computation, a concept that he had heard about at Cambridge and which was then beginning to be more widely known. Through Simmons's advocacy, in May 1947 two members of the group were despatched on a fact-finding expedition to the USA (already recognized as the home of computing) to learn what they could. The pair encountered the two principal US projects of the time, ENIAC in Princeton and the Harvard Mark 1 machine sponsored by IBM. From both sources they heard that, ironically, the work of Maurice Wilkes back in Cambridge on the development of the EDSAC, influenced by ENIAC and EDVAC, might well provide the solution that they sought.

The Lyons board decided that they would indeed carry out their own computer construction work, based on Wilkes's EDSAC design, but only after the EDSAC had been shown to work. And work it did. In May 1949 Simmons was given the go-ahead to proceed with the development of what would be the first computer developed explicitly for commercial purposes – the Lyons Electronic Office, or LEO.

The team that Simmons founded to work on the project was truly staggering: the alumni of the project went on to create almost the entire information technology industry in Britain. In later years, LEO old boys were responsible for the airline reservation system for British Airways; the Camelot infrastructure to run the

National Lottery; the National Computer Centre; the computerization of the Freeman's catalogue business; the online systems for the London Stock Exchange; and the information systems at Sainsbury's. Even a young Miss Roberts, a chemistry graduate working in the Lyons laboratories, only narrowly avoided becoming involved, going on instead to marry one Dennis Thatcher and become the country's first woman prime minister.

LEO I followed the Cambridge EDSAC design almost perfectly, working with punched cards, paper tape and over 6000 electronic valves housed in 21 racks and covering roughly 5000 square feet. On 17 November 1951, the new computer ran the first of a weekly batch of bread and cake valuation jobs. LEO I was the world's first computer to run a live, time-sensitive office application. Even more importantly, in February 1954 this was extended further when LEO I became the first computer to calculate payroll and produce pay cheques directly.

With payroll functioning, the project team turned their attention to improving the LEO machine. In May 1954 a new computer design was published. Not only was it approved in June of that year, but the Lyons board went a crucial step further. They declared that they wished to 'sell or hire' these LEO II machines, and a new company – LEO Computers Ltd. – was born. In 1957 the LEO II machine was ready.

LEO Computers had two elements to their business plan: the sale of the computers themselves (to the Ford Motor Company, amongst others, in 1957), and a 'bureau service' to provide the computerized payroll solution in particular. Kodak and Tate & Lyle, for example, were early users of this service. The bureau was not, however, limited to this single application. For the Inland Revenue, LEO II calculated taxation tables for the PAYE system following the budget; and for what was then British Railways, LEO II calculated timetable data. Through to the early 1960s, the LEO Computers bureau in Bayswater, London, provided services to some of the largest British companies of the day, including Dunlop and Standard Motors, and even ran the payroll for the Ministry of Pensions.

In 1961, LEO III was developed with a relatively new technology, the semiconductor transistor – a tiny, solid-state device that permitted or prevented the conduction of electricity depending on its configuration. Developed by William Shockley at Bell Laboratories in 1947, the transistor was a tiny, relatively cool, relatively low-power unit when compared to the vacuum tube or valve technology that had been used up to that time. It allowed computers to be substantially smaller and lighter; indeed, in 1949 a popular electronics magazine had predicted that future computers might well weigh 'no more than one and half tons'. Transistors had initially proved difficult to work with, as Zuse KG had found in their work in Germany, so the LEO team had at first been nervous of working with them. By the turn of the decade, though, experience was beginning to be gained in this new technology and LEO put it to good use.

LEO III received a warm reception, and throughout 1962 and 1963 sold well. Indeed, LEO Computers even won a stiff battle with IBM to provide a LEO III mainframe to Dunlop. Unfortunately, the Lyons board had plans of their own, and in February 1963 LEO Computers Ltd. was merged with English Electric to form English Electric LEO Computers. The LEO Computers senior managers were replaced in favour of staff from English Electric; and a notably home-grown and particularly special company began to change its appearance and flavour. The company became a more aggressive computer-sales company – perhaps just in time, as in April 1964 IBM announced their System/360 mainframe and with it their intention to dominate the nascent commercial computing industry.

In October 1964, the Lyons board sold the last of their interest in LEO to a company formed from the merger of English Electric

LEO Computers and Marconi; this in turn ultimately merged with International Computers and Tabulators in July 1968 to form the famous International Computers Ltd. ICL was for decades *the* British computer company: a business that owed its existence to a tea shop company that wanted to calculate its bakery bills and payroll more efficiently.

The growth of the minicomputer

Until the middle of the 1960s, computers were large, monolithic constructions, dedicated to the service of serious organizations, usually from a single, expensive computer-room facility. In 1964, though, IBM broke this mould with the launch of the System/360. This was not only important from a technical perspective, it was also an important commercial statement for IBM. Just 20 years earlier, Thomas Watson Senior had declared that there was a world market for 'maybe five computers'. His son, who took the helm of the company in 1952, quickly realized that his father had been wrong.

Then as now, IBM was the mainspring of a lot of technical advances, closely studying developments made elsewhere. Watson Junior could see that computers could only become cheaper, faster and smaller – and with it, increasingly important to businesses. He decided that IBM would focus almost all of their prodigious resources in that direction – which they did to great effect, as they had a huge impact on the growing industry. Descended from Hollerith's revolutionary 19th-century work on punched-card technology, IBM had funded the development of the Harvard Mark 1 computer and developed a number of scientific computers throughout the 1950s. By 1956 they had introduced magnetic disks for storage and had made a large number of technological innovations in many other areas, including both commercial and scientific computing and, much later, home computing.

It was at the end of the 1960s, however, that IBM had its most important impact on the industry, with the introduction of the notion of 'unbundling'. In the System/360, IBM introduced a computer that was modular. Customers could select from a range of increasingly powerful processors, a variety of different sizes of memory, a collection of different power supplies, peripherals, and so on. The computers themselves, now using dense arrays of transistors on ceramic circuit boards, could also be smaller and therefore much cheaper to run. This modular approach to hardware was important in itself, but in 1969, pursuing the unbundling strategy still further, IBM introduced the concept of software modularity. This allowed customers to buy just the packages that they wanted. Instead of buying a computer with built-in payroll, accounting or scientific programs, requiring support technicians to maintain and manage the monolith, customers could now buy these elements separately and in a way better suited to their businesses. With tailored computers, bespoke programs and cheaper, cooler and increasingly reliable machines, IBM came steadily to control the growing worldwide market for automatic calculation.

Throughout the 1960s and 1970s, these large systems (collo-quially called 'mainframe' computers) and the programs and services associated with them dominated the world of computing. And so it remained until increasing expertise with transistors allowed the development of so-called 'minicomputers', most notably by Digital Equipment Corporation (now owned by Compaq).

DEC was established in Massachusetts in 1957 and for many years occupied a former woollen mill. They developed a variety of electronic devices and plug-in modules for simple control processes. In 1960, though, the company began to move into the world of computer construction, despite the objections of its board. A few years earlier, a study had shown that the world market for computers was at most only 100 machines. Convinced that the study was mistaken, chairman and founder Ken Olsen was determined that his company should not allow the opportunity to pass them by. So, in an audacious move, he chose to ignore the prejudices of his board and begin developing computers. However, he chose not to call them computers. Instead, they were 'Peripheral Data Processors', known more widely as the PDP family.

The PDP-1 went on sale in 1960 at a cost of just 100,000 dollars, at a time when mainframes were routinely selling for 10 times that amount. By 1962 Olsen's team had designed and built computers that ranged from the PDP-4, which was a real-time control system, to the PDP-5 and 6, which were general-purpose computers for customers such as the Massachusetts Institute of Technology. As they became more experienced, Olsen's engineers were creating in that old woollen mill computers that were increasing in power and shrinking in size and in cost. By 1965 DEC's expertise had progressed to the point where they were able to make a small, powerful computer (the PDP-8) that cost just 16,000 dollars. It was not only a fraction of the cost of mainframes, it was also a fraction of the size. The minicomputer had arrived.

Mainframe computers at that time needed an air-conditioned room with a dedicated power supply and a team of system managers and maintenance engineers to keep them running. The computer itself consisted of several large, separate cabinets (the 'frames') to house the different elements. The processor and power supply were in one frame; main memory boards in a second; disk or drum storage in a third; peripheral interfaces in a fourth, fifth or even a sixth. Some mainframe computers could have as many as 20 different elements, not even counting the main control console where the system manager would sit. DEC's minicomputer ranges consisted of at most two cabinets plus a teletype console. Everything was integrated into small units housed in metal-frame cabinets about the dimensions of a single wardrobe. More importantly, there was no longer a need for a dedicated, air-conditioned room. As the technology used in the minicomputers progressed, it became possible for the computer to operate in an ordinary office environment. The computer was being democratized and made available to anyone who could afford it.

Perhaps the most important of the computers that DEC developed was the PDP-11 range, launched in 1970 and costing just 10,000 dollars. Cheap and very flexible, this basic computer design went through a variety of further developments and was widely bought by university departments and medium-sized businesses around the world. It became the staple computer for academics when the UNIX operating system was made available on the platform free of charge to universities in 1973, and it reinforced this in 1975 when the PDP-11/70 machine was launched. Over the years that followed, the PDP-11 went from strength to strength, eventually evolving into one of DEC's most popular and powerful computer ranges – the VAX-11/780 so-called 'superminicomputers'. These were physically the same dimensions as the minicomputers but provided mainframe computing power, running the popular and accessible UNIX operating system.

With one series of computers launched in the middle of the 1960s and stretching over 20 years, Olsen revolutionized the computing industry – not bad for a man who had had to hide from his board the nature of the machines he was building. Even these small machines, though, would come to be seen as oversized in comparison to the computers that began to appear at the end of the 1970s. The computer revolution proper can be thought of as beginning with the emergence of the *personal* computer.

Personal computers

The seeds of the personal computer revolution and ultimately of the computerized, online world of today were many and varied, sown quietly throughout the second half of the 1960s. In 1965, for example, the computing language all too familiar to teenage programmers of the time – the Beginners All-purpose Symbolic Instruction Code, or BASIC – was created at Dartmouth College in the USA. Also in 1965, Douglas Englebart of the Stanford Research Institute was granted a patent for the very first mouse. And in 1969 the first small portion of what would grow to become the internet was established by the US Department of Defence. The single most important step, however, was the creation of the 'silicon chip'.

Transistors had slowly replaced valves throughout the 1950s. These much smaller, plastic-covered semiconductors were initially wired onto the circuit boards in almost exactly the same patterns as the bulkier valves. Gradually electronics engineers began to realize that the transistors could be packed much closer together, since they produced much less heat and so were less inclined to interfere with one another. Then a wholly novel idea appeared: entire circuits of electronic semiconductors all embedded within an individual slice of silicon.

Credit for this important invention goes to two companies and two engineers working wholly independently: Robert Noyce at Fairchild and Jack Kilby at Texas Instruments. In July 1958, shortly after starting work at the company, Kilby realized that, since all the semiconductor elements were made of the selfsame material, germanium, they could in fact all be created *in situ* on a single fragment of germanium: there was no need to separate the individual transistors and package them discretely. Noyce, independently, realized the same thing, though it is believed that Kilby was the first to demonstrate his invention, to the Texas Instruments chairman on 12 September 1958. It was a sliver of germanium fixed to a glass slide and connected to an oscilloscope.

The 'microchip', as it was called, was not an instant success. The management at Texas Instruments struggled to find an application for what was obviously an ingenious solution in need of a problem. Finally, in 1961, the microchip began to find a niche, first of all in compact computers used by the US Air Force in the Minuteman missiles; and then in the first range of pocket calculators developed and sold by Texas Instruments. Gradually the idea of a tiny processor began to be more and more attractive.

The silicon chip, as it came to be called, was a crystal of pure silicon treated (or 'doped') with small germanium impurities that acted as semiconductors, allowing tiny electric currents to be manipulated within the 'integrated circuit' of the chip itself. In 1972, Large Scale Integration (LSI) allowed around 500 distinct components to be embedded in a chip; by 1977, VLSI (Very Large Scale Integration) allowed a staggering 10,000 distinct electronic components to be embedded in a chip of silicon about the size of the letter 'm' on this page. Sealed inside black plastic modules resembling Lego blocks, these silicon chips have revolutionized the electronics industry. The microscopic circuitry that they now contain is measurable literally in terms of the individual atoms of the silicon crystal lattice itself.

Though he was perhaps beaten to the winning post on the invention itself, the company that built its fortune and much of the present computer age on these silicon chips – Intel – was founded in 1968 by Robert Noyce and a small group of friends. It is now one of the most famous names in the computer industry. While at the time others, in particular IBM, questioned what the early, simple silicon chips might be good for, Intel began energetically discovering the answer for themselves. In 1970 they began selling the world's first memory chip, providing 1024 bits of storage; and in November 1971 they produced the very first 'microprocessor chip', the 4004.

Modern microprocessor chips are called '32-bit' processors because they handle data, memory addresses and instructions in words that are 32 bits wide. Thirty-two bits can specify a range of values from 0 to $2^{32}-1$, or about 4 billion different values. As a result, they can specify a huge address range, handle large numbers, and carry out a wide variety of instructions. The 4004, by comparison, was a 4-bit processor and so was much more limited. It could specify values from 0 to 2^4-1, or just 16 different values. In fact, it was not destined to become a part of a computer but was instead developed as the control element for washing machines and similar automated devices. The 4004 was followed, however, in April 1974 by an 8-bit microprocessor called the 8080. This was used in the very first personal computer, the Altair 8800, released in kit form in December 1974 at a price of less than 400 dollars per kit.

The home computing revolution was about to begin, and in 1976 the most important bricks were laid: MOS Technology launched the inexpensive 8-bit 6502 microprocessor; Zilog launched their equally inexpensive 8-bit Z80 microprocessor, a processor compatible with the more expensive Intel 8080; and most importantly, Steve Jobs and Stephen Wozniak founded Apple Computers. The following year Ken Olsen of DEC made his first and only mistake in the computer industry, when he pronounced that there was 'no reason' why anyone would want a computer at home. How wrong he was.

Steve Wozniak was a 26-year-old engineer at Hewlett-Packard and a member of a Palo Alto amateur electronics and computer group called the Homebrew Club. Having played with the 8080-based Altair computer, Wozniak felt that he could build much better and much cheaper computers by using the 6502 micro-processor that had only just been announced. He designed and created a sophisticated home computer kit for the members of the Homebrew Club to play with; and he persuaded a 21-year-old friend and fellow club member, Steve Jobs, to come into business with him to develop and market the computer throughout local electronics shops. Apple Computers Ltd. was officially formed on 1 April 1976.[4] The Apple 1 went on sale in July of that year at 666.66 dollars, dropping to around 500 dollars the following year.

The Apple 1 had a keyboard, an interface to a standard television set, and a socket to allow programs to be loaded from an ordinary cassette-tape player. It came with an implementation of BASIC, developed by Wozniak from the original Dartmouth College system. It even supported some simple games, including *Mastermind*, *Star Trek* and the *Lunar Lander* program. It was a first step along the road to successful home computing. But it was only a fraction of the journey to come, as Apple introduced the much more powerful Apple II in May 1977.

By 1980 there was a host of computers serving the fast-growing home market. The Acorn and Commodore machines were all based, as the Apple-1 and II were, on the 6502; and the Atari ST was based on the new 6800 microprocessor launched by Motorola. Finally, based on the Zilog Z80 microprocessor, there was the first of the home computers launched by Clive Sinclair, the ZX80 – now remembered as something of a novelty but for a time the fastest-selling computer in the world. Home computing was a thriving, energetic market, and that was enough to attract IBM's attention, who saw it beginning to eat into their corporate computer revenue as these 'home' computers began to be used by businesses for small-scale accounting and office administration tasks. They decided that they too would produce a home computer.

Development of the IBM Personal Computer began in October 1980, based on the Intel microprocessor range. The first IBM PC went on sale on 12 August 1981, and by Christmas of that year, a phenomenal 100,000 had been sold at a price of 2880 dollars a unit. It had competition, of course, and quite stiff competition at that: from the Z80-based ZX81 in 1981; the 6502-based BBC Micro in 1982; the 6502-based Commodore 64 in 1982, along with the ZX Spectrum; and finally, in January 1984, the Motorola 6800-based Apple Macintosh.

With the sole exception of the Apple Macintosh, the IBM PC beat off all competition, going from strength to strength with a variety of increasingly powerful models such as the XT in 1983 and the AT in 1984. What helped this computer model to succeed, however, was not the technical specification; arguably, the Apple Macintosh, based on the Motorola microprocessor, was (and still is) much more sophisticated. Rather, it was the fact that the specification was an 'open' one, so that any other company was free to develop an IBM PC-compatible computer. In 1982 Compaq were the first to market with a PC clone, the Compaq Portable.

The pattern of computer development for the rest of the 1980s, the 1990s and the first few years of the 21st century was essentially set. As Motorola produced increasingly powerful versions of the basic 6800 microprocessor, new versions of the Apple Macintosh appeared under a variety of names: the Macintosh Plus, II, SE, LC, Classic, and so on. As increasingly powerful Intel microprocessors appeared, such as the 8086, 80286, 80386, 80486, and the Pentium range, then IBM PC clones from a staggering variety of companies implemented them – in units ranging from a desk-side tower module to a laptop, and then even a palmtop-sized module.

The home computer market has grown on the back of the IBM PC clone, as has the 'workstation' market within companies. Where simple, unintelligent or 'dumb' teletype terminals with just a keyboard and a screen were used to communicate with the original mainframes, these cheap PCs are now used as workstations. They are wonderfully flexible, able to perform local processing tasks but also to interact with the company's central servers and with one another over network connections. The whole thrust of computing has changed. As the motto of Sun Microsystems has it, 'The Network is the Computer' now.

From the room-sized monsters produced by Konrad Zuse and Mauchly and Eckert, computers have shrunk to the point where even slim IBM PC clone laptops might be considered bulky and entire computers can now be squeezed into pocket-sized devices complete with miniature screen, keyboard and stylus input. The progression, though, is a logical one, as processors have shrunk and the features of the systems have become increasingly sophisticated. However, perhaps the greatest impact on the way that computers have developed – or at least in the way that computers are now used – was made not by Intel, IBM or Apple, but rather by a company more usually associated with printers and photocopiers, Xerox.

In the 1960s, at the Stanford Research Institute in California, Douglas Englebart developed a dramatically different idea for the interaction of humans and computers. In place of the text-driven command–response interfaces typical of the time, Englebart envisaged a flexible interface of multiple windows and a pointer based on his invention of a wheeled device he dubbed a 'mouse'.

Called the 'online system' (abbreviated to NLS), this interface was demonstrated by Englebart in December 1968 on an immense 20-foot video screen in San Francisco. NLS included graphical user interfaces and hypertext links between documents, following a model for textual information display that had been developed by a Harvard graduate student, Ted Nelson, in 1960 and made public in 1965. Whole documents, or in some cases paragraphs within documents, were linked to others, the links being displayed on the screen as lines between the documents concerned. The user could explore the texts and navigate between them, following their own particular interests and using the mouse to select where they wanted to go. It was recognizably a primitive form of the modern interface and hyperlinks of the World Wide Web.

The NLS was farsighted and original, but it was immensely complex to use. As a result, it was never destined to be a research success, let alone a commercial one. The same, unfortunately, was true of the system developed by Nelson. His hypertext environment was called 'Xanadu', and though Nelson has continued to work on it right up until the present day, it too has always been overshadowed by the systems that it inspired. However, Englebart's central ideas of a collection of windows and a pointing device controlling hypertext were taken by SRI researchers when they moved across the road to the Xerox Palo Alto Research Centre at the end of the decade.

Xerox PARC was, for a short time in the 1970s, *the* leading innovative research centre for computer use and interaction. The modern ball-style mouse (as opposed to a wheeled version created by Englebart) was developed there, as were graphical user interfaces, local-area networks, laser printers, and even so-called WYSIWYG (What You See Is What You Get) text editors. Almost *every* aspect of modern computer use was created at Xerox PARC at that time, as elements in the production of one of the earliest desktop computers, the Xerox Star, in 1981.

The Star was intended to be part of a total office environment (hence the laser printer and the network capabilities), so extending the influence that Xerox had in business-information processing, thanks to its dominance in the printer and photocopier market. Unfortunately, the Star was a long way from being a success, with Xerox lacking the marketing belief to push the technology as hard as they might. A chance visit by Apple's Steve Jobs in the late 1970s, however, resulted in many of the Xerox WIMP (Windows, Icons, Mouse and Pointers) ideas being introduced into the new Apple Macintosh computers and from there into the IBM PC clones running the Microsoft Windows system.

Other common features of the modern computer world slipped almost unnoticed into our day-to-day experience through equally opportunistic events. The floppy disk was invented in Japan in 1950; the compact disc in 1979. LaserJet printers first appeared in 1984, and CD-ROMs in 1985. Sophisticated colour monitors were produced in 1987, as were sound cards to support computer games. And the World Wide Web was invented in 1989.

In many ways, it seems as though the computer has appeared almost overnight; in other ways, that is has had a long, slow germination. It is sobering, though, to realize that at the time my father was born on 30 October 1936, a young engineering student in Berlin was building a cumbersome and noisy calculator and a young mathematician in Cambridge was producing the first computational model. On my father's birthday there were quite literally no computers in the world. The development of those huge, cumbersome, complex machines during my father's lifetime has been *unimaginably* staggering. From non-existence to world domination in one man's lifetime is quite an achievement.

3

How do computers work?

'Okay, now I know the answer is likely to be, "It's magic, Dad!"...
But I really do want to know how this thing actually works. Not
simply how I work it, but how it works! And of course, what all
these numbers are that the people in the computer shops keep
throwing at me... all these "megabits" and things...'

'Well, first of all, it's definitely not by magic...'

One of the most pernicious myths about computers is that they
are impossibly complicated, well beyond the ability of all but a
PhD-qualified computer scientist to understand. This is simply
not true. Computers are actually among the simplest devices that
we have ever developed, doing just one thing: they allow a small
electric charge to be passed from one storage cell to another.

Viewed under an electron microscope, a silicon chip is like an
aerial view of a busy city at night. Some parts are dark, others are
lit up where a charge is being stored; and a stream of light (like
the city traffic rushing from junction to junction) flows from place
to place as the electric charges are shunted around the storage and
processing components.

A computer carries out this single, simple task of allowing
electric charge to flow. It does so, however, in a very regulated
way, driven by the heartbeat of an internal clock; and it does it
very quickly and an enormous number of times. It decides
whether the charge is going to flow or not by applying a small set

of very simple rules, the *logic* of the computer operation. What makes computers so powerful is the complex combinations of these very simple-minded tasks so as to perform ever more sophisticated activities and actions. In many ways, a computer can be thought of as a 'stupid-smart' machine, a name dreamt up by the philosopher/computer scientist Douglas Hofstadter at the dawn of the microprocessor era.[1]

Representing numbers

One of the few things that everyone knows about computers is that they work with just two numbers, 1 and 0: they are *binary* devices. Given that people normally count and do arithmetic in decimal, with a full 10 digits, this might well seem something of a restriction. There is, though, definitely method in this apparent madness.

For mathematics performed in decimal (base 10), a number is written out in what is called 'positional notation', where each position represents 10 to an increasing power. For example:

$$5689 = (5 \times 10^3) + (6 \times 10^2) + (8 \times 10^1) + (9 \times 10^0)$$

Notice that 10^0 is 1 and that 10^1 is just 10. Counting the positions in this notation from 0 at the right-hand side, the number written in that index position is multiplied by 10 raised to the index. The final feature of decimal notation is that only 10 distinct number patterns are required; all the other numbers are formed by combinations of these.

Binary (or base 2) notation is similar but with only two distinct numbers, 0 and 1, the binary digits or 'bits'; and the positions correspond to powers of 2. So, taking a four-digit binary number such as 1011:

$$\text{binary } 1011 = (1 \times 2^3) + (0 \times 2^2) + (1 \times 2^1) + (1 \times 2^0) = \text{decimal } 11$$

Binary can represent any number, albeit with a greater length of digits, and is used in computers for one very simple reason: to solve the problem of *discrimination*. Numeric values inside a device need to be represented by some physical property of the device. In the days of mechanical calculators, these values were represented by the position of a series of cogwheels. In electronic computers, they must be represented by some other property: the presence or absence of an electric charge, voltage or current; a particular magnetic value; a colour of light; an intensity or frequency of sound; and so on. Once these properties have been determined, however, there is then a corresponding problem for the computer, that of discriminating between the two possible values when the actual property detected is not an exact match. For example, if voltage is used as the property for the value, with 0V for the number 0, +1V for number 1, +2V number 2, and so forth up to +9V for 9, then an obvious question arises: what if the actual voltage recorded is discovered to be +2.5V? Is this a number 2 or a number 3? Worse, what if the voltage is fluctuating rapidly between +2.4V and +2.6V? Which should the computer actually choose?

To work effectively, the computer's electronics would have to be engineered to a high degree of tolerance if this type of representation were used. That high tolerance would make such a device very expensive. Using binary values solves the problem elegantly and neatly. With only two widely separated voltage values, discrimination becomes easy and tolerance need not be a problem. If 0V represents number 0 and +9V represents 1, for instance, then there is little or no chance of confusion between the two unless the computer electronics are wildly inaccurate. The binary operation of computers means that two widely different values of some physical property can be applied easily and with the minimum chance of confusion between the two values.

So as to ensure that numbers are not confused with one another, computers therefore work with binary-number representation. However, computers seldom work with single bits but rather with fixed-width collections of binary digits called 'words': for example,1011 is a word that is four bits wide. The very first microprocessor produced by Intel, the 4004, worked with just 4-bit words. A larger word made up of eight binary digits is called a 'byte',[2] while larger words are usually formed from multiples of bytes – 2, 4 or 8 bytes, for example.

In these words of 8, 16 or 32 bits, a sizeable and useful range of numbers can be represented, though some form of representation scheme is required. In fact, computer engineers have used three different schemes for representing numbers in binary. The first was a superficially appealing scheme called 'binary-coded decimal', used most extensively in some of the early IBM computers. In this, the decimal digits 0 to 9 are represented by their binary values. Since decimal 9 is binary 1001, each decimal digit requires only four bits for storage. Decimal numbers of multiple digits are then represented by joining these together, so that in this scheme decimal 11 would be 00010001.

This coding scheme is possibly the most wasteful imaginable. With it, a one-byte word can only hold values up to decimal 99. The second scheme is much more efficient, using a 'pure binary' representation, so that decimal 11 is 00001011. With pure binary, one byte can hold values from 00000000 to 1111111111 – decimal 0 to 255. This is certainly an improvement over 99 and a more appropriate use of the byte storage in almost every case.

This scheme allows the byte to give the widest possible range of numerical values expressed in 8 bits, but it is not without its problems, most obviously that it cannot represent negative numbers. One simple way to solve this is to use the 256 patterns slightly differently, so as to give instead the numbers from −127 through 0 to +127. To do this, the bit at the far left-hand side of the word (called the 'most significant bit') can be used as the +/− sign. For example, the bit pattern 00001011 is decimal 11, whereas the bit pattern 10001011 is −11. This is called 'signed binary' because it uses a binary number with a sign to show whether it is a positive or negative value.

Although this is a simple and appealing idea, it suffers from one rather embarrassing flaw: simple arithmetic with pure-binary numbers does not work correctly when positive and negative numbers are added together. For example, −11 plus 11 should be 0, but in this notation it is actually −22, the 11 added to the 11 with the negative sign. This is a huge problem for any computer because the most efficient way of performing the subtraction function is by simply adding the negative of the number, so 5 minus 3 is actually done by 5 + (−3). If this simple number representation is used, then a dedicated subtraction module is required as well as the addition module, again adding to the complexity and cost of the machine.

A second, though much less important problem is that this simple sign scheme has *two* representations for binary 0: it has 00000000 and 10000000; a positive 0 and a negative 0. In most computers that have ever used this scheme, the −0 value is used as an error value to indicate when something has gone wrong.

A better representation for negative numbers is to use a scheme called '2's complement', in which the negative of a particular value is produced by inverting each bit and then adding 1. Decimal 11 is 00001011; inverting each bit − turning each 1 to a 0 and each 0 to a 1 − produces the pattern 11110100; and adding a 1 gives 11110101. So −11 in 2's complement is 11110101.

To see that this is indeed the negative, it is necessary to understand how binary arithmetic is done. It follows a very simple set of rules:

- 0 + 0 is 0;
- 1 + 0 and 0 + 1 is 1; and
- 1 + 1 is 0 but with 1 to carry to the next column.

A carry is produced when the result is greater than 1, just as in decimal addition a carry is produced when the result is greater than 9; otherwise the carry value is 0. Following these rules to add 00001011 to 11110101 produces 00000000, with a carry (which we can simply throw away) from the most significant bit position at the far left-hand side of the byte.

The 2's complement scheme for numbers in the pure-binary representation satisfies many of the important criteria. Negative numbers all have the most significant bit set, so that they are easily recognized, and they satisfy the basic rules of addition. As with the simple signed-binary scheme, it allows numbers from −127 to +127 to be represented, though interestingly there is no −0 value, since the 2's complement of 0 is in fact 0. There is therefore a bit pattern left over: the 10000000 pattern that was decimal −0 in the signed-binary scheme. Again, it can be used as an error value, or it can represent −128 if the computer designers prefer.

Other than that a 16- or 32-bit word rather than an 8-bit word is used, this 2's complement arithmetic is exactly the scheme used for simple arithmetic in almost all computers, including the powerful microprocessors of today. The scheme is fast, flexible and arithmetically correct – everything that could be hoped for in a binary representation. Unfortunately, though, whether in 8-, 16- or 32-bit words, the scheme only allows for the representation of whole numbers lying between the minimum negative value and the maximum positive value. What about larger numbers? What about fractions? To represent these, an altogether different scheme is applied: 'floating point', first used in the early machines designed in Germany by Konrad Zuse.

The floating-point scheme is often called 'scientific notation'. It represents values using a fixed number of digits and a specification for where within the string of digits the decimal point is to be placed. A pattern of digits such as 13579, for example, can be anything from 0.13579 to 13,579.0 – or an even wider range of values if the decimal point can be placed further to the right or the left.

To position the decimal point, the usual scheme applied is to 'normalize' the fixed digits (called the 'mantissa') so that it is of the form 1.3579 — a single leading digit followed by the decimal point and then the remaining digits of the fixed-length string of values. To shift the decimal point to the right (so as to make 13.579 or 135.79, etc.), the mantissa simply needs to be multiplied by 10 or 100 or 1000 as required. Conversely, to shift the decimal point to the left, so as to make a fraction, the mantissa needs to be divided by 10, 100 or 1000 as required. This shifting can be achieved by multiplying the mantissa by a power of 10: 10^0 if the decimal point is to stay where it is; 10^2 to move it two places to the right; 10^{-1} to move it one place to the left; and so on. The 0, 2 or -1 is referred to as the 'exponent'.

To represent a floating-point number, over a vast range of different values, it is only necessary to store the mantissa, the exponent, and whether each of those values is positive or negative. For example, in an eight-bit word, a floating-point number might be represented by three bits for the exponent (a sign bit and two exponent-value bits) followed by five bits for the mantissa (again, a sign bit and then four mantissa-value bits). In this way, the size of the numbers represented can range from fractions in the region of 10^{-3} all the way to larger numbers in the thousands, 10^3. The values themselves, with four mantissa bits, can range from decimal 0 to 15, positive and negative. This clever scheme can therefore be used to represent decimal fractions in the range from +/−0.0015 up to +/−1500.

Floating-point numbers, however, cannot be handled by the simple arithmetic operations of whole binary words, such as the bit-by-bit addition of 2's complement used above. Instead, more complex activities need to be carried out by the computer. The mantissa and exponent elements have to be separated out of the word and handled differently, before being recombined in the result. This is a complex and time-consuming activity for the computer, so most modern microprocessors now have dedicated 'floating-point processors', either as an entire second processor (called a 'co-processor') or built into the main processor, as in the Intel Pentium microprocessor. Although this makes for a substantially more complex processor unit, it has the advantage of making the computer significantly faster. It is one of the primary reasons why modern personal computers are so very good at handling the graphics processing required for computer games, for example.

In practice, modern computers use words much larger than 8 bits to represent the floating-point numbers. Word sizes of 32 bits allow a truly phenomenal range of numbers to be handled, with large exponents and very precise mantissa values. It is important to recognize, though, that *still* only 2^{32} different numbers on the number line can be represented. The floating-point scheme provides a means of specifying a selection of numbers (around 4 billion with 32 bits), but they are still just widely separated beads along the whole number line. The numbers that can be represented are clustered together in small bunches of values along the number line, representing no more than a tiny subset of the infinity of values in reality.

Despite this limitation of only being able to represent a small fraction of the available numbers, computers are of course remarkably successful calculating devices – astonishing given that they only actually perform four different types of operation. These are represented by three 'gates' and a 'shift'.

Processor gates

All that computers do is to allow a minute electric charge to pass from one place to another according to the rules of 'logic' that they have been designed to apply. These rules of logical operation are actually implemented by three types of gate that control

whether or not the charge is allowed to pass: **AND**, **OR** and
NOT gates.

The **NOT** gate is the simplest. It has one path into it and one
path out of it. If there is an electric charge on the input path, then
no charge is put on the output path; conversely, if there is *no*
charge on the input, then the output *does* have a charge. The
NOT gate acts to invert the signal, turning a binary 1 into a 0 and
a binary 0 into a 1.

By contrast, the **OR** and the **AND** gates have two paths into
them and one path out. For the **AND** gate, both input paths have
to be carrying an electric charge for the gate to put a charge on
the output path. If neither input or only one input path has a
charge, then the output does not carry a charge. For the **OR** gate
to put a charge on the output path, one or both of the input paths
must be carrying a charge.

Computer scientists and mathematicians usually describe these
two gates with the following tables:

AND	0	1
0	0	0
1	0	1

OR	0	1
0	0	1
1	1	1

For completeness, the **NOT** table is:

NOT	0	1
	1	0

These gates can be combined to give a very simple addition
facility for a computer, called a 'bitwise adder'. The adder has two

inputs and two outputs: the inputs are the two bits that are to be added; and the two outputs are the *result* and the *carry* value. These two output values can be described with a pair of tables:

RESULT	0	1
0	0	1
1	1	0
CARRY	0	1
0	0	0
1	0	1

The adder can create these output values by combining **AND**, **OR** and **NOT** gates appropriately. First of all, notice that the CARRY table is identical to the **AND** table above, so the carry output can be produced simply by combining the two input values with an **AND** gate:

A **AND** B

Next, the RESULT table is almost the same as the **OR** table, except for the '1 + 1' item, which is inverted. So the result is A **OR** B unless A **AND** B is 1. This can be written as:

(A **OR** B) **AND NOT** (A **AND** B)

Mathematically, this is a simple expression (though it undoubtedly looks frightening at first glance to a non-mathematician), and the earliest computer pioneers found it straightforward to implement mechanically or electromechanically through switches. The simplest to construct is the **OR** gate. If the binary values 0 and 1 are expressed as voltage levels (0V and 1V, say), then the switch can be engineered so that it only requires 1V of input before it opens to allow a 1V electric circuit to be completed. The **AND** gate is only slightly more complicated. This can be constructed so that it completes a 1V circuit only when its input is 2V. Finally, the **NOT** gate is simply a switch that opens to break the 1V circuit when it receives 1V on its input, or closes to complete the 1V circuit when the input is 0V.

Electromechanical switches were very simple to apply to logical operations and to calculation. They were first proposed by Claude Shannon in 1938 in his doctoral thesis at the Massachusetts Institute of Technology. He described how the symbolic logic developed by the British mathematician George Boole in 1848 could be used to analyse complicated telephone switching circuits. From this basis, Shannon quickly realized that the inverse was true – that Boolean symbolic logic and hence arithmetic on binary numbers could easily be *implemented* by switches. Interestingly, as well as for this and for his achievements in the fields of cybernetics and information transmission, Shannon is also remembered as the man who first coined the word 'bit' for a binary digit.

Other than being noisy, slow and unreliable, switches worked well.[3] But while the application of electromechanical switches in this context is straightforward, the purely electronic elements are perhaps more difficult to understand. The first of the electronic elements to be used in computers was the 'vacuum tube' or 'valve', a glass bulb from which air had been pumped. A vacuum is an excellent insulator, but a sufficiently high voltage allows an electric current to 'jump' the gap from one electrified plate to a second plate at a distance from it. This was exactly how the early valves worked, with two plates separated from one another inside a vacuum. When the voltage was below the threshold value for the current to jump, no current passed between the plates; when the voltage was high enough, it did. In this way, the valve could act as a crude switch.

Implementing the logic gates was simple in these early valve computers, though the valves themselves were prone to breaking, became very hot, and required high voltages actually to work. Little wonder that when William Shockley and colleagues at Bell Laboratories in New Jersey invented the transistor at the end of 1947, computer engineers were keen to exploit the smaller, more reliable and much less power-hungry units.

'Transistor' is a corruption of the original name for these electronic items, which were at first called 'transfer resistors'. When he discovered them, Shockley had been experimenting with materials called 'semiconductors' — crystals that act as conductors but only under certain circumstances. For example, some semiconductors were known to pass no current at all until their temperature reached a particular threshold value. Once at that threshold, the crystals allowed current to pass; they are conductors, but only if their temperature is correct. Other forms of semiconductor were also known, including crystals that passed a current only if exposed to enough light, or which passed current in one direction but not in another.

Before Shockley, such semiconductor crystals were seen as scientific curiosities for which no really useful application had been found. Working with two different forms of germanium crystals, N-type and P-type, Shockley discovered that he could put these two different forms together in a sandwich arrangement (NPN or PNP) and then pass a current along the 'filling' between the two outermost semiconductor elements. When he did this, the semiconductor changed abruptly from one state to another: with no current to the filling, the semiconductor behaved as a resistor; with a current, it behaved as a conductor. Even more usefully, this 'transfer resistor' worked with a threshold current. It could be switched on and off as required, the ideal property for a switch.

At first glance, it might appear that the transistor is broadly similar to the vacuum tube, but there is a curious and very important difference. In the vacuum tube, the resistance to the current presented by the gap between the plates remains constant. This means that, when the threshold value for the current to jump across the gap is reached, only a trickle of electricity flows across and needs to be boosted (or 'amplified') at the far side of the valve. By contrast, in a transistor the current affects the *resistance* of the unit: below the threshold, the transistor has a very high resistance, but when the current reaches the threshold value, then the resistance changes abruptly to a new value. Because of this, there is either a circuit or no circuit; there is never only a 'trickle current' needing to be amplified.

The benefits in computer technology were enormous. The electromechanical circuits acted as switches to control a circuit. There was a fixed circuit representing the binary 1 value (say, 1V) that was established or broken depending on the setting of the switches. In this way, a binary 0 was represented by no electric current in the circuit and a binary 1 by the presence of an electric current. The switches, though, were slow, noisy and unreliable. By contrast, the electric-valve circuit used a vacuum as a threshold switch to pass or to block as appropriate an electric current (representing binary 1), but once the current had been passed, it needed to be amplified. The transistor switch, however, passed current just as a vacuum tube but without the requirement for the current to be amplified. More importantly, it did this with very small currents and proportionally less heat.

Transistors were perfect for creating the **AND, OR** and **NOT** gates so as to allow or prevent the flow of minute electric currents from place to place within a computer. Implementing the simple adder described above is then merely a question of connecting those gates together – an **OR** gate, a **NOT** gate and two **AND** gates:

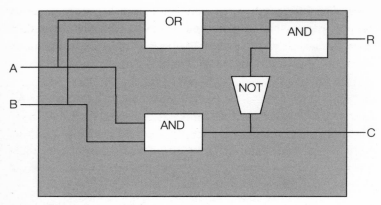

A simple half-adder with logic gates

This simple adder is actually called a 'half-adder' because, although it produces a carry value, it does not include a possible carry as a part of its input. A 'full adder' can be created from two half-adders:

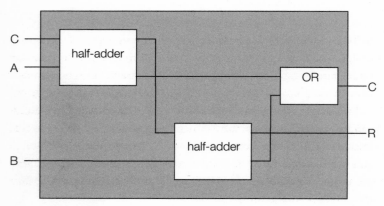

A full adder created from two half-adders

Finally, two words of any bit length can be added together simply by 'daisy-chaining' a sequence of these full adders together, with the initial 'carry-in' value being 0 and the final 'carry-out' value being used to indicate an 'overflow' condition.

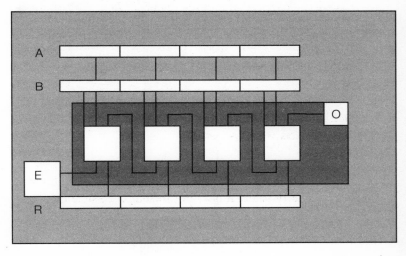

Adding two 4-bit words with full adders

These examples illustrate an important principle of computer design: build complex things from simple things that you already understand. Logic gates are the most fundamental building blocks, from which half-adders can be constructed; from these, single-bit full adders can be created; and from these, whole-word full adders can be made. This principle of increasing complexity from simple building blocks is followed again and again in computer design and is the single most important reason why understanding how computers operate simply requires a little knowledge rather than the intellect of a genius.

Full adders can be chained together to handle words of any bit length. Where the input words are expressed in the 2's complement scheme, they can support both addition and subtraction. They can even support multiplication, but only by the strategy of repetitive addition of one number to itself. A much better, faster, efficient and elegant solution to multiplication – and hence also to division – is achieved by the use of the fourth basic arithmetic device in a computer, the 'binary shift'.

To show how this works, take a simple multiplication: $12 \times 4 = 48$. In binary, these values are:

- $12 = 00001100$ $(8 + 4)$
- $4 = 00000100$ (or 2^2)
- $48 = 00110000$ $(32 + 16)$

Notice that the result is simply the original number shifted two places to the left; and that 2 is also the exponent of the power of 2 by which it was multiplied. Multiplication by powers of 2 can be achieved simply by shifting the original number (called the 'multiplicand') an appropriate number of places. Second, notice that *every* value (or at least every value that can be represented in a computer) is the sum of a finite number of powers of 2. For example:

$$9 = 8 + 1 = 2^3 + 2^1$$

This means that, for example, 9×12 is also $8 \times 12 + 1 \times 12$. Each of the multiples of 12 simply needs the binary for 12 to be shifted to the left three times for the 8 and not shifted at all for the 1. Multiplication can be achieved by a combination of shifting and adding the multiplicand, which makes the implementation of a binary multiplication device straightforward. The shift operation simply requires a skew connection between the input and the output.

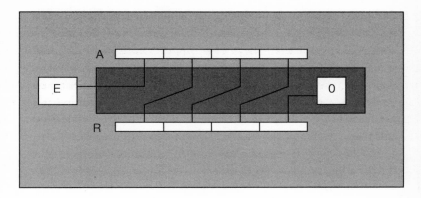

A shift gate between 4-bit words

In practice, the actual multiplication unit is more complicated than this. To support multiple shifts, corresponding to the power of 2 required, the result has to be fed back into the top of the shift unit; a counter has to be maintained of the number of single-bit shifts performed; and the shifted value has then to be added to the other results in order to create the final answer. This creates a complex and truly terrifying diagram, but following the principle of 'complicated things from simple things', it can be achieved through the use of adders, 2's complement values, and the simple shift gate shown above.

These three gates and a shift provide a simple, flexible set of building blocks from which an arithmetic unit for a computer can be constructed. With the 2's complement or the floating-point representation scheme for numbers, this gives the potential for a computer to perform any mathematical operation. Computers, though, do not simply handle numbers, they also need to handle *characters*.

Computer data

In English, there are 26 lower-case and 26 upper-case letters; 10 digits; a space and a tab character; and around two dozen punctuation symbols in regular use. In addition, there are some more specialized characters, such as the 'e acute', the 'c cedilla', and other accented characters in various European languages. All told, there are around 100 characters that a Western computer might routinely be expected to handle. This means that the character set can be easily represented by the 256 possible patterns of bits within an 8-bit byte. Indeed, the original definition of a byte was just that – the number of bits required to store a unique character in the computer's internal character-representation scheme.

The most popular character-representation scheme is the all but universally used ASCII scheme, the American Standard Code for Information Interchange. ASCII was devised in 1963 by one of the most irrepressible and creative individuals in computer history, Bob Bemer. Bemer has worked for very nearly every major computer company and has a list of inventions and radical ideas longer than most. In 1959 at IBM he proposed the idea of word processing; he coined the name COBOL for the business programming language developed initially as FLOW-MATIC by Grace Hopper; and he invented the concept of users 'time-sharing' access to large computers. He was even, in 1971, the first person to warn of the year 2000 problem, later called the 'millennium bug'. Perhaps his most important creation and certainly the one that has had the widest impact is the specification of ASCII.

This standard character code uses seven bits of an 8-bit byte to store all of the printable characters, along with the non-printable 'control' characters such as ESCAPE and DELETE.[4] Seven bits allow 128 characters to be represented, but it leaves the most significant bit (the bit furthest to the left) in the byte unused. Some clever strategies have been developed over the years to put that eighth bit to good use. One idea is to use the eighth bit to provide an extended character set, so as to encode lines and boxes for drawing simple shapes, or to represent Chinese, Russian or other non-European alphabets. When the eighth bit is 0, the remaining seven bits encode the 128 characters of normal ASCII; but when the eighth bit is 1, they encode these extended alternatives. This is perhaps the simplest scheme, but an alternative is to use the eighth bit as an 'error-detecting' bit.

Occasionally when a byte of information is transmitted (or even simply when it is stored in a faulty portion of memory), an error can occur in which a bit that should have been a 0 is flipped to become a 1, or vice versa. Characters can then become garbled and text can even end up being completely illegible. An error-detecting bit is a scheme for recognizing that a mistake has been made, so that faulty characters can then be retransmitted, for example. The simplest way to do this is through a 'parity bit'. In a byte there are several 1s: if there is an even number of 1s, then the parity is said to be even; otherwise the parity is odd. The eighth bit of the byte can be used to ensure that the parity is always even, say, by being set to a 1 or a 0 as appropriate to balance the existing parity of the seven ASCII code bits. This parity-correcting bit can detect a single-bit flip but not multiple errors. Nonetheless, it is a clever way of using the 'spare' bit at the end of the byte.

Computers can therefore represent numbers and characters as binary values, and can perform any arithmetic operation on the numbers. There are also schemes for storing pictures and for storing sound. For pictures, just as in a television, the image is divided into an array of 'pixels', or 'picture elements' – all the dots that make up the image. For colour pictures, a red, green and blue value is then given for each of the pixels, recorded either in one 8-bit byte (to give the 256-colour display mode), or in two or four bytes (16-bit or 32-bit colour).

For storing or transmitting pictures as files, this pixel colour map can be stored as a simple array of binary values, one line of pixels at a time. The simplest and oldest scheme of this kind is called 'bit-mapping' and was developed by Texas Instruments in the 1970s. It uses no compression scheme at all, simply storing the pixel values exactly as they are presented. This is sufficient for medium- to low-quality monochrome pictures, but for the now widespread high-quality colour pictures (particularly those stored and transmitted over the internet), a better scheme is needed. In 1987, CompuServe introduced a graphics code called GIF (Graphics Interchange Format) for its online users to download pictures. This scheme compresses the data and uses a clever inter-leaving of lines so that a partial, fuzzy image is displayed even before the picture has been fully downloaded. This partial display was introduced so that CompuServe users could abort the download if the picture was not the correct one.

Although it provides very high resolution and clear pictures, the GIF format uses only a very simple compression scheme, so it produces relatively large files. The alternative scheme used on the internet is the JPEG (Joint Picture Experts Group) format, invented in 1991 and standardized in 1992. JPEG uses a particu-larly sophisticated compression algorithm, allowing clear pictures to be represented in relatively small files.

As well as photographs, encoding schemes exist to represent sounds (either as individual frequency values or in some more compressed way) and moving pictures. In fact, every imaginable type of information that might be considered useful as data for a computer program can be represented by some binary encoding scheme. It is not enough, though, to be able to represent the values; it is also necessary to be able to *store* them.

Computer memory

Computers work by allowing a small electric charge to flow from one place to another, subject to the application of logical rules such as those embodied in the **AND**, **OR** and **NOT** gates. That charge, however, has to be stored somewhere, in a 'memory cell'. The earliest form of electronic memory cell was a pulse of noise reflecting through a tube of mercury about 5 feet long, called a 'mercury delay line'.

A pulse represented a binary 1 and no pulse represented a 0. The pulse would echo through the thin tube of mercury, reflecting off the back of the tube, in about one-thousandth of a second. The noise was created, detected and reinforced by electronics at the front of the tube, from where it could be read into the main processing elements of the CPU (central processor unit). Other kinds of delay line were also developed, including circuits in which an electronic pulse was bounced through a complex structure of valves.

Although this sounds awkward, clumsy and prone to problems, not to mention being physically gargantuan, with a veritable church organ's worth of piping to be maintained, it was the basis of the registers for many of the computer systems in the 1940s, including the original British computers at Manchester and Cambridge. The computer developed at Cambridge by Maurice Wilkes was actually called the Electronic Delay Storage Automatic Calculator; and Williams's computer at Manchester was specifically developed around the 'Williams tube' invented there.

Mercury delay lines were soon superseded by faster, smaller and much more reliable devices using a simple electronic component called a 'capacitor', an element that acts as a container for electric charges and allows the charge to bleed out slowly. Originally capacitors were made from two electrically charged sheets of metal placed close together. Charge ran into the plates until it reached a maximum level, at which point it bled back out again. Modern capacitors are embodied in germanium impurities in silicon chips, but the principle is the same.

A capacitor works as memory in a very simple way. If the charge contained in the circuit is more than half of the capacity, then the contents represent a binary 1; if less than half, a binary 0. The charge in the capacitor, however, is of course bleeding away at a known rate of flow. To correct this, every few fractions of a second the capacitor needs to be topped up with roughly the amount of electric charge that can be expected to have bled away. This is called the 'refresh cycle' and works constantly while the computer is turned on. When the contents of the memory cell are read, a simple detector circuit determines whether the capacitor is half or fully charged, so allowing it to be topped up as its charge passes to the appropriate part of the computer.

Inside a computer's CPU there is a small group of words made from these tiny capacitors. These words are used by the arithmetic and logic elements for 'scratch' storage and are called 'registers'. These register words contain the various operands for the operations to be performed (in the earlier diagrams of shift units and adders, the input and output values were read from these registers). Early microprocessors such as the Intel 8080, for example, typically had seven registers, each of eight bits. By contrast, a modern Intel Pentium microprocessor has 32 registers, each one 32 or even 64 bits wide. In many ways, the 'power' of a particular processor can be determined by how effectively it handles the rapid shuffling of data words between these several registers and the operation units.

In the very earliest computers these registers were the total memory available to the computer. They were hand-set (either directly by turning cogwheels or read from punched cards, paper tape, etc.) and the processor unit only had these few portions of storage to manipulate. Working with only a minute number of register words is not enough, however, and computers need an additional quantity of memory that is separate from the CPU registers and from which those registers can be filled and to which they can be saved as required. This additional memory is the computer's 'main memory', sometimes called the 'store'. It is an array of several thousand words of data, each one of which can be read directly into any one of the CPU registers, where it can be manipulated. This is RAM – memory that can be 'randomly accessed'. When they were first introduced, capacitor-based memories were simply too expensive to be used in this 'bulk storage' manner, so alternative forms of memory were considered.

One of the earliest forms of main memory was invented in 1949 by an MIT researcher, Jay Forrester, who was working on Project Whirlwind for the US Navy. Whirlwind was a digital computer system that was intended to provide the first true flight simulator for training bomber crews. In fact, the Navy decided to withdraw their funding, so instead in 1949 Whirlwind became the centrepiece of an even more ambitious project for the US Air Force, the SAGE automated air–defence system, which was used throughout the Cold War to protect the US homeland. For Whirlwind, Forrester proposed and refined a mechanism for storing binary values within a collection of ferromagnetic rings, called 'cores'.

The idea of using such cores to store binary values had first been proposed by a young Chinese American immigrant called An Wang of Harvard University as a part of his 1948 PhD in applied physics. But Wang, who would go on in 1951 to establish the still thriving Wang Laboratories, had proposed using the cores as a form of magnetic delay line. In this, in place of a mercury tube within which a physical pulse was echoed and stored, Wang proposed a string of ferromagnetic cores along which a magnetic pulse could be transmitted. It was certainly a 'core memory', but nothing like as sophisticated as the mechanism that Forrester proposed. His scheme was for a mesh of wires with a small ferro-magnetic core threaded where each pair of wires crossed. If that core was magnetized, it was read as a 1; otherwise a 0. The mesh of wires allowed a particular core to be detected or to be changed, allowing the memory value to be read or written.

These core memories were very successful, being faster, smaller and much more reliable than the cumbersome delay tubes that they replaced. A magnetic-core mesh of around 1000 16-bit words looked rather like a beekeeper's honeycomb in shape and size, in contrast to the unwieldy, jet engine-sized delay lines. They allowed computers to be made much smaller than the monsters of the 1940s, and until well into the 1970s, they were the staple of computer main memories (main memory is still often referred to as the 'core'). Unfortunately, magnetic-core memories were *very* difficult to construct, so they were expensive. In time they were replaced by the capacitor model, as these proved easier and cheaper to create in transistor form.

An unfortunate aspect of these capacitor-based memories is that all of their contents are lost once the computer is turned off and the refresh cycle is interrupted. For the transient data involved in specific calculations, this is not a problem, but for the data required to operate the computer, it can be devastating. The entire set of operating programs and information need to be recopied into the memory every time the computer is restarted, a process called 'booting' the computer. To achieve this, a second type of memory is available – read-only memory, or ROM.

In ROM, the binary values within the words are established by permanent circuits, which are either connected to indicate a 1 or broken to indicate a 0. When electricity is applied to the ROM unit, it will always then be seen to contain those values. The values themselves are set when the ROM is first created, in a process called 'blowing'. Some ROM can even be reprogrammed, though only in a special way. For example, Erasable Programmable ROM (EPROM) resets all of its contents to 1 if exposed to ultraviolet light; the values can then be re-blown in a special programming unit. There is also Electrically Erasable Programmable ROM (EEPROM or E-squared ROM), which can be reset directly by applying a control signal.

ROM and RAM are the two components of computer main memory. ROM holds the fixed contents which tell the computer how it is to work; and RAM holds the contents which are used as temporary storage as the computer operates. However, simply being able to *store* data is not sufficient. The computer must also be able to specify and to retrieve that data, and to write data back to memory at a specific location. The memory needs to be 'addressable'.

Computer memory works in a very simple way. Presented with a valid address, the memory responds with the contents of the specified word. The word is copied by the memory unit from the specified location to a register within the CPU – an operation called 'loading'. The address that is specified to the memory for the load operation is a number, and like every other number within the computer, it is specified in binary. The microprocessor has a specific 'address register' which holds the address value of the current memory element of interest. This register, like every other register in the processor, is of a fixed width. In the old 8080 microprocessor, it was actually formed of two 8-bit registers concatenated; in modern microprocessors, the register is 32 or 64 bits wide. The width of the address register determines the largest possible 'addressable memory' that the computer can contain. A 16-bit address register can contain 2^{16} different bit patterns – 65,536, or 64 (2^6) times 1024 (2^{10}), possible values. This is usually expressed as 64 Kb. By contrast, a 32-bit register can contain 2^{32} different patterns – 4 (2^2) times 1,073,741,824 (2^{30}), or 4 Gb.

These computer terms for the large numbers expressible in binary can often appear to be impenetrable, but they are actually quite simple to follow. Notice that 2^{10} (1024) is roughly a thousand – the Kb stands for 'kilobyte', a thousand bytes. 2^{20} is then 2^{10} times 2^{10}, roughly a thousand times a thousand, or a million – a 'megabyte', a million bytes, or Mb. So 2^{30} is then roughly a thousand million, or a billion – the Gb stands for 'gigabyte'. Finally, 2^{40} is a trillion, or a 'terabyte' (Tb).

When computer magazines or product specifications talk of a '32-bit processor', it is the width of the CPU registers that are being quoted. These registers determine the maximum addressable memory that the computer can contain; they also determine the size of different data elements that can be held in that memory and handled as a unit by the processor registers. This is a raw measure of the processor's power. By analogy with a car, this would be comparable to the cubic capacity of the engine, for example.

Although a particular processor might have an address register of 32 bits, it can be fitted with considerably less memory than this. Even though silicon chip-implemented memory is cheaper than the old magnetic cores, it is still expensive. The laptop on which these words were written has a 32-bit wide address register but only 128 Mb of memory, so only 27 of the 32 bits available in the address register are actually being used – since 2^{27} is 128 Mb. Again, when computer magazines or product specifications talk of a '128 Mb laptop', it is this capacity that is being considered. The amount of memory determines how much information the computer can handle at a given time. This is a measure of the computer's efficiency. Again by analogy with a car, this would be comparable to the fuel economy.

128 Mb is a lot of information. To give some idea of scale, 1 Mb is roughly the amount of text contained in a 250-page novel – a full 2-inch deep packet of A4 paper would be required to print out 1 Mb. The information that could be held in 128 Mb would therefore produce a good wall's worth of paperback books and would require a pile of paper about as tall as two-storey house if it were to be printed out. Even though this sounds like a lot of information, it is nowhere near enough for a computer. No matter how much memory a computer has, it always needs more. This problem of always needing to use more memory than is

actually provided in main memory has dogged computing since the very earliest days. To solve it, computer engineers came up with the notion of a 'secondary memory'. This is a larger, cheaper but slower alternative memory that can be used to fill up the main memory as required.

Initially, on the old EDVAC-era computers, this secondary memory was implemented with either punched cards or paper tape shuffled manually by the operators. Faster mechanisms were required, though, as computers developed, and these were again provided by using magnetism: this time, not of ferromagnetic cores but rather of magnetized areas on some surface that could be accessed with a sensitive read/write head. Magnetic tapes were one of the earliest solutions.[5] For a whole generation, the picture of spinning tapes and of flashing lights is *the* image of a computer in operation.

Unfortunately, tapes suffer from two particularly difficult problems in the context of computer use. First of all, stopping and starting the tape inevitably results in the tape becoming stretched and damaged. Making tapes out of stronger, heavier materials helps, but that makes the tapes cumbersome, expensive, and even more difficult to stop and start. Some solutions were proposed and implemented to address this. For example, in 1950 IBM patented a scheme for retaining a *loop* of tape in a tube containing a partial vacuum, providing enough slack for the tape not to tear as it was stopped or started. Again, that image of the tape loop became emblematic of computers in operation.

The second problem is slightly more difficult to solve. Magnetic tapes are purely *sequential* storage media, so to reach an item of information at the end of the tape it is necessary to run through the entire tape – a process called 'spooling'. This makes tapes ideal in situations where information is to be read or written in a long stream, but far less satisfactory where the information is to be transferred to and from main memory in smaller, non-sequential chunks. To solve this, a magnetized surface that can be accessed wholly randomly is used. The first invention to provide this technology was a spinning drum, invented in 1948 by Andrew Booth of Birkbeck College, London.

Booth was another von Neumann protégé. He visited the Institute for Advanced Study at Princeton between March and September 1947 to see the work on the first stored-program computer. He was accompanied by his research assistant, Kathleen Britten, and both of them in fact got much more out of that visit than simply an understanding of and a fascination for the stored-program concept, since Kathleen became Mrs Booth shortly afterwards. The pair worked on the development of a series of stored-program computers, the APEC (All Purpose Electronic Computer), throughout the 1950s. This was a series of computers which were eventually produced and marketed by the British Tabulating Company, in time to become the International Tabulating Company and thereafter ICL.

Booth produced his prototype magnetic-drum storage device in January 1948, only months after returning from Princeton and all too aware of the problems of memory. It was not, however, his first idea about how to implement magnetic memory. Initially, Booth experimented with a flexible disk covered with a magnetized coating – a 'floppy disk'. Unfortunately, he found the reliability of this mechanism a long way below his requirements, and he abandoned the floppy disk in favour of the magnetized, spinning-drum idea. In retrospect, had Booth experimented for longer with the magnetic floppy, then we might have credited him with the important invention of this ubiquitous disk. As it is, credit instead goes to a researcher at the Imperial University in Tokyo, Yoshiro NakaMats, who perfected the magnetic coating in 1950 and licensed the resulting technology to IBM. In 1970, IBM began to market the original 8-inch floppy disks, originally for use on their System/360 mainframe computers.

Booth's prototype drum memory was tiny at 2 inches in diameter and just 2 inches long, holding 10 bits per inch. Though it looked like a spinning desk toy, the machine actually worked. Bigger drums followed hard on the heels of this prototype. Booth created drums with 32 concentric magnetized bands along the outer surface, each divided into 32 words of 32 bits. A read/write head was placed on a spindle that ran the length of the drum. The spindle could be moved up or down the drum length so as to be positioned over a particular band. Then it simply read off the magnetic values as the drum spun beneath it. It was simple, fast and effective. Booth implemented this device for all the computers that he built at Birkbeck throughout the 1950s.

The magnetic-drum idea clearly worked and so was inevitably copied by others working in the field. At Manchester University, for example, Frederick Williams and his team working on the Mark 1 took Booth's basic idea and implemented it as an important element of the machine. It became a secondary memory to supplement the delay-line main memory (the Williams tube) that had been invented specifically for the machine.

Over the years that followed, this basic magnetic drum became the staple of computer secondary memory until it was slowly supplanted by hard platters (as opposed to floppy disks). The first hard disk was developed by IBM and launched on 4 September 1956 for use with the IBM 350 range of mainframe computers. The RAMAC was the Random Access Method of Accounting and Control, a six-foot tall tower of 50 spinning disks two foot in diameter, mounted one above the other on a spindle. Each metal disk had a ferromagnetic coating arranged in a series of 100 concentric tracks on the top and bottom surfaces. An array of read/write heads were able to move as a unit across the disk surface so as to read the tracks on every disk. It was quick and, for the time, high-capacity – the entire RAMAC unit could hold 5 Mb of data.

The first RAMAC unit was sold to a San Francisco paper mill in 1957. At an annual leasing cost of 35,000 dollars, the RAMAC was by no means a cheap storage option, so drum storage continued to be widely used throughout the 1960s. The hard-disk platters had one huge advantage over the drum solution, however. Though they were more expensive, they provided a greater 'data density'. In a given floor space within a computer room, more data could be stored on a disk array than could be stored on a drum. As the data-storage requirements of computer users continued to escalate, the advantages of disk storage gradually became more important until eventually drum storage was completely superseded by vast disk farms of multi-platter disk drives.

These disk drives were enormous devices. Each drive was roughly the dimensions of a top-loading washing machine, into which a heavy module of 8 or 16 multi-platters was fitted. The disks themselves came in clear plastic carriers with twist-release handles on the top. They were heavy, delicate and prone to problems. Perhaps the most disastrous of the problems that could beset a hard disk was a 'head crash'. The read/write heads had to ride within fractions of an inch of the surface of the fast-spinning disk, cushioned by a layer of compressed air blown across the surface. The slightest trace of grease, dirt or even a human hair was enough to drag the head down onto the surface, gouging a circle of damage across the disk and destroying the head.

To solve these problems, IBM engineers began to look for ways of making sealed-unit disk drives. This meant that they had to make the drives themselves much smaller than the washing-machine size of the time, so that whole drive units rather than disk-platter packages could be swapped and moved as required. The codename for the development project was 'Winchester'. The result was the Winchester disk, ancestor of all modern hard-disk drives, launched in 1973.

By 1980, Winchester drives were being sold by several manufacturers and had become standard packages in a sealed unit
roughly the size of a shoe box, containing a read/write head and
a single 5½-inch hard disk holding 5 to 10 Mb of data. In
comparison with the six-foot tall RAMAC drives of the previous
generation, the Winchester drive seemed like a miracle. Perhaps
even more than the silicon-chip microprocessor, the Winchester
drive is responsible for the way in which computers gradually
came to be small and cheap enough to be used at home.

Modern computers use capacitor memories implemented in
silicon chips, supported by secondary hard-disk storage on units
that are the direct descendant of those Winchester drives – but
which now typically contain some 40 to 160 Gb of data storage.
Floppy disks have also become standardized on the 3¼-inch
format first developed by the Sony Corporation in 1980 – though
these are gradually disappearing in favour of high-capacity
'memory sticks'. And first CD-ROMs, developed by Sony and
Philips in 1983, and now DVDs have become the higher-capacity
storage of choice. For larger systems, tape drives are now used
purely as a tertiary storage system, to back up the hard drive in
case of a now very rare hard-disk failure.

The memory structures themselves have also developed in
sophistication. Modern microprocessors have a large set of local
high-speed registers used to hold the current instruction and the
most immediate data elements to be worked on. They also have a
larger set of memory locations within the processor itself, acting
at the same speed as the registers. This is called the 'on-board
cache' memory, where recently executed instructions or recently
modified data are copied in anticipation that they might shortly be
needed again. The main memory, where programs and data are
stored awaiting the processor's attention, is divided into RAM

and ROM: RAM for the variable elements and ROM for the fixed elements of the operating-system program. Because RAM and ROM are limited in size, a dedicated part of the main disk drive (called the 'swap space') provides yet another form of memory and is used to make it appear as though there is even more main memory.

Instructions and data are shuffled rapidly and dizzily between each of these storage locations. Programs exist on the main hard-disk drive in a dedicated file. When the program is to be executed, the contents of this file are copied to the disk's swap space. From there, as much as possible of the program file is copied into the main memory. The first instruction is then loaded into the processor's registers, and in anticipation that they will soon be needed, the next few instructions are also copied across to the processor cache. The result is the fastest-possible execution of programs, with as much of the data and instructions retained as near to the microprocessor as can be managed.

The technology has moved on dramatically from the clumsy, slow electromechanical devices of two generations ago. Naturally, though, it is still necessary to have some way of telling that technology what it is supposed to be doing. There needs to be some way of instructing the computer, and that requires a program.

4

How are computers programmed?

'Let me check I understand this… Pascal was named after Blaise Pascal? Fortran means Formula Translator? Cobol stands for Common Business Oriented Language? But C is called C for no better reason than that it's the letter that comes after B?'

'Hey, I never said it had to make any sense, did I?'

As described above, computers work by simply allowing small electric charges to flow from storage cell to storage cell according to certain rules of operation. This flow of electricity has to be directed in some fashion – it has to be *programmed*.

The basics of programming

The computer memory holds the initial state of the data that is to be processed in some way. This could be a collection of numbers to represent air pressure, wind speed and temperature; or characters in a document; or perhaps data items in a database. To the computer hardware (the electronic devices handling the binary data patterns), the actual *meaning* of the bit patterns is irrelevant. The computer program is a series of instructions that direct the processor in the precise operations and alterations that are to be performed on that data, piece by piece until the work is completed. The weather is forecast, the document is edited or the database is analysed. The computer program gradually changes the initial state of the data collection in memory until it has reached a final state, the result.

In a von Neumann computer, which is what all but a handful of modern computers actually are, this process of change is called a 'locus of control'. The computer reads an instruction from memory; it follows that instruction to make a tiny change to the data collection; and then it selects another instruction. Incidentally, it is also the computing model developed by John von Neumann that is responsible for the spelling of 'program'. With such heavy American influence on the development and operation of computers, British engineers adopted the American spelling in computing terms, even though the British spelling of 'programme' was retained in other contexts.

These program instructions, just like the data on which they operate, are stored in the computer's memory. In some early computers, such as the older DEC PDP machines, the instructions and the data were held in wholly separate computer memories. This was called 'split I and D' storage. In modern computers, instructions and data share the same memory and are often intermingled with one another, with the programs themselves keeping track of which memory locations are to be used as data to be modified and which are instructions to be followed. This means that the instructions are simply binary patterns represented in the memory words. The representation scheme is called the 'instruction set' of the computer. In the instruction set, different bit patterns within an instruction word (16 or 32 bits in modern computers) cause the processing unit to handle the words in memory in slightly different ways.

Some instructions make the processor copy words from memory to the processor registers; other instructions make the processor add, multiply or alter the contents of a specific register; yet others make the processor read instructions from a different memory location than before. The instructions achieve this by opening gates that allow the data and address word contents in the registers to flow from place to place within the computer. These control gates are placed on the conducting paths between storage cells and the AND, OR and NOT gates that make up the different processing elements within the computer. Between each register and each processing element (performing a distinct and different task within the computer) are data paths interrupted by gates, themselves operated by the instructions. In most processor architectures and therefore in most instruction sets, this is achieved by a 'decision tree' structure of branching data paths. If the data is to be handled by the arithmetic unit for add or multiply, the data path goes in one direction; if the data is to be handled by the logic unit for OR, AND or NOT, then it goes in another. If the data is destined for the arithmetic unit, then the next gate makes the 'add or multiply' decision, sending the data in the correct direction for processing.

In the instruction words, these decisions are represented by 1s or 0s in different places in the instruction. The first bit might be a 1 for arithmetic operations and a 0 for logical; the second bit might then be 1 for an add or for an AND depending on the data route being followed. An example 8-bit instruction word might then have the following structure:

- Arithmetic or Logical : 1 bit
- + / × ; AND / OR : 1 bit
- 1st operand register : 3 bits
- 2nd operand register : 3 bits

In these forms of instruction sets, typically the result is directed back into the first operand register when completed. This instruction type would allow a computer to have an architecture of eight data registers and to carry out simple operations on the contents of those registers. For example, 11010001 can be interpreted as 'Using the arithmetic unit, add register 2 to register 1 and put the result in register 2'.

Modern instruction sets are of course more complicated than this, though the original instructions for the Zilog Z80 microprocessor were not much different. In modern 32-bit instruction sets, there are one, two and three-operand instructions. These, for example, perform a NOT on a specified register (one-operand instruction); put the contents of a specified register in the memory word specified within the second register (two-operand instruction); or add the contents of two specified registers together, putting the result in a third register (three-operand instruction). In 32 bits some very complex combinations of operations can be specified and followed by the computer.

These instructions, however, need then to be *sequenced*. The computer needs a way of controlling the timing of different operations so that the necessary data is in the correct place when it is actually needed. If this sequencing is not carried out, then the processor might well find itself adding two old values together while the correct value is still being transmitted along a data path to the arithmetic unit. To carry out this sequencing, the processor follows the strict heartbeat of an internal clock, so that gates are opened or closed only when the clock 'ticks'. The rate at which the clock ticks then determines how rapidly different operations can be performed − or rather, the time taken to move operands and instructions from place to place within the computer determines how quickly the clock should tick.

Modern computers have clocks that tick *very* quickly. For example, Pentium 4 processors routinely now operate at 3GHz frequencies − that is, the clock ticks over *three billion* times a second. Not every tick equates to an operation, rather to the action of a gate or series of gates. It may take several gate sequences for an operation to be performed, but the more rapidly the gates can be opened and closed, the faster the computer. Again in car terms, this clock speed is roughly analogous to the acceleration figures.

The programmers' task is therefore to direct the operation of these control gates, through a complex sequence of carefully selected instructions. This is now done in sophisticated high-level languages, but originally the exercise was an awful lot more difficult, when the machine had to be directed explicitly in 'machine code' – its native language, binary.

Machine-code languages

The first computers were programmed directly. The instruction values (in these early days, the specification of which switches were to be opened and closed in a given order) were entered directly by the engineer. In his Difference Engine, Charles Babbage devised switching and control sequences to carry out various tasks; and Ada, Countess Lovelace devised even more sophisticated sequences. The Difference and Analytical Engines, however, were at best only approximations to stored-program computers. Since they were never actually built in Babbage's time, it is a moot point whether they were ever actually programmed in reality.

The first *true* professional programmer is now widely recognized as being a blind German mathematician called August Fast, employed by Konrad Zuse to program instructions for his Z3 machine in 1941. Fast lived in an institute in Berlin and was considered useless for the German war effort, but Zuse was confident that Fast, as a mathematician, would be invaluable to him in directing the operation of his computing device. Also, as Zuse himself later confessed, he was also confident that Fast would not suddenly be rushed into the army and therefore snatched away from him.

Zuse and Fast called their programs for the Z3 (and later for the Z4) *Rechenplane* or 'reckoning plans'. Between them, the pair devised a flexible scheme for representing numeric calculations (which was the extent of Zuse's computing ambitions in this period), using a mathematical scheme called 'reverse Polish notation', created in 1920 by the Polish mathematician Jan Lukasiewicz.

Lukasiewicz was born in 1878 and was professor of logic and twice rector of Warsaw University in the years between the World Wars; he was even the Polish minister of education in 1919. In 1946, he fled Poland for Belgium and eventually settled in Ireland, where in 1949 he became professor of logic and was awarded an honorary PhD by University College Dublin. Lukasiewicz worked on a staggering variety of subjects which have only recently begun to be useful in computer science. One in particular was 'fuzzy logic', in which the *true* or *false* state can be partial rather than absolute and which is proving invaluable in studies of artificial intelligence. His lasting work, however, was in the reverse Polish notation, developed primarily as a tool for analysing logical expressions; it only later became useful for arithmetic calculation.

In this notation, instead of writing '3 + 4', one would write '4 3 +'. This might not seem like a wonderful development, but it produces a structured description of mathematical expressions in which brackets for grouping terms are not required. This makes the expressions much easier for computers to handle and was adopted by Zuse and Fast for application in their *Rechenplane*. Zuse's true genius, however, lay in devising a sophisticated programming language quite unlike any other – until the relatively recent development of more mathematical, non-von Neumann languages.

Zuse called this language 'Plankalkül' – 'Plan' as in *Rechenplane*, and 'kalkül' from the German word for calculus. Plankalkül was a calculus of computing plans. Plankalkül supported a rich variety of concepts in what we now call 'high-level' programming languages. It allowed for repeated sections of code; it had support for complex data structures formed from structured combinations of bits, or *Ja-Nein-Werte*, as Zuse called them; and it even had reusable procedures. Astoundingly, Plankalkül even had support for some programming operations that have only recently appeared in the most modern 'object-oriented' programming languages: for example, a single operation that selected individual entries from a large table of values depending on some specified property.

At a time in the 1940s when the most advanced computing developments in the USA and Britain amounted to clumsy calculators 'programmed' by the direct setting of relay-switch circuits, Zuse was creating and working with a sophisticated language easily the rival of the most modern. Zuse even developed a program to play chess on his early computers.

Unfortunately, Plankalkül was not publicized until a busy Zuse finally took the time to record the language's specification and details in a 1972 research paper. As a result, the programming language is often overlooked by historians of computer programs, who concentrate instead on the story of British and US developments. In truth, although Konrad Zuse's progress *was* astounding, it has had only the most peripheral impact on modern computer science, which has been influenced far more heavily by von Neumann and by the programming languages developed in that tradition.

Assembler languages

Of the computers in the tradition of the EDVAC specification,[1] the Manchester Mark 1 machine is considered to be the first to run a program. In July 1948, the Mark 1 computer ran a simple series of instructions programmed by Tom Kilburn. His first computer program for the Mark 1 was a simple mathematical routine to find the highest factor of two numbers.

The most striking aspect of this simple program is that it was written as a sequence of binary numbers forming the instructions for the computer to execute. The first computers were programmed directly in binary – not simply by entering the binary values into the computer's array of switches as on/off states, but by *thinking* of the program instructions as the switch settings required. These early computer programmers in the von Neumann tradition were battling not simply to express their requirements in machine instructions but also to formulate their thought processes in the necessary switch control sequences. Programming on these first clumsy and awkward computers was itself a clumsy and awkward exercise.

Not surprisingly, those tasked with instructing the Mark 1 (and a few months later, those working on the EDSAC machine for Maurice Wilkes in Cambridge) began to follow the route that, unknown to them, had been blazed by Zuse and Fast in Berlin half a decade earlier. They began to formulate their program instructions in a more stylized manner, now called 'assembler language'. Credit for the first assembler-language programming is given to Maurice Wilkes, who began to work with instruction symbols rather than binary values in 1950.

In many ways, it is at this point that the science of programming began. Before Wilkes and assembler language, computer engineers understood the capabilities of their hardware constructions to the most intimate degree possible. They had built the device and knew *exactly* what it was doing and what it was capable of. They also understood the finer details of the computing task that they wanted to have the machine perform. Assembler language, however, enabled them to begin to separate their programming tasks from the detail of the machine implementation it was to run on. As they began to work with an abstract language to express these instructions, the first programmers were therefore working with an idealized abstraction of their computing machines. They began to think in terms like *move register 1 to register 3*, instead of tasks such as *set the switch to open control gate 27 so as to allow the contents of register 1 to flow into register 3 when the clock next completes a cycle*.

The difference was immense. If the computer changed at all, if a new data route or a new control gate was introduced, then in the old style of thinking the computer operation would need to be quite dramatically reconsidered. In assembler language, though, the program was an 'abstract machine' that could then be implemented by binary instructions. This concept of *abstraction* is now central to computer science. Computers, programs and networks are all now thought of as layers of abstraction, with the detailed implementation of a given layer hidden from the layers above it. We think of an arithmetic unit rather than an adder; we think of an adder rather than a set of gates; and we think of gates rather than a set of transistors. Abstraction is what makes the science of computing achievable. Without abstraction, modern computers would not be possible and would certainly not be understandable and programmable. They would simply be too complex for anyone to understand.

The introduction of symbolic assembler instructions by Wilkes was the first and most important step in that abstraction process for the programming of computers. All the subsequent development in the science of computing proceeded from that simple first step. Although Wilkes and his team were unwittingly following the path already pursued by Zuse and Fast, they also made one particularly crucial advance that had not been achieved in Berlin: they told the world of their work and they made the emerging art of 'software development' into something of a science.

Throughout 1950, with a collection of computer programs to their name, Wilkes and the team at the Cambridge Computer Laboratory had begun to realize that a vast amount of their time was being spent in tracking down errors in those programs. This came to a head through the long vacation when Wilkes began to run the very first summer school in programming and had to address the issue of teaching relative novices about the necessary discipline. To make the task of teaching programming easier,

Wilkes devised the idea of reusable portions of programs. These were routines that had been tried and tested in other programs and could be relied upon to work correctly if used in a new program. In modern programming terms, Wilkes had invented the 'subroutine' – building blocks that were a slightly further abstraction of programming tasks and which could be combined into more complex structures. It was the beginning of the 'library' of reusable code at the Cambridge Computer Laboratory – a library used in all subsequent programs and one of the most important facilities provided by the laboratory as it began to offer general computing services to the university.

Wilkes formulated his approach to developing programs through the use of these general subroutines and wrote the world's first programming textbook, *The Preparation of Programs for an Electronic Digital Computer*, published in 1951. Though it would not come to have the name for another decade, Maurice Wilkes had invented the science of software development.

As the 1950s dawned, those programming computers were beginning to think in terms of the first level of machine abstraction. This was an idealized version of their hardware creation in which data words were copied and manipulated by instructions rather than by direct control of the switching gates; an abstraction in which these instructions were not specified as binary words but as slightly more meaningful expressions. While the physical computer was a 'binary machine', this first level of abstraction was an 'assembler-language' machine, and it allowed computer engineers to create some interesting concepts.

The basic elements of the assembler-language instructions were already in place by this time. Most obviously, the computers supported *jumps*. The von Neumann computer works by reading instructions sequentially from memory, in such a way that an instruction is copied into the processor, decoded and executed; the instruction that follows it is then copied into the processor. The address of each of the instructions is stored in a dedicated register called the 'program counter'. As each instruction is copied from the memory, this counter is increased by one so as to point at the next instruction. With a jump, however, an entirely new memory address is copied into the program counter, so that execution leaps abruptly from one sequence of instructions to another. On its own, this ability to shift execution from place to place in a computer program is not particularly useful. However, jumps are commonly determined by an instruction which tests the value of a specified register. If the register is not zero, for example, then the jump is executed; if it is zero, then execution continues along the original path. A 'conditional jump' like this allows the computer programmer to implement two important program building blocks – branches and loops.

In a *branch*, some condition is tested, such as whether the number in register 1 is greater than the number in register 2. If the condition is true, then one block of instructions is performed; otherwise, a whole alternative block of instructions is followed. In a *loop*, by contrast, a block of instructions is executed a number of times. For instance, a 'loop count' might be kept in register 1 and decreased every time the block of instructions is executed. The conditional-jump instruction tests the value of register 1, and if it is still greater than zero, jumps back to the beginning of the block of instructions.

To implement this, the assembler-language programmers used a 'label', a marker attached to a program instruction, usually at the top of a block of instructions. The jump instruction could then be given that label as the destination to be jumped to if the test is true. So, a loop might look like this:

```
Start:  loop-body instructions
        loop-body instructions
        loop-body instructions

        counter − 1
        test counter
        jmp nz Start:
```

The label at the start of the loop–body instructions here is 'Start'. The loop counter is decreased by one and then tested at the end of the loop body. The 'jmp nz' is a typical assembler-language instruction and means 'jump if the tested value is non-zero'. The location to jump to is specified by the label 'Start'.

There are two important things to notice in this fragment of assembler language. First of all, the use of a name ('counter') for a variable data item used in the program; the second is the label itself. Neither of these things actually *exists* in the binary computer that supports this assembler-language program; they are convenient abstractions in the assembler-language 'virtual' computer, there simply to assist the programmer. In the reality of the underlying binary computer, the variable called 'counter' is actually the contents of some register. In reality, the jump instruction is either an *absolute* jump to a specified instruction number or a *relative* jump backwards or forwards by a specified number of instructions.

The assembler-language virtual computer is an abstraction away from the physical machine itself and could provide useful facilities not actually supported in reality. This allowed the computer scientists emerging from the ranks of the computer engineers to create even more interesting concepts for their virtual machine. Following the lead set by Wilkes and his team at Cambridge to develop reusable 'library code' collections of instructions, computer scientists began to create some very general solutions to the specific problems that they faced. The result was ideas about how these abstract machines were to work, and these ideas are still the foundations of computer operations today.

The first of these foundation ideas is a simple but surprisingly powerful way of managing the memory used by a program, a *stack*. There is no particular reason why data should not be written to *any* part of the computer's memory, since RAM is, after all, random-access. What computer scientists developed was a structured way of using at least some of that memory. In principle it is like a stack of paper on a desk, in which the topmost item is visible but those below it are obscured. When a new piece of paper is added, it always goes on top of the pile; and when it is removed, paper is always taken from the top of the pile. Computer scientists called this form of memory 'last in, first out' (LIFO). To implement this in a computer, all the programmers needed to do was to put a range of computer-memory addresses to one side for the stack and to keep a record of the address in memory of the 'topmost' item on the stack. When data is written to the stack, this address is increased by one (so that the stack grows) and the data is copied into the memory word that the address now points to; when data is read from the stack, the address is decreased by one (so that the stack then shrinks). This address record was called the 'stack pointer' and was actually implemented in most computers as a dedicated register in the processor.

In itself, this is no more than one of several ways in which the data stored in the computer memory could be maintained. In conjunction with the second important development, however, it gave computer scientists a powerful new abstraction tool – it gave them the ability to implement *procedures*.

Through the work of Wilkes at Cambridge, the idea of reusable subroutines had been developed. At least initially, these subroutines were used by being copied bodily into new programs where and when they were actually needed. If the task performed by a subroutine was needed in five places in a particular program, then it would be copied five times. By contrast, a procedure to carry out some specific task is included in a program only once and can be accessed from anywhere within the program. As long as the programmer knows the label for the start of the procedure, the jump instruction can shift the locus of control to the procedure code. However, whilst getting *to* the procedure is straightforward, returning *from* it is slightly more difficult. How does the computer know which address in the main body of the instructions should be copied into the program counter?

A crude way of solving this is to put the return address in a register or a specific memory location when the procedure is first jumped to (or 'called') by the main body of the program. This would ensure that the return address was available to the procedure when it completed its task. Unfortunately, if the register option is taken, then only one procedure can be called – subsequent procedure calls would overwrite the return address and so lose the thread. If the memory option is chosen, then only one call of a particular procedure can be made, since subsequent calls to that procedure would end up with the return address again being overwritten and lost.

The solution is to place the return address on the stack. This allows arbitrarily many procedures and arbitrarily many copies of a given procedure to be called. When the procedure finishes and needs to return to the instruction that called it, all it need do is to remove the topmost address from the stack (called 'popping') and then jump to that location. If procedures are called from within procedures, then each address will have been placed in turn on the stack (called 'pushing') and will appear at the top of the stack in the correct order.

Stacks provided programmers with a very flexible solution to the issues of 'nested returns' to the calling section of code. The stack also neatly solved a second issue in the handling of procedures – *arguments*. A procedure can be called from many different places within a program but will then carry out exactly the same instructions in each case. If it is to do something different – to perform a loop seven times rather than three, for example – then it has to be informed of the value for these variable elements. Again, this could be done by using a register or a specific memory location; but again, this is too restrictive, so the stack is used once more. The procedure arguments – the variable values that control how the procedure is to behave – are themselves placed on the stack where they can be accessed. When a procedure is called, therefore, the return address and the arguments are all placed on the stack so that they can be used. This allows the most flexible way possible of reusing subroutines in programs, and it quickly became a key part of the Cambridge Laboratory library of code.

The assembler-language virtual computer supported a variety of useful developments. By working in a simple abstract language, programmers were able to explore a range of different algorithms (that is, techniques for solving problems) that would have been too complicated to have simply written in binary. However, the abstract assembler-language commands still had to be translated into the corresponding binary code if they were to be executed. This is where the next fascinating development occurred: the automatic translation of assembler instructions into binary machine-language instructions; the invention of a program to create programs – the *compiler*.

The first compilers

Assembler language added three things to the basic machine language of binary instructions that supported it. First of all, reasonably meaningful terms (like 'jump', 'load' or 'move') replaced obscure binary-code numbers for instructions. Second, meaningful names for the values used within a program (like 'counter' or 'result', for example) replaced the raw memory address or register holding the value. Third, labels as the destination for jump instructions (like 'start') replaced the raw instruction number.

Translating those programs from assembler into the binary machine-language instructions was then a simple if tedious, time-consuming and error-prone task. Each assembler-language instruction corresponded to a single machine-language instruction, so the assembler could be translated one-to-one. Each instruction of an assembler-language program was written on a separate, numbered line so as to give the instruction number and therefore the actual location of the jump destination. Similarly, the named data values were held in a separate collection of memory locations so as not to be confused with the program instructions; and equally easily the memory locations could be deduced from the line numbering. Finally, having replaced labels and variable names with specific memory locations, the programmer would transliterate each instruction in turn into binary. The first person to realize that this rote task of transliteration could be carried out by a computer program was Grace Hopper.

Computer science seems always to have been a male-dominated field, yet two of the most famous names in the development of computer programming were women: Ada, Countess Lovelace in the 19th century, and Rear-Admiral Professor Grace Murray Hopper in the 20th. Both were women; both were mathematicians; and both were interested in automatic calculation. But there the similarity ends. Ada was the daughter of the 'mad, bad and dangerous' Lord Byron; a society beauty who married well and for whom calculating engines were never anything more than a hobby. By contrast, Grace was a career teacher and naval officer, the eldest daughter of a struggling, handicapped insurance broker. She divorced and died childless, and would never have been described as a beauty, even as a young woman. For all that, she had an even greater impact than Ada and was one of the most remarkable figures in the development of computer science.

Grace was born the eldest of three children in New York City in 1906. From an early age she showed a talent for mathematics and was encouraged by her father not to settle for the traditional 'women's roles'. She studied mathematics and physics at Vassar College in Poughkeepsie, New York, graduating with a BA in 1928 and winning a scholarship to nearby Yale, where she gained her MA degree in 1930. Married to an English professor at New York University, Grace returned to a teaching post at Vassar and was awarded a PhD from Yale in 1934.

Her future in academia seemed to be well mapped out as she rose through the college teaching ranks to become, like her husband, a professor and faculty member. In 1941, however, the USA joined the war against Nazi Germany, and Professor Grace Hopper's life changed dramatically as she chose to serve her country as a naval officer. It was not an easy option for her. At 35 she was considered to be too old, not to mention undersized, and as a mathematician, she was working in a protected occupation vital to the country's war effort. Nonetheless, following her father's encouragement to overcome opposition, Grace finally succeeded in persuading the navy to enlist her in the Naval Reserve in December 1943. In June 1944 she graduated first in her class and was appointed as a junior lieutenant in the US Navy.

Until this time, Grace Hopper had never encountered a computer. Her mathematical work was in the specialized field of solving algebraic problems through geometry, a 20th-century version of the mathematics practised by the ancient Greeks. She had never done any 'number crunching' in her life, and other than to teach her Vassar students about the use of logarithms, she had never used tables in calculation. Nonetheless, as a mathematician she was despatched to Harvard University, where the

US Navy had funded the development of the Harvard Mark 1 computer under the direction of Howard Aiken.

By her own account, Grace fell in love immediately with the Mark 1 and was soon grappling with it to produce programs to calculate elevation and firing trajectories for naval gunnery tables. She became only the third programmer to use the computer. Fortunately for computer science, 'grappling' was the most accurate description. The task of programming the cumbersome machine was fraught with problems, encouraging Grace to begin thinking of ways to improve the task. The machine itself would often break down (once, as mentioned above, because of a moth becoming stuck in one of the relays), and Grace and the other programmers would make mistakes in translating their instructions into the necessary binary code. Often, Aiken would come through the rooms holding the Mark 1, Grace and her colleagues, demanding to know whether they were 'making numbers', only to find that they were instead poring over faulty programs or trying to fix broken machinery. Grace herself, following the moth's intrusion in the summer of 1945, coined the word 'de-bugging' to mean that they were solving the computer problems. It is the term used to this day.

At the close of the war, Grace was 40 and considered too old to remain on active duty in the navy. She had also divorced her English professor husband, and though she had the formal offer of a permanent appointment at Vassar College, she had no reason to move back to New York. Instead, she chose to remain at Harvard and to join the Naval Reserve force as a lieutenant. Grace continued to program the Harvard Mark 1 and then the Mark 2 machine, still working alongside Howard Aiken and collecting together a range of different binary-coded routines to perform standard tasks on the computer. Just as they had been before the end of the war, the programs continued to be prone to error. Like any good mathematician, Grace was lazy enough to hate the repetitive and mundane task of transcribing the binary programs and of then poring over them to 'debug' them. Eventually in 1949 she had the opportunity to approach the problem from a fresh angle when she joined the Eckert-Mauchly Computer Corporation set up in Philadelphia to exploit the ENIAC and EDVAC designs.

It was a brave move on her part, to leave the protection of an academic position for the rigours of a free-market existence. The general belief at the time was that there was only a market for at most a dozen computers in the entire world, so the prospect of a company being able to make a business of it was laughable. Grace herself later joked that Mauchly and Eckert had chosen their building perfectly. It was between a junk yard and a cemetery, so if it all went wrong, she said, they could throw the UNIVAC out of one window and themselves out of the other.

It did not go wrong, although the company had to be rescued by Remington-Rand in 1950. For Grace, even though the financing was precarious, the working conditions were much easier than when she had been struggling with the clumsy binary code used for the Harvard machines. Following the work of Maurice Wilkes and his Cambridge team, Grace and her colleagues had begun to code their programs in an assembler language. What was more, Grace began to work on a program that would translate the assembler into binary automatically. It was the world's first 'compiler'.

Grace published her first paper and gave her first public talk on the design of automatic compiling programs in 1952. The initial programs were not what we would now consider to be compilers; they were what we would call 'assemblers' or 'loaders'. They were programs that had as their input data the crude assembler code of the time and which produced the binary numbers corresponding to the instructions for that assembler code on the UNIVAC computer. That output could then be loaded into the UNIVAC itself and executed. For Grace, it was a marvellous step. Instead of having to transliterate each and every program that she wrote, she now had only to transliterate the compiler program (called A-0) and have it perform the transliteration of each further program. The A-1 and A-2 translators that followed were increasingly powerful but were all met with scepticism by those who heard of them. It took until 1956 for Grace to convince her colleagues that the program was really as powerful as she claimed.

The development of the assembler language and of the automatic translators went hand in hand through the years from 1952 to 1956. Over that period, Grace came to harbour an idea that was remarkable even for her. The A-0, A-1 and A-2 languages were crude − single words that corresponded to the basic UNIVAC operations. However, enthused by the success of the initial translating programs, Grace began to believe that she could, quite literally, teach the UNIVAC computer to 'understand English'.

If the description of a simple transliteration program had been met with disbelief, then this idea was met with outright incredulity and scorn. Grace Hopper, however, was nothing if not determined. By the end of 1956, she had a B-0 compiler for a language that she christened 'FLOW-MATIC' and which contained some 20 English-like expressions that could be trans-lated automatically into a form that the UNIVAC computer could execute. FLOW-MATIC was not the first high-level pro-gramming language, though it was the first one deliberately designed to be as close as possible to English. In 1954, John Backus of IBM had designed a language for programming scien-tific calculations. This was FORTRAN (Formula Translator), and it became the most widely used scientific language of the period. In 1959, FLOW-MATIC evolved into the business programming language COBOL (Common Business Oriented Language). For much of the 1960s, programming was performed in COBOL for commercial software and in FORTRAN for scientific. The 'high-level' language was born.

⁌

Grace Hopper went on to even greater things after her work on these first programming-language concepts. She served on very nearly every major committee considering computer development and was granted professor status at the University of Pennsylvania. At the end of 1966, Grace was formally retired from the Naval Reserves with the rank of commander. Just seven months later, though, the navy recalled her to active duty with the task of rewriting their payroll system in COBOL. She continued to serve as a uniformed officer specializing in software development for the navy, lecturing at the George Washington University and training new programmers throughout the 1970s and 1980s. She was promoted to captain in August 1973; to commodore in November 1983; and to rear-admiral in 1985, the first woman to gain flag rank.

The oldest serving officer in the US forces, Grace Hopper finally retired as a rear-admiral in August 1986 aged 79 in a formal ceremony on the deck of the USS *Constitution* which included an award of the Defence Distinguished Service Medal, the highest peacetime award in the US forces. Despite her age, Grace continued to work. She was appointed as a senior consultant by DEC and showered with almost 50 honorary degrees, uncounted fellowships and a variety of academic medals. She continued to teach enthusiastically and to work on a variety of projects.

The 'Mother of COBOL' finally died on New Year's Day 1992 and was buried with full military honours in Arlington National Cemetery. The US Navy even named a ship after her, the USS ('Amazing') *Grace Hopper*.

John von Neumann developed the first understanding of how a computer could be made to work; but Grace Hopper was responsible for showing the world how a computer could be *used*. Without her disregard for received wisdom, her conception of automated program translation and her creation of a non-scientific programming language, computers would have continued to be simply expensive calculators for formulating mathematical tables. She will also be remembered as a witty and warm teacher, whose personal motto is perhaps best summarized in a quote: 'It's better to ask forgiveness than it is to get permission.'

High-level languages

Assembler-language instructions are separated from the machine-language binary instructions by the concept of abstraction; high-level language instructions are separated from assembler by an altogether more important concept, that of a *grammar*. The year 1957 saw the publication of the official FORTRAN documentation by John Backus, a milestone in the development of high-level languages. It also saw the publication of an even more important document that would come to underpin the development of all subsequent programming languages: *Syntactic Structures* by Noam Chomsky.

Chomsky was a linguist who had analysed a huge variety of languages, current and historic, pure and pidgin. He came to believe that a formalized structure underpinned them all. He believed, with good cause as we now know, that languages expressed some underlying mental structures that are intrinsic to human brains. Chomsky wanted to pursue those structures, which he called 'formal grammars', so as to produce the *rules* of all different human languages. Ironically for someone trying to clarify the rules of languages, Chomsky's own writing and explanation of his work was all but impossible to follow. Though his ideas were revolutionary and have served as the mainstay of academic linguistic research since that time, they were virtually impenetrable. Also, his rules of grammatical structures seemed to describe 'ideal' languages well but to fail at the hurdle of describing a 'natural' language such as English, with its special cases and inherited attributes. The notion, however, of describing ideal languages through grammatical 'generators' (rules that allow the production of grammatically valid statements) was vitally important in the production of *new* languages. Computer scientists immediately adopted Chomsky's ideas. The work with the most lasting impact on the development of programming languages was, once again, produced by John Backus of IBM.

Born in Philadelphia in 1924 to wealthy parents, Backus had joined IBM in 1949 after a turbulent youth and a patchy education. His school grades were poor and his attendance was poorer still, but his father insisted on the young Backus following him into a career as an industrial chemist. Backus went to the University of Virginia to study applied chemistry in 1942, but again he did so poorly that he was expelled and joined the army that summer. Even his army career was marked by the same restlessness as his education. He served as a corporal in an anti-aircraft battery, before moving first into engineering and then into medicine. He might have been destined to live a life of such unfocused lassitude had not a chance medical examination discovered that Backus was suffering from a brain tumour. It was removed, and in 1946 he retired to civilian life with a medical discharge and a pension.

At just 22 and financially secure, John Backus was fortunate in that he did not *need* to work. He took a small apartment in New York City and, wanting to build a wireless set for himself, enrolled on a Radio Technicians course. There, in carrying out the calculations necessary to compute amplifier coefficients, Backus finally discovered his true calling: mathematics. He enrolled at Columbia University and graduated with a BSc in 1949, joining IBM in New York that summer. FORTRAN grew out of a proposal that Backus made in 1953 to improve the programming of the latest

IBM models. In truth, although FORTRAN was a substantial step forward in the art of programming, it provided very little in the way of abstraction away from the underlying assembler code itself. It simply made the expression of loops and of complex calculations a little easier.

FORTRAN was a successful language and is used to this day. Important though its contribution to the development of programs was, however, its contribution to the development of programming *languages* was even greater. FORTRAN inspired ALGOL (Algorithmic Language), and with it, the concepts embodied in almost every major programming language since. FORTRAN simplified the production of programs to calculate mathematical formulae; FLOW-MATIC, and hence COBOL, simplified the production of programs to perform business calculations. By contrast, ALGOL invented the foundations of grammar, abstraction, expression and structure that are the true currency of programming languages. In ALGOL we see the first *truly* high-level language.

Before ALGOL, computer programming languages were effectively specific to the computers on which they were developed to run. The languages reflected the characteristics of the machines and were essentially the creation of the small set of individuals who had worked on designing the computer itself. By contrast, ALGOL was designed by an international committee of computer scientists to be as abstract as possible. Because of this, the language embodied a wide range of ideas from different schools of computer development, creating a flexible and very abstract language. ALGOL introduced two very specific ideas, the notion of a *data type* and of a *block structure*.[2]

All data stored in computer systems is actually represented as binary words at the machine level. Within assembler language, these data words can be specified by giving them a label to act as a name that can be used anywhere within the program. This is an abstraction but not a huge one – the labelled memory word is still simply a memory word. True, the memory word can be interpreted by arithmetic operations as a number or by binary operations as an alphabetic character. This is a property of the *instructions*, however, rather than a property of the data.

By contrast, 'data typing' associates a property with the data item itself. A memory word, or perhaps even several words, are given a name to act as a label for them and a property that specifies how they are to be handled. Typical data types might be *character* for an alphabetic character, *integer* for a number, and *float* for a floating point value. Once a data item has been given a name and a type (called a 'declaration' of the variable), then it can only be used in ways consistent with that type: a character cannot be multiplied or divided, for example. In a 'typed' language, character and integer data types cannot be combined; and in a 'strongly typed' language, even integer and float variables cannot be multiplied together.

These distinctions do not exist as any property of the computer or of the assembler language in which the program is to be compiled. They are purely features of the high-level language, and they made it substantially easier to discover mistakes in computer programs. If a programmer inadvertently combined two incorrect variables in an assembler-language program, this would be all but impossible to track down. In a high-level language program, though, it would be easy to discover – and in fact the compiler would almost certainly produce an error message.

These high-level languages went further still, introducing complex new data types called 'structures', in which several different data types could be handled as one unit. For example, a structured data type might be a personnel record, a series of characters to represent the individual's name, and a collection of integers to represent details such as their salary or employment number.

The abstraction that was provided by the introduction of strong typing into ALGOL became a key feature of every subsequent programming language. The principle of a program block structure was equally influential. In assembler code, instructions could be collected together into useful sections of code, but that collection was not a part of the *language* but rather of the programming practice adopted by an individual. By contrast, in ALGOL the language featured specific blocks, bracketed between the keywords 'begin' and 'end', that were handled as a unit by the computer.

To make the block structure work, ALGOL introduced the concept of 'reserved words' – key words that were part of the language's structure rather than words that were either variable names or program comments as used in assembler. Words like 'begin', 'end', 'if', 'then' and so forth were the skeleton of the programs and could be combined into meaningful block structures. Again, the concepts of blocks and reserved words made the process of debugging faulty programs substantially easier. The blocks had to have a particular format and be laid out and used by the programmer according to very specific rules. This made the analysis and the generation of the programs very much easier.

These specific rules, however, had to be expressed to the programmer in the form of a rule set or manual and to the compiling program so that it could analyse and translate valid programs. This was where John Backus made his most lasting contribution to the field of programming languages.

The ALGOL language was completed in 1958, but it was so complex and so unlike any language that had gone before that it was difficult to understand. At a conference in Mainz, Germany, in December 1959, John Backus presented a paper on the grammar of the language using a notation that he had invented based on the expression of formal grammars in Chomsky's linguistics. It was a *production* grammar, allowing correct programs to be produced by applying the rules. The notation became known as Backus Normal Form, but unfortunately it used symbols that had to be handwritten since there were no keyboard characters for them to be typed. A Danish programmer called Peter Naur, who had the task of writing up the notes for the conference, simplified the notation so that he could type it up, and BNF (Backus–Naur Form) notation was born. When it was finally published in 1960, the formal ALGOL language specification was in BNF, and all subsequent programming languages have used BNF to specify their syntactic structure. In fact, a so-called 'compiler compiler' was even produced by Bell Laboratories in the 1970s that would transform a BNF language specification into a compiler for that language.[3] Backus's contribution to programming languages through the formal specification of their grammar was so significant that, in 1977, he was awarded the Turing Prize for this achievement.

Because of its precise specification and its powerful expressions, ALGOL became the founding ancestor of an impressive dynasty of programming languages. Not every programming language in modern use is a direct descendant of ALGOL. LISP was developed in 1958 at MIT to allow the creation of artificial-intelligence programs; BASIC in 1964 to be a simple and easily learnt language; and COBOL, of course, in 1959 to provide a flexible and English-like business language. Each of these went on to be popular and widespread – and even to create their own mini-dynasties in some cases. For example, LISP inspired LOGO, beloved of schoolchildren playing with the still-popular little turtle robot controlled by it; and BASIC led to Visual BASIC, used to create simple programs on the World Wide Web.

None of these languages, however, not even COBOL, had the widespread impact that ALGOL and the BNF specification can claim. ALGOL itself developed into the monstrously powerful, near-infinitely flexible super-language ALGOL 68, a language that was specifically designed to embed *every* theoretically possible programming technique and remains unsurpassed to this day. From ALGOL 68 a simplified language called PASCAL was produced by Niklaus Wirth, a renegade from the ALGOL committee. And from PASCAL and ALGOL 68 came the military programming language ADA (named in honour of Ada, Countess Lovelace) in which missile, flight and even satellite control systems are written.

Perhaps the most important child of the ALGOL dynasty, though, was a small, often overlooked programming language developed by the Cambridge Computer Laboratory and the University of London in 1963. Called the Combined Programming Language (CPL), this combined much of the ALGOL block structure and strong typing into a language that could also control the computer hardware directly. It was ideal for programming everything from the most abstract processing algorithm to the most time-critical hardware control. Unfortunately, it was difficult to program effectively because of this complexity and flexibility, so a simplified version, called Basic Combined Programming Language or BCPL, was produced in 1967. In turn, BCPL was further simplified in 1969 by a US programmer called Ken Thompson at Bell Laboratories in Murray Hill, New Jersey. Thompson called this language 'B', and in 1971, when it was developed further, it evolved into the most widespread and popular programming language in the world, the C programming language.

Almost every component of the modern computer age has been developed in C. UNIX was written in the language, as were huge parts of Windows, the World Wide Web and a host of other environments. Modern programming languages such as Java and Perl equally trace their ancestry back to Thompson's simple little language evolved from ALGOL. Not as grand as ADA nor as baroquely complicated as ALGOL 68, C has nonetheless proved to be the programming vehicle of choice for the modern world.

Until, that is, even more powerful models were developed – in particular, the 'object-oriented' approach to programming.

Object-oriented programming languages

In traditional, linear programming languages such as C, a collection of data structures is defined and populated. For example, a structure representing a person might have a variable-length string of alphabetic characters to store their name; an integer to store their age; and a single character to store their sex. The program itself is then created from a number of procedures which receive the data structures (perhaps as arguments, perhaps as global items) and carry out some transformation on the contents. To achieve this, a procedure might do the transformation itself or it might pass some or all of the data structure to a further procedure. When the transformation is complete, the original procedure passes the data structure back to the part of the program that first asked for it.

A traditional, linear program might be thought of as a factory in which bolts of raw cloth are washed, stretched and dyed. The 100-metre bolts of cloth are passed from stage to stage within the factory, and at each location a small team of people performs a single, simple transformation on the cloth. At one place, the team runs the cloth through a washing machine and then folds it into a trolley tub for transport to the next stage. Here, the still-wet bolt is dipped into a tub of dye before being passed on to the stretching and drying machines, and then on to the final press and the rolls. At each stage in the factory the team carries out a distinct process, using their local resources (the dyes, the machines, the people) on the bolts of cloth that are passed to them.

In a linear program, the data structures are like the bolts of cloth passed from place to place; the procedures are the distinct stages through the factory; and the local variables are the resources available at each stage. The data structures are moved and transformed, but the procedures remain in place. In object-oriented programming, the basic elements of the program are no longer structured collections of data passed from procedure to procedure. Instead, the basic elements are collections of data *along with* the procedures that are permitted to act on that data, and it is the data and the procedures that move from place to place within the program. In the cloth factory, this is like each bolt of cloth being accompanied around the factory by an employee who washes it, colours it, dries it and presses it. The advantage of this approach is that the programming style can be either linear or functional, depending on the nature of the problem to be solved. The data and functions can both be encapsulated in a structure that hides the internal details so that the object can be passed from processor to processor if required.

The ideas of object-oriented programming styles grew out of the work on ALGOL and the other block-structured languages in the late 1960s and early 1970s. One of the first languages to introduce the principles of encapsulated data and procedures was Modula, developed in 1975 by Niklaus Wirth as an extension to his own language, Pascal. In its turn, Modula encouraged the development in 1983 of object-oriented versions of the C programming language, in particular the currently most popular development language, C++, by Bjarne Stroustrup at the former AT&T Bell Laboratories.

The most widespread and successful implementation of the object-oriented approach, however, is Java, which has taken advantage of an interesting feature of the object-oriented style. With procedures and data encapsulated together, the objects can be distributed to independent processors within a network, particularly over the internet. The Java language was developed by Sun Microsystems for exactly that purpose.

Sun Microsystems was founded in February 1982 in Santa Clara by four Californian graduate students, specifically to market a UNIX-based workstation which had been developed for the Stanford University Network – hence the name. Throughout the decade, the company prospered, growing rapidly from the initial four founders into a huge multinational with a reputation for technical excellence, particularly in the arena of cooperative networks. This is indeed reflected in the company motto, 'The Network is the Computer'.

By the end of the 1980s the Sun founders were keen to ensure that the company stayed at the forefront of technology, particularly as the internet and ever smaller microprocessors made a range of things possible. They therefore established a wholly separate, entirely undirected group of their most creative people to think about and plan for the 'next wave' of technology. The 'Green Project' was established in December 1990 and housed in a separate office building in Menlo Park, a few miles northwest of the Sun head office.

The most important trend that the Green Project team members could identify was towards computerized, distributed control of household appliances. With tiny, inexpensive microprocessors embedded in washing machines, microwaves, video recorders and the like, the team anticipated that soon *every* appliance would be computer-controlled. This, they believed, provided an opportunity for the development of a single control facility for the 'networked home'. To provide this control facility, however, they recognized that they needed a way of programming and distributing instructions to each of the appliances and that an object-oriented programming style was ideal for the purpose.

In June 1991, the leader of the Green Project team, James Gosling, produced the first version of a network-mobile programming environment that he dubbed 'Oak'.[4] This was used to program the team's first product demonstration, a controller for TV, video and audio entertainment centres called '★7' ('Star Seven'), first shown in September 1992.

Although the ★7 device itself did not take off, the Oak programming language, and the notion of network-mobile code in particular, was quickly recognized as an ideal product for the company. Renamed Java, the programming language was a huge success. In 1994, the Green Project (itself renamed First Person) developed a crude web browser in Java, called WebRunner. Demonstrated for the first time in early 1995, it allowed programs to be downloaded to a browser over the internet and executed locally. For the first time, the pictures on a web page could be made to move and sophisticated programming tasks could be carried out on a user's PC by tiny, network-mobile segments of code called 'applets'.

Launched unofficially to the internet developers community in March 1995, Java was immediately popular – there were tens of thousands of downloads within the first few days. At the official product launch on 23 May 1995, Sun Microsystems CEO Scott McNealy and Marc Andreessen of Netscape Communications Corporation announced that Java would be a key component of the then most popular web browser, Netscape Navigator.

Since then, Java (and the rival Microsoft system, ActiveX) programs have made the Web a dynamic and interesting environment and have helped (as we shall see) to create the facilities for the development of electronic commerce. Not bad for a programming environment that was originally developed as a means of controlling microwaves, video recorders and fridge freezers.

Programming languages like C, C++ and Java have allowed developers to move away from the physical machine of binary digits to an idealized platform of complex data types, flexible operations and network-mobile applets. Key to this is the notion of abstraction, so that the physical device that runs the programs can be safely ignored and programmers can deal in the virtual world of data structures and general-purpose algorithms. However, even with the most sophisticated programming language possible, developers still need a way of conceiving, designing and implementing their programs. They need a methodology for programming.

Writing computer programs

Even with the most sophisticated of modern programming languages, writing a computer program is a daunting prospect. This is true whether it is a simple routine to balance a cash book, a hugely complex system to play a network adventure game, or an artificial intelligence. However, all computer programs can ultimately be boiled down to the single, simple task of transforming input data into output data. All that a programmer needs to do is to work out the structure and nature of the data to be introduced into the computer; the changes that must be made to it; and the structure and nature of the result that must be produced.

Designing a computer program therefore usually begins with the specification of input data and of output data. This design specification can be either a 'back of the envelope' scribble for a quick program, or a hugely formalized design exercise and document-ation for a multi-programmer project. The way in which the data formats are expressed can be either informal ('a series of characters typed by the user') or specified by a formal grammar to show what is or is not valid data. With the specification of data to be input and a similar specification of the required output, the task of the programmer is then to create a series of instructions to achieve that transformation. For even the simplest of programs, though, this process of transformation can be immensely daunting.

As an example, take one of the computer games provided with

the Windows operating system. Minesweeper is played on a grid of covered squares behind some of which mines are hidden. The user can move the mouse to click on each square. If the square contains a mine, then it blows up and the game is over; if there is no mine, a count is displayed, showing the numbers of mines adjacent to that square. By a combination of luck and deduction, the user has to discover where every mine is without getting blown up.[5]

The program could hardly be simpler, but the task of developing it, at least at first glance, is hugely difficult. The user chooses the square to uncover by moving the mouse around the screen, so the program must keep track of where the mouse is and where it has moved. A square is selected by clicking on it, so the program must analyse every mouse click to determine whether the mouse was over a square at that time or whether it was over some other part of the display, such as the Help button. If the mouse was not in the Minesweeper window at the time of the click, then the program must know that it should ignore it. Assuming that the mouse click was indeed over a valid square, the program must then determine whether there is a mine at that point and alter the display as appropriate.

Although this *is* a complex task, it can be hugely simplified. The basic tool of the programmer is a method called 'functional decomposition', in which the 'hugely difficult' main task is broken down into a series of several, merely difficult tasks; each of these is then broken down further into complex tasks, which can then be broken down further still into very many simple or even trivial tasks. The simple or trivial tasks can be programmed directly or can be created from standard library routines. By combining these simple tasks to follow the program design, the complex and difficult tasks can be completed. Not only does this make the exercise of creating programs possible, it also makes the description of the programs easy as well.

In the Minesweeper example, for instance, the series of 'difficult' tasks might be expressed as:

1. Set up the initial state of the display.
2. When the mouse is clicked, look for its location; ignore it if it is not somewhere relevant to the program.
3. If the mouse was over a button such as Help, then perform the action associated with the button.
4. Or, if the mouse was over a square, then reveal that square's contents.
5. If the square is revealed to be a mine, perform the 'explode' action.
6. Update the state of the display.

Decomposition turns the overall task of 'running the Minesweeper' into a series of repeated tasks which can be expressed as subroutines such as 'initiate', 'explode', 'reveal' and 'display'. Programmers typically express this stage of the design as 'pseudo-code' – simplified programs, with a combination of general programming syntax and English for the elements yet to be refined.

```
Minesweeper()
begin
        InitiateMines();
        while ( no mine has yet exploded )
                        DisplayMines();
                wait for mouse click;
                if ( click was on a button)
                        DoButtonAction( Button );
                elseif ( click was on a square )
                        Reveal( square );
                        if ( square was a mine )
                                Explode();
        end
```

This top-level, functional design gives the programmer the basic 'shape' of the program to be created, while hiding the details of the precise way in which the subcomponents are to be implemented. The next stage in the development process is to design the data structures with which the program is to be implemented. In many ways, the design of these structures is *the* central task of programming; well-defined data structures make programming easy.

In most programs there are three types of data structure usually manipulated by the instructions: global data; local, temporary variables; and procedure arguments. The global data variables are those which are available to every part of the program. In the Minesweeper example, the collection of squares possibly containing mines and the current state of the display of those squares would be a global variable available to all subcomponents. Local, temporary variables are those used by individual procedures for their own, private manipulation of data. The variables and their values are not visible outside the procedure; they can be thought of as 'scratchpad' variables. The procedure arguments are the values which are passed to the procedures when they are called, allowing the procedure to work in a different way for different values. In the pseudo-code example above, the 'square' in the line 'Reveal (square)' is the procedure's argument value. Not only can procedures be called with these arguments, they can also 'return' a value to the part of the program where they were called. A procedure which returns a value is often called a 'function'. This gives the third category of data element that must be considered – the values that are passed backwards and forwards between the component procedures.

Taking the global data structure of the mine grid itself, this would usually be expressed as an element called an 'array' – a fixed number of data elements arranged sequentially in memory. These data elements can then be selected by the programmer using an 'index' value to select the required entry. Because the entries are sequential, a simple loop can be used to step through each entry in turn. In the case of the Minesweeper program, the grid of covered squares has both columns and rows; the array data structure is therefore a two-dimensional arrangement of columns and of rows. So the procedure used to 'reveal' the appropriate square can be created simply by reading off the value in the array at the (X,Y) coordinate of the mouse click point within the display grid.

In designing this aspect of the program, the programmer needs to consider the best type of two-dimensional array to be used, probably an array of integer numbers. Each entry in the array will correspond to a square on the grid, and the value stored in each entry might be expected to correspond to the value to be revealed. For example, 0 would denote that the square has no neighbouring mines; values 1 to 8 would show the numbers of mines in the adjacent squares; and a value of 9 would be used to show that the square contained a mine.

The fragment of code above, 'if (square was a mine)', can therefore be decomposed further into something like:

```
X = FindMouseX();
Y = FindMouseY();
value = ArrayOfMines[ X, Y ];
if ( value is 9 )
        Explode ( X, Y )
```

The other elements of the program design follow much the same approach of decomposition and definition of data structures. The mouse click provides an (X,Y) coordinate position which can be mapped onto the locations of the squares and the buttons; the procedures such as 'display' take the global data structure and draw it on the screen; the 'reveal' function returns the value located within the global data structure; and so on.

Programming is never simple, but it can easily be seen as something that is constructed in simple steps using simple elements and based on simple principles. Nowhere is this more apparent than in the most complex programming task of all, the creation of the computer's operating system.

5

What do operating systems do?

'So, did you make your mind up, Dad? Was it Windows in the end?
Or did they manage to sell you a computer with a different
operating system on it?'

'You know, I'd feel so much happier if I even just understood the
question…!'

Few car drivers *really* need to know how the ignition system,
automatic gearbox or differential traction works; few drivers, in
fact, even need to know what a spark plug is. All of them,
however, need to know how to use the steering wheel, accelerator and indicators. In the same way, although it is useful to
understand how a computer really works, most PC users will
never see the inside of a computer and will never need to know
about the 'von Neumann bottleneck' of sequential execution.
Though it is interesting, most will never need to know about
programming languages, algorithms and data structures. All
computer users, though, will come into contact with the
operating system, be it Microsoft's popular Windows range or the
variants on the UNIX system.

Even though cars and lorries are quite different, there are gross
similarities in the way that they are driven. The pedals are in the
same place; there is a steering wheel, mirrors, indicators, gear
lever and so forth. Even though a car driver might not know how
to drive a bus, they can expect to recognize the basic mechanisms

involved. In the same way, even though different operating systems work in dramatically different ways, there are many similarities. The screen presents a view of a 'desktop' on which icons are arranged to represent documents, programs or folders, which in turn contain documents, programs or further folders. The mouse is used to select icons. Clicking on an icon activates it, to open a document or to run a program. Even the programs now have broadly similar ways of operating, with almost all, for example, having drop-down menus from which items are selected.

This collection of icons and functions, however, is not actually the operating system. It is the 'user interface', the surface aspect of the incredibly complex series of programs that truly make the computer usable. Although this is important, the operating system does *much* more than simply providing a means of displaying colourful icons. Just as the hardware does one single, simple task of shuffling electric current from place to place, operating systems do one single, simple task: they provide a cushion between the user and the computer. Or rather, they provide a cushion between the *programs* that the user runs and the underlying hardware on which those programs are executed. Operating systems provide an abstract, idealized computer for the programs to use, hiding the specific details of just how the physical computer itself actually functions.

Achieving this 'single, simple task' is no mean feat. Operating systems must provide an interface to all the computer peripherals – the printers, keyboards, disk drives, screens and so forth. They share the processor evenly between all the programs that must run, which even in a single-user laptop can be dozens of distinct processes. They provide the interface to users so that they can direct the computer's operation. And they provide a degree of separation between programs and users, so as to give protection and privacy.

These, though, are simply the most obvious tasks that operating systems perform. Behind the scenes, operating systems do much more even than this.

The role of the operating system

Operating systems are easily the most complicated programs ever to be designed, developed and run. To understand how they work, it is necessary to divide their activities into a small set of distinct functions that they provide. The most natural place to start this is in the deepest and most machine-dependent part of the operating system, the 'device drivers'.

Every disk drive is different; every different make of CD-ROM has slightly different characteristics; every printer has a different type of interface and expects a slightly different stream of control characters to be sent to it. These differences, dramatic or minute, are invisible to the user and to the application software that they run. It is the operating system's role to disguise these differences, using the device drivers that make this 'virtual machine' work.

A disk drive, for example, has to be controlled in a very precise manner. The hard-disk platter has a mass that gives it an angular momentum, which determines how long it takes to 'spin up' from rest to full speed. Once it is spinning, the disk-drive hardware has to move the read/write head over the disk surface so as to select the appropriate track. Again, this head has a particular mass and a particular 'lag' before it can be moved into position. Once in position, the head then has to wait for a short time for the data bits themselves to spin into place underneath it before it begins to read the data.

Controlling the disk is a nastily detailed activity. Each different disk has a slightly different control sequence and a slightly different timing detail for the transfer of data between the processor and the disk drive. The operating system uses the device drivers to mask this detail. All of the messy task of interfacing with the hardware is given to the device driver, which presents a simple interface to the operating system. The operating system merely requests that a block of data bytes (say, 512 characters, a typical unit of transfer from the disk) is read from or written to a specific part of the disk. It then relies on the device driver appropriate to that specific disk drive to carry out the function.

This principle of masking the messy details of particular devices behind a standard interface by means of device drivers is true of *all* parts of the computer. There are specific device drivers for every different screen, keyboard, mouse, printer, scanner, modem, network connection, and so forth. Operating systems come with a vast array of different device drivers already available. When a new piece of hardware is bought, it will generally come with a specific device driver ready to be installed. The purpose of that device driver is to mediate the detailed interaction with the hardware, allowing the operating system to treat all devices in a single, simple way.

Device drivers need to interact with specific memory locations and specific processor registers and to generate and handle very specific control signals. Their operation is very time-critical. While most programs can be run as and when the operating system chooses to allow them access to the processor, device drivers have to be able to do very specific control activities timed to the microsecond. Key to the successful operation of this device-driver structure is the concept of a control signal (called an 'interrupt') between the disk-drive unit and the central processor unit when the data is available. Handling these interrupts is the second important task of the operating system.

~🖱

Imagine a computer that is running a program to read characters typed by the user – a word-processing application, for example.

As each character is typed, it must be passed to the program so that it can act upon it: simple characters might be placed directly into the document being edited; arrow keys or control characters might move the cursor position within the document or might make the application perform various other tasks.

When each key is pressed, a binary number (as specified in the ASCII code set devised by Bob Bemer in 1963) is placed in a buffer that lies between the keyboard and the processor. This character is then passed from that buffer to the application by the operating system's keyboard device driver. Until that buffer contains a value, however, the word-processing application cannot do anything. It must simply wait, and even with the fastest of human typists busy filling that buffer, the program is going to spend significantly longer waiting than it is in actually doing something with those characters.

In the earliest computers, the program would simply perform a very short loop. It would look to see if the next character was ready in the keyboard buffer, and if it was not, the program would wait a few microseconds and then try again. This was called a 'busy-wait'. Obviously this meant that the computer was waiting for the user for substantial periods and so for the vast majority of time was idle. The early computer designers realized that this idle time could be fruitfully used if the machine was being shared between a large number of different programs. One of the earliest tasks for an operating system was solving the problem of how this could be achieved.

When one program is waiting for user input, others might well be able to proceed. However, the program that is in the busy-wait while waiting for the keyboard character to appear is actually blocking access to the processor. Worse, when it *does* receive the expected character, it will still be blocking the processor while it handles the character. The computer can only process one program at a time, so all others must wait until that one program has finished. Unfortunately, this means that the computer is not truly being shared – it is being monopolized. To solve this, the operating system 'halts' the program: instead of allowing the program to execute a busy-wait, the operating system puts it to one side and allows it to 'sleep' until the character appears. When the character does finally appear in the keyboard input buffer (at the glacial speed of a human typist), the operating system wakes the program and allows it to read and act upon the character. The signal that makes the sleeping program wake up when the character is ready to be used is called an 'interrupt'.

In even the simplest personal computer, the operating system is usually running several dozen different programs at any one time, only one of which is actually allowed access to the single central processing unit of the computer. The operating system shares the processor between each of these active programs, called 'processes'. All but one of the processes is waiting for some event to occur – for a keyboard character to appear, for the disk drive to spin into the correct position, or perhaps simply for it to be the process's turn. When that event happens, the operating system loads the process and executes it. The program is then running and can deal with the event for which it was waiting.

Of course, this simple description covers a multitude of detail. First, how is the process that is waiting for some event 'put to sleep'? This is actually the easiest of the details to manage. The operating system maintains a table of 'active processes', programs that are currently being run by the computer. That table contains all the detail necessary to describe the process: where it is held within the computer's main memory; what the current values are for all the processor registers; what the program-counter and stack-pointer values are; and what event it is actually waiting for. When the process is the currently active one, all the operating system must do is load the register, stack and program-counter values into the central processing unit and allow it to run.

The next detail is the question of how the operating system ensures that the process does not block access to the central processing unit. A program that read no keyboard input, did not need access to the disk, printed nothing out, and so on would never need to go to sleep. It would remain the 'current process' until it finished, perhaps after many minutes or even hours; indeed, it might *never* finish. To solve this problem, the operating system issues a special 'time-out' interrupt to processes that are running without any form of waiting. Every microsecond or so, the computer-hardware clock generates a 'tick' which is counted by the operating system. Any single process is only allowed a few of these ticks in the central processing unit before the operating system puts it to one side in favour of another process. When it is timed out, the process is put into a waiting state exactly like any other process, with the single difference that it is waiting its turn rather than for a specific external event to occur.

A third detail is then the question of how the operating system decides which of the many eligible processes is next to have a turn at using the central processing unit. At any one time, the list of active processes maintained by the operating system will have several that can be run immediately, called the 'ready' processes. There are a number of ways in which the operating system can select the next process from the list of ready ones. The simplest mechanism is a straightforward 'round robin' scheme, in which each process has a turn and then relinquishes the processor to the next, either when it runs out of time or when it has to wait for some external event such as a key to be pressed. Alternatively, more complex schemes can take into account the resources used by a given process and the amount of time that it has taken already. 'Expensive' processes can be penalized; those that might be nearly finished can be favoured. Every different operating system has a different way of selecting the next process. Of course, no method is ever the perfect one – all have flaws and all are compromises in which the operating system tries to predict the future behaviour of the processes it runs.

This issue of predicting the future is not the only problem faced by the operating system. The fourth important detail of this process management is an even more fundamental one. The operating system is itself a program which must gain access to the central processing unit if it is to perform these process-management tasks. How can the operating system relinquish the central processor to one of its flock of ready processes and be sure of having control returned to it in due course? The answer again lies with the interrupt mechanism, this time not between the operating system and the process, but between the computer hardware and the program that is the operating system. This is called a 'hardware interrupt'.

Modern computers have two modes of operation: a normal one called 'user' mode and a special, privileged one called 'executive' or 'supervisor' mode. In supervisor mode, all the computer's registers and instruction set are available to the running process, including those instructions for accessing the hardware components directly. In user mode, only a restricted subset of registers and instructions are accessible. In particular, the process is not allowed to execute instructions to control the hardware directly. Supervisor mode is restricted to the operating system; user mode is for the ordinary programs.

When a physical event occurs in the computer (a key is pressed or the clock ticks, for example), then a hardware interrupt occurs. This interrupt makes the computer do two things. First, it changes the operating mode to supervisor; second, it makes the computer jump to a special set of instructions that are the very heart of the operating system. These instructions are called the 'scheduler' and allow the operating system to regain control of the computer's central processing unit from the currently running process. These scheduler instructions do a very simple series of tasks. The very first thing that they do is to issue a privileged command called an 'interrupt mask', which disables interrupts and ensures that no other event will interfere with the execution of these special instructions. Secure from further interruption, the scheduler next looks to see what type of interrupt actually caused the instructions to be executed – a keyboard, mouse, disk or clock event, for example. The process waiting for that event is informed that it is now ready to run and the scheduler selects the process which will be run next – hence the name 'scheduler'. The registers, program and stack-counter values are copied from the process table into the central processor registers and, just before the scheduler passes control to the selected process, the interrupt mask is disabled and the operating mode is changed from supervisor back to user.

This sequence of scheduling instructions is performed every few microseconds when the clock ticks, every time a key is pressed, every time the disk produces data for a file, and so on. In fact, the scheduler is executed in a continuous flurry of repeated activity. A few instructions from an individual program are interrupted by the scheduler, which executes and then allows another program its brief foray into the CPU before once more grabbing control back again. In many ways, the scheduler *is* the operating system – everything else is simply additional functionality or flavour in the way that the individual computer actually works.

The operating system hides the different underlying mechanisms by using standard interfaces to device drivers; and it coordinates the scheduling of individual processes through the interrupt handling procedure. The third thing that the operating system must do is to manage the way in which programs request services from the hardware.

Individual programs must be able to read data from the disk or the keyboard, and all must be able to write the data on the screen, a printer or the disk. Programs must be able to send data to one another, and programs must be started or stopped. All of these things require the programs to control the computer devices directly. An important role for the operating system, however, is to *protect* the computer hardware from clumsy manipulation by the programs that might, for example, cause damage. The operating system must therefore provide a safe means of achieving these tasks.

As described above, programs are executed in user mode within the computer. Only a restricted set of instructions are available in user mode. Those that access the devices directly are not included in this selection. The purpose of this restriction is to ensure that programs can access and control the hardware only through the carefully controlled functions provided by the operating system's device-driver interfaces. To make this work, the operating system provides a small set of special-purpose functions called 'system calls' that can be used by any program to make the operating-system device drivers perform these sensitive tasks on its behalf.

System calls appear to be ordinary program procedure calls. The program gives the name of the system call such as 'write', for example, and an indication of what is to be written and to where – the screen, a printer or a specific part of the disk. Unlike ordinary procedures, however, the programmer does not have to then specify the details of just what the system call is to do. Instead, the instructions are part of a standard library of special-purpose procedures that are loaded into the computer along with the program itself. These system-call procedures all start with a special instruction that shifts the operating mode from user to supervisor so that the system call can access the hardware. In this way, the sensitive operation of the computer can be protected from clumsy programmers.

To the programs that use it, the operating system is defined by the interface to these special system-call procedures. They provide the means of controlling the computer itself and dictate the ways in which programs can interact with users. For example, the nature of the system calls provided by the operating system for controlling the computer screen determines whether the interaction is to be conducted through simple textual commands (as in the earliest computers) or through windows (as in modern machines).

One whole class of these system calls is particularly important, giving in many ways the truest flavour of modern computers, These are the system calls that between them create the 'file system', the fourth important task of the operating system.

Data has to be stored in some structured way if it is to be retrieved and used appropriately. Modern computers do this by storing data in a hierarchical arrangement of 'files' and 'folders' (or 'directories') on the computer's hard disk.[1] If the computer has several disk drives (or a single disk drive divided into several smaller ones), then the drive can be a further level of hierarchy.

To the operating system, however, a file is simply a collection of bytes that is stored on the disk and which is accessed and altered by the programs. Such a collection is referred to as a complete unit. On the disk, data is arranged in fixed-size units called 'clusters' or 'blocks'. Typical cluster sizes are 512 or 1024 bytes, numbered from zero up to whatever the maximum might be for a given size of hard disk. At the lowest possible level within the operating system, a file of information is simply the list of cluster reference numbers indicating where the file contents are stored on the disk. Users, however, do not think of files as being arrangements of clusters; rather, they think of a file in terms of a *name*. It is the operating system's task to provide the link between the names and the clusters. To provide this link, for each file the operating system keeps a data record at the start of the disk. This is variously called a 'file allocation table' or an 'inode table', depending on the operating system, Windows or UNIX.

In UNIX, the inode table has one inode (or 'information node') for each of the files held on the disk. This inode has a variety of information about the file, including how large it is, when it was last changed, whether the file is a program to be executed or a document to be edited, and so forth. The inode also has a set of 13 cluster numbers which, in effect, point to clusters (or 'blocks', as they are called in UNIX) spread around the disk. The first 10 of these pointers are to the first 10 blocks of the file. This allows files to be easily managed up to 10 blocks in size. As a file grows further, however, the operating system begins to handle the block pointers in a slightly different manner. The eleventh pointer is not to a file *data* block; instead, it points to a block which contains only further pointers to the data blocks. The twelfth is to a block that contains pointers to blocks that contain pointers. And the thirteenth adds a third level of 'indirection'. This mechanism allows UNIX files to grow to a very large size, yet also to be retrieved quickly.

The Windows file systems have always used a slightly different mechanism. The file allocation table (FAT) contains blocks with two addresses. The first is the cluster address that points to the file data block, and the second points to the FAT entry for the next cluster in the file. In effect, the FAT provides a 'daisy chain' of entries which point to the file blocks. The FAT structure is simple and allows files to grow without limit. It is also very powerful when programs proceed linearly through a file from the start to the end. It is less flexible, however, when a program (such as a word processor, for example) must jump to the middle of a particular file. The UNIX inode structure is much more useful in that case; conversely, it is less powerful at proceeding through files linearly. Operating systems are always compromises of this kind, although there are variants of file systems which attempt to combine the best of both these mechanisms.

The operating system locates and accesses a file by means of the FAT or inode reference, using specific system calls which take a reference number and perform read or write operations on a specific place in the file. This allows the operating system to 'spool' through the file to a desired byte and then either to overwrite it with a given number of specific characters or to read characters from that point onwards. Users, however, do not refer to a file by an inode or FAT reference; they specify the file's name. So the operating system has to translate the file name into the reference number. This is the role of the directories (in UNIX) or folders (in Windows), which contain a list of file names and a corresponding list of reference numbers. When a user gives the name of a file, the operating system simply looks in the directory or folder for the reference number corresponding to that file name, which is then used for the system calls to manipulate the file contents.

Perhaps the most important aspect of the file system, though, is not this obvious fact of files within directories within further directories. Rather, it is the way in which the file system is handled within the operating system. The operating system maintains a collection of data-structure entries corresponding to each file that is being used by a particular program, including the file that contains the program itself. These data structures provide the details of the files' inode or FAT reference blocks. A particularly clever aspect of both UNIX and Windows is that the operating system maintains exactly these data structures for access to other elements of the computer as well – the keyboard for input; the printer and the screen for output; and even the communication between individual processes and the network connections. All of these are provided with file-access data structures, so that *everything* is presented to the running programs as though it were just another file. The device drivers and the file system conspire to hide the implementation detail, giving the most general interface imaginable to every aspect of the computer.

In sum, operating systems provide carefully controlled mechanisms for accessing the physical computer; they provide an interface to the user; they provide a structured file system; and they provide a means to coordinate and run several processes simultaneously. The final two things that they manage are the protection of users from one another and the presentation of the computer's main memory.

User protection is part of the operating system's 'security management' role. The objective of these controls is to ensure that the computer maintains the confidentiality, integrity and availability of the information stored. Confidentiality ensures that information is made available only to those who should be permitted to see or use it; integrity, that the information is changed only in specific and well-understood ways; and availability, that the information is accessible to those who should be permitted to use it. Operating-system security measures are there to provide these features; and hackers and virus writers try to undermine them.

The basis of the security measures lies in the reliable identification of computer users. Individual users of a computer each have a unique identifying number, assigned to them when they are first registered on the computer. This registration associates a user name with the identification value. To prevent illicit users masquerading as valid ones, a password is also required. This is a word known only to the legitimate user, who gives it along with their user name when they log in to the computer. Assuming that the name and the password are correct, the operating system creates a process associated with that user identification number. The identification is then a part of the information attached to processes by the operating system, so that it can audit activity and ensure that no unauthorized processes are run.

To protect users from one another, the operating system maintains a strict control over the individual processes and files, so that only the processes associated with an authorized user can manipulate the files or other processes belonging to that user. Protecting users from one another is a straightforward exercise, though of course the main activity of hackers is to try and subvert this in a variety of clever ways.[2] This subversion is usually possible because of programming errors. The hackers' target is almost always to gain the most privileged status on the computer, that of the administrators or 'super users' of the computer, who alone are able to ignore or bypass the user-to-user restrictions imposed by the operating system.

The final task of the operating system is to manage the computer's main memory. Just as the operating system is responsible for mediating access to the disk drives and the other hardware facilities, the main memory is considered to be a manageable resource. The operating system achieves this management through a very clever mechanism called 'virtual memory'.

Any computer has a limited amount of real main memory, usually much less than can be accessed through the addresses supported by the computer in a 32- or 64-bit word. This means that the computer can potentially access much more memory than is actually available. Also, programs are written to be independent of the computer on which they might ultimately be run. With no way of knowing in advance how much main memory might be available, programs usually now assume that they have no limitation in memory availability and use as much main memory as they actually need.

Virtual-memory schemes allow the main memory that *is* present to be used in the most efficient manner, by allowing programs and users to assume that the total addressable memory is indeed present. This complete 'virtual' address space is divided into fixed-size blocks, usually the same size as the blocks stored on the hard disk. These are called 'pages'. All of these pages are stored on the hard disk, in an area called the 'swap file'. As a program runs, the first of the pages containing the program's instructions and data is copied bodily from the disk drive into the main memory, a process called 'paging'.

As the program runs, the locus of control that steps through the instructions and modifies the data will perhaps move on from this first page to another one. As it does so, the operating system receives an interrupt called a 'page fault', which makes the operating system suspend that program long enough to copy the required page into the main memory. This means, though, that one of the pages that is already in the main memory must be 'swapped' back out to the disk drive so as to make room for the new page. As with the issue of predicting which process is the best one to run at any given moment, this again is an opportunity for operating-system designers to try a number of different strategies to decide which page is the best choice. Some systems choose to swap out the page which was used the least recently; others the one that has been used the least frequently. More sophisticated schemes involve collecting complex usage statistics on each page to establish 'page weights', with the lightest being swapped.

These kinds of virtual-memory management schemes have a number of advantages. Most obviously, they allow programs to be written without regard to the actual physical form of the hardware on which they are to be run. This is a further development of the abstraction seen throughout the development of computer technology. Second, it provides a useful balance between using inexpensive hard-disk memory and the more expensive main memory storage. In fact, abstraction and the balance of costs against functionality are again the common themes running through all operating-system development.

An operating system is therefore the 'shell' that sits between users and their programs on the one hand, and the physical hardware on the other. It hides the details of the devices; supports a flexible interface to the user; provides access to files containing data or programs; and coordinates the execution of programs.

The development of these sophisticated computer operating systems was one of the key events in the history of technology.

The creation of operating systems

The earliest computers had no operating system at all. Instead, users accessed the computer directly, one at a time, booking their time slot well in advance. Research students, for example, often found that the only time slot available to them was the early hours of the morning. Each user was responsible for loading their own program, usually from paper tape or from punched cards, and then for overseeing its execution. In time, the inefficiency of this system became obvious, and instead of individual programs, operators would load a 'batch' of programs into the computer. Each program would be run, and then the computer would automatically jump to the next program in the batch. The 'operating system' was the simple loading routine run by the operator in order to copy the programs into the computer and to allow them to run.

Throughout the 1950s, this mode of computer operation was the norm. Programs were prepared and then delivered to the computer operator, who ensured that they were collated and executed and their results delivered back to the user. Tended by these acolytes and housed in a dedicated and separate room, the computer was a remote machine with which the ordinary user had no direct interaction.

Towards the end of the 1950s, however, a growing interest developed in 'time-sharing' access to the computer, so that several users could gain access concurrently, with the processing power shared dynamically between them. One of the first projects in time-sharing operating systems was the 1961 development of CTSS (Compatible Time-Sharing System) at the MIT Computation Centre in Cambridge, Massachusetts. CTSS was developed to run on a modified IBM mainframe computer, providing support for at least 200 users. It became the basis for one of the most important peacetime computer development programmes, Project MAC.

Project MAC grew from work proposed by Professor Joseph Licklider, one of computer science's greatest pioneers and second only to John von Neumann in terms of his impact and influence over the development of the subject. Known almost universally simply as 'Lick', he was the man who sowed the most important seeds that grew into the modern, interconnected world of user-friendly, point-and-click, windows-and-mouse-driven personal computers. He was the father of the operating system, the internet, and a host of other developments. In fact, without Licklider's work there would not even have been any PhDs offered by US universities in the emerging discipline of computer science.

'Lick' was born in St Louis, Missouri, in March 1915. He was undoubtedly an imaginative and creative genius, showing an early talent for science. Unusually amongst geniuses, he was also socially successful. He was well liked and modest, with a great skill at persuasion and 'people management' – a truly well-rounded individual. Licklider took no fewer than three degrees at nearby Washington State University – Mathematics, Physics and Psychology, an unusual combination of disciplines but one that prepared him for seeing relationships between several different fields of activity. His PhD research was in an equally unusual cross-disciplinary area, the psychology and physiology of the human auditory system. This examined the way in which people make out meaningful phrases and sounds even in the presence of substantial background noise. His results were immediately useful to the US Air Force, so the young Licklider moved to Harvard in 1942 to work on the USAF-sponsored problem of ensuring that crewmen in bombers could safely hear their orders.

Licklider's association with the USAF and his wide-ranging field of interests meant that in 1950 he was invited to MIT to join a particularly prestigious Air Force project, the SAGE system for integrating radar air-defence systems. SAGE (Semi-Automated Ground Environment) was envisaged as a sophisticated, computerized system to provide real-time interception information to an operator able to direct USAF fighters to Soviet bombers. Research and development for SAGE had started in 1948 when US military planners had begun to consider the integration of information collected from a number of different radar sites around the country. The Cold War threat of nuclear bombers from Russia, perhaps many of them flying quickly and low, was far too great for the simple command-and-control structure then in place. Operators would have to place telephone calls to one another, discussing the information that each was seeing on their screens. Information, recommendations, analysis and orders would all then have to flow through the system to the intercepting fighters. By that time, the bombs could well already be falling on US cities.

George Valley was a physicist at MIT who had been asked to consider this problem. The choice of a physicist may perhaps seem surprising at first, but in the Manhattan Project the US military had come to rely on scientists (physicists in particular) to solve their problems. In this situation, the military wanted science to help them not just in the problem of *creating* nuclear weapons but also in defending against them. Valley's solution was to adopt the then wholly new concept of information automation and to rely on computerized communication between the various radar sites; the data would be integrated into a single, coherent presentation that could then be acted upon by the interception operators directing the fighter aircraft.

In an age in which computers were typically operating exclusively on piles of punched-card data sets, remote from the user and tended by expert system managers, SAGE called for a wholly new form of user interaction. The flight operators had to be able to interact directly and immediately with the computer system, entering data and questions and getting responses almost immediately. Also, in an era when computer output was exclusively 'hard copy' (paper, punched card or tape), the operators needed to see the results displayed on a screen. SAGE introduced the concept of real-time interaction and was the first use of teletype and cathode-ray-tube displays.

So successful was SAGE that it became the basis for US air defence for 20 years throughout the most frightening period of the Cold War. The first SAGE division became operational in 1959 and continued until it was finally replaced in 1979 – though one SAGE division continued to operate up to 1983. Although eventually replaced, SAGE continued in a civilian form: the American Airlines SABRE system for flight reservations was created as a civilian implementation of the SAGE system in cooperation with IBM engineers who had worked on the military version.

As a psychologist and a mathematician, Licklider was ideal to provide the basis for the 'human factors' aspect of this development work. From 1950 to 1957 he contributed to the SAGE project while teaching both psychology and computer science to graduate and undergraduate students at MIT. Most importantly, during this period Licklider began to develop a series of ideas culminating in a 1960 paper, 'Man-Computer Symbiosis', which anticipated the concept of user-friendly interfaces to computers.

In 1957, Licklider left MIT to join the company Bolt, Beranek and Newman (BBN), based close to the MIT buildings in

Cambridge, Massachusetts. Before Licklider's arrival, BBN was a firm of consulting engineers in Licklider's first academic interest, the control of noise. The company had been formed in 1948 by two MIT professors, Richard Bolt and Leo Beranek, who were joined a year later by a former student, Robert Newman. They had provided advice on the acoustics for the United Nations Assembly Hall in 1948 and had spent many years analysing the noise aspects of jet aircraft. Licklider's early work on noise levels in USAF bombers was clearly of interest to the company.

Licklider, however, had plans in another direction, and he persuaded them to invest first 25,000 dollars and then a further 150,000 dollars on two computers. He worked at BBN for six years, rising to the post of vice-president and moulding the company into one of the US's leading computer consultancies. Beginning with those first two computers, Licklider hired a series of talented computer engineers as they graduated from MIT. He developed computer programs to help BBN in the business of acoustical studies of buildings for public performances, but he also worked on developing his own ideas of how time-sharing computers (rather than 'batch processing') could be managed for large numbers of users. In 1960, as his key paper on using computers was published, Licklider and his team of engineers were able to implement an interrupt management subsystem on a PDP-1 computer, allowing the demonstration of a working time-sharing system. In 1962, BBN were able to give the first public demonstration of several users simultaneously accessing and using a single computer.

Licklider moved on to greater things at the end of 1962, but his legacy at BBN was enormous. Although they continued to have an involvement in acoustical analysis (working, for example, on an audio tape for the Kennedy assassination inquiry), BBN moved almost wholly into computer science. BBN specialists invented the Logo programming language, developed the first network email program, introduced the use of the @ symbol for email addressing, and even implemented the first four nodes of what would become the internet. They are now one of the leading research and development companies in the world. Licklider himself, however, left BBN in October 1962, headhunted to join the organization where he would have his greatest influence, the Advanced Research Projects Agency.

On 4 October 1957, Americans woke to the news that the Soviets had successfully launched a Sputnik satellite into orbit on board a modified missile. It is hard to overstate the shock that this news produced. A nation which had come to take their leadership in science and in technology for granted had been humbled by their greatest adversary. Worse, they had been humbled in a way that had immediately obvious military implications, since an adversary that could launch a Sputnik could equally easily launch a spy satellite or even a nuclear warhead. The sense of outrage at the loss of security felt by US citizens would not be repeated until the infamous events of 11 September 2001.

The result of this shock was a programme of research and development, principally into aerospace and defensive technologies. It resulted in Kennedy's commitment to put a man on the Moon; and it led to the aptly named MAD (Mutually Assured Destruction) stand-off with the Soviet bloc. The first and most important step in all this, however, was the establishment of the Advanced Research Projects Agency in February 1958.

ARPA was established to fund and carry out research into areas of technology and science that would directly assist the military effort. ARPA, indeed, was subsequently renamed DARPA, the *Defence* Advanced Research Projects Agency, to reflect this focus. One of the keys identified early on for this advanced research was the use of computers. Their role was not simply to perform complex mathematical calculations but, as shown in the experience with SAGE, to provide communication and analysis capabilities in real time, and to provide a reliable and robust command-and-control network for the US military. Licklider's work within SAGE and his writing and research while at BBN had shown him to be ideal for the exercise. In October 1962 the director of ARPA, Jack Ruina, persuaded Licklider to join the agency.

Licklider was initially given two ARPA departments to run – Behavioural Science and Command and Control. He was also given a donated computer along with instructions to 'find something new' to do with it. He began immediately to find new things to do, though not simply with the operation of the computer. Instead, he began to explore new ways of performing research and development in the field of computing.

During World War II, the US military had funded research projects in the universities. This had led to the creation of computing technologies at a variety of different places – MIT, Stanford, Princeton, Harvard and so forth. After the war, however, computer companies had been established to exploit these developments, and the military had become used to placing their development requirements with these companies. The result was that the military received those technologies and developments that were in keeping with the computer companies' requirements. These companies were more interested in making traditional, offline, commercial batch processing work efficiently than they were in exploring wholly new ways of accessing and using computers.

Licklider began to seek out a group of researchers and individuals at the universities, directing funds into those projects and programmes most likely to have the impact that he wanted. Under Licklider, ARPA established a wholly new department, the Information Processing Techniques Office, or IPTO. This funded, amongst many other projects, the work at Stanford carried out by Douglas Englebart which led to the creation of the mouse, windows and icons of graphical user interfaces. It was as a direct result of this funding focus that US universities began to offer PhD research programmes in computer science. Licklider also proposed that the research groups he had funded (which he jokingly referred to as the 'Intergalactic Computer Network') should be provided with a means of communicating computer-to-computer. This became the internet. Finally, he agreed to fund a broad research programme at MIT that would encompass operating-system design and user interaction with time-shared computers. This last became Project MAC; the 'MAC' element variously stood for 'Man And Computer', 'Machine-Aided Cognition', and 'Multi-Access Computer', depending on which element of the total programme was under consideration. The project was initially run by Robert Fano, but in 1968 Licklider himself took over its management after a brief period of working for IBM.

Project MAC was a particularly ambitious programme whose aim was to research and to produce some wholly new, flexible and powerful ways of interacting with computers, ostensibly so as to support the military use of command-and-control systems. MIT was home to Marvin Minsky's Artificial Intelligence group, as well as various groups looking at man–machine interfaces, computer networking, computer-aided design, and (as shown in the development of CTSS) novel ideas in operating systems. It was the ideal location, and the project flourished in the period from 1963 to 1970, when it received some 25 million dollars' worth of support from Licklider's IPTO at ARPA and substantial funds from the American National Science Foundation.

Joseph Licklider retired from MIT in 1985, and he died of complications from an asthma attack in June 1990. However, he lived long enough to see many of the ideas that he had proposed and funded come to fruition. Licklider's genius and far-sightedness in steering both IPTO and Project MAC through the 1960s produced a series of vitally important ideas, from which almost every aspect of the modern computer world can be traced. The Xerox PARC work on graphical user interfaces grew from ideas formulated in Project MAC and pursued by alumni from the programme. Spreadsheets, word processing, local-area networks, expert systems, and computer-aided design all benefited from the well-funded hot-house atmosphere of Project MAC during those years.

Perhaps the most important development, however, was in operating systems.

The UNIX operating system

The MIT-developed CTSS was originally chosen as the base operating system to support the Project MAC activity. Although it supported several hundred concurrent users, however, it was not as powerful, simple or secure as the researchers required. So in 1965 work began on an improved operating system to resolve these problems and to explore the limits (at that time) of operating-system design. The result was MULTICS, the Multiplexed Information and Computing Service, developed as a collaboration between Project MAC, AT&T's Bell Laboratories, and General Electric.

It was a hugely ambitious project, which established a lot of the concepts that would come to be crucial parts of all modern operating systems. MULTICS was one of the first operating systems to be written in a high-level language (PL/1) so as to be more easily portable between computers and more easily modified; it featured flexible handling of files and of computer devices such as keyboards and printers; and it was designed with an intrinsic security model so that only file *owners* were able to access or to change the contents. Unfortunately, it was also cumbersome and very complex, so the Bell Labs researchers felt that a simpler structure was more likely to be successful.

Although the Bell Labs contingent withdrew, MULTICS did in fact go on to be a success. It ran on the General Electric 32-bit mainframe until bought out by Honeywell (later Honeywell Bull, after a merger with the large French national computer company). About 80 sites used the Honeywell Bull MULTICS operating system, particularly in French universities and the government marketplace, until development was finally halted in 1985 in favour of a more robust operating system called GeCOS. Even after development had finished, however, MULTICS had a long and fruitful life, with the final platform eventually turned off only on Halloween 2000.

The two key members of the Bell Labs MULTICS team were young but gifted computer programmers Ken Thompson and Dennis Ritchie. They were not withdrawn from the MULTICS project to work on another exercise, certainly not to develop a new operating system specifically for AT&T. They were, at least initially, at a loss as to what to do with their time. The most popular story (though it undoubtedly has apocryphal elements) for what the pair did involves a discarded DEC PDP-7 computer that they found in a storeroom and decided to 'liberate' in order to write documents and to play a 'space explorers' computer game.

Had they not already had the experience of working on the baroquely complicated MULTICS system, it is likely that Thompson and Ritchie would have contented themselves with simply porting the game and the text editor to the PDP-7. They would have been able to play their game sooner, but the world of useful computer systems would have been all the poorer for it. As it was, the pair decided to apply some of what they had learned on the project (and some improvements of their own) to creating a simple operating system on the platform before porting the two programs.

The most important step that the pair took in designing their operating system was to concentrate on simplicity. Where previous systems such as MULTICS and CTSS had featured huge, complex programs, Thompson and Ritchie designed a simple, slim-line system. In particular, they created a single central program to run much of the functionality in the 'supervisor-privileged' mode – they called this the 'kernel'. In the kernel were the interrupt, device, process and file-handling facilities. Everything else was constructed on top of this foundation and operated primarily in user mode, save for the necessary function calls to those services.

It made for a fast, flexible and simple environment. This basic kernel structure (now referred to as a 'monolithic kernel') has been the basis of all operating systems since that time. As a play on the name MULTICS, Thompson and Ritchie called the operating system the '*Uni*plexed Information and Computing System', or UNIX,[3] because on the PDP-7 it supported at most only two simultaneous users, one of whom had to run as the privileged 'super user' of the system.

This very first, very simple UNIX system was written in PDP-7 assembler code and was completed in 1969. By 1972, UNIX had progressed dramatically. Dennis Ritchie had devised a powerful programming language (the C language) specifically for tasks such as operating-system development. Together with another Bell Labs programmer, Brian Kernighan, Ritchie and Thompson moved the operating system onto a more powerful DEC PDP-11/20 and rewrote it in C with no assembler code. They now had a simple, portable and flexible operating environment, which was built on the foundation of handling everything as a file (even including interaction between individual processes) and was remarkably reliable. It even supported arbitrarily many users and could be easily understood by anyone able to program in C.

Ritchie and Thompson's new operating system also introduced the concept of a structured file system. This was a hierarchical structure of directories, subdirectories and files arranged as a tree from a single, common root. Although this feature was first developed in MULTICS, it was UNIX that made the principle commonplace. Before UNIX, file systems were arranged in a simple, flat arrangement of drive, directory and file. Now, every operating system has adopted the tree hierarchy, although Windows retains the distinct drive letters as much for backwards compatibility as for any other reason. UNIX also introduced small, constantly running programs called 'daemons' which provide operating-system facilities (such as access to the printer or to the network services) through simple interfaces.

UNIX also developed the idea of the 'command line interface', called the 'shell'. Many earlier operating systems had a 'job control language' to allow the user or the operator to direct the sequence of execution of different programs. Indeed, the invention of operating systems for the earlier generation of shared-computer systems arose as a way of supporting this control language's operation. Earlier computer operating systems also supported an interactive way of directing operations from the computer console or from separate teletypes. These two forms of interaction were essentially distinct, however, and a different syntax, command structure and interface were used for each. In the shell, UNIX provided a command interface subsequently copied by nearly every other operating system until the Xerox PARC invention of the 'windows, icons, mouse and pointer' interface became more widespread. Commands were specified by a single keyword ('copy', for example) followed by a list of arguments. Individual commands could take their input from a file or from the output of other programs, chained together by 'pipes'. Everything was handled simply as though it were a file, even including input/output devices such as keyboards and screens.

Finally, Ritchie and Thompson deliberately created the UNIX kernel (the most basic, central element of the operating system) to be portable from computer to computer. First, it was written wholly in the C programming language, a significant achievement given that (except for MULTICS) all previous operating systems had been written in assembler. Second, the machine-dependent elements, principally the device drivers, were separated from the rest of the kernel by simple, standard interfaces behind which they could be rewritten for each different computer. In UNIX, a lot of (then) very new ideas of operating-system design came together in what was a remarkably simple system. Rather than being designed by a committee, the system was designed by two very skilled programmers; and rather than being designed to show off particular features of the underlying hardware, it was designed to do a simple job of work.

Interest in this novel environment began to stretch throughout Bell Labs and to the various universities and research establishments working with them. At first, the developers distributed the source code of the operating system freely (or at least for the cost of the tape and postage) to every university or establishment that asked for it. UNIX spread rapidly around the world in the mid to late 1970s. Because UNIX was distributed with the source code, other developers were equally able to extend, improve and modify the operating system. At the University of California at Berkeley, the BSD (Berkeley Systems Development) version was produced and distributed, and subsequently adopted by many of the computer manufacturers. At AT&T, an official release called 'System V' was developed and marketed through most of the other computer companies. This eventually evolved into a version of UNIX that combined the AT&T and the BSD developments, and which was ultimately adopted by almost every computer manufacturer, even including Apple for the most recent of their systems.

As well as these official versions of the operating system, a number of unofficial, free implementations were also produced. The most important of these is the Linux operating system, developed by a Finnish university student, Linus Torvald, as a hobby in 1991, but now popularized around the world as a powerful, free operating system that is compatible with the standard UNIX system. For personal computers, Linux is *the* alternative to the other important operating system, Microsoft Windows.

Beyond these immediate members of the UNIX family tree, the operating system had an even wider impact on the field of operating-system design and programming philosophy. It introduced the concept of 'open systems', in which an operating system can be run on different manufacturers' platforms and operate in a well-publicized, well-understood and agreed manner. It popularized the C programming language, now effectively the standard language in which almost every major program is developed. It also introduced the basic philosophy of combining several simple, distinct programs in different configurations to create more powerful processing options. UNIX helped to create a legacy of small, flexible and powerful operating systems able to run on different computers. On the surface, it introduced elements such as the command line for users to direct the computer's operation; it popularized the nested hierarchy of directories and subdirectories; and it developed the concept of a small kernel at the heart of the operating system. These were all elements that gained even wider attention in the range of operating systems produced by Microsoft.

The rise of Microsoft and Windows

Microsoft is now *the* dominant company in the computer industry. The overwhelming majority of personal computers run a Microsoft operating system; the Microsoft office automation tools are the most popular choice for word processing or spreadsheets; and Microsoft has come to influence large elements of the World Wide Web over the internet. However, this dominance came about in part as a result of a mistake on the part of an all but completely forgotten company called Digital Research Inc. (DRI) and a contract to supply the operating system on the IBM PC.

The original, most popular operating system on the first generation of personal computers was developed in 1973 by Gary Kildall, who founded DRI (originally called Intergalactic Digital Research) when he left the US Navy in 1976 to pursue the system's commercial possibilities.

As an instructor in the navy, Kildall had begun development on the system to provide a support environment for his implementation of the PL/1 programming language on the newly emerging 4- and 8-bit microprocessors from Intel. He called this implementation of the language 'PL/M' (Programming Language for Microcomputers) and the operating system to support it 'CP/M' (Control Program for Microcomputers).

Sold originally through classified advertisements in computer magazines, by 1977 CP/M was the most common operating system on the 8080 and Z80 microcomputers which were then becoming popular. Although small and simple, CP/M had a lot of features that Kildall borrowed from the UNIX operating system – in particular, the command-line interface, a hierarchical file system, and the separation of hardware-dependent and hardware-independent elements. Arguably, CP/M went even further than UNIX in this separation: it provided a low-level, machine-dependent set of routines called the BIOS (Basic Input/Output System) upon which an abstract BDOS (Basic Disk Operating System) was built. The BIOS handled the device drivers to interface directly with the computer's disk drive, while the BDOS provided the abstract functionality of a file system. On top of this file system, the CP/M command line (the CCP, or Console

Command Processor) operated to interpret the user's requests in the form of keywords followed by a list of files and control instructions, just like the UNIX shell on which it was based.

CP/M was widely successful at the end of the 1970s. The original personal computer office automation tools (WordStar and dBase, the first small-system word-processor and database applications) were originally written for CP/M, and it became the operating system for the popular personal computer the Atari ST. No surprise, therefore, that when IBM elected to enter the fast-growing personal computer market with their 1980 development of the PC, their first call was on Gary Kildall to seek a licence to use the operating system. Unfortunately for Kildall, the IBM lawyers were unsuccessful in negotiating an acceptable contract and turned instead to a small, eager company called Microsoft.

Originally called Micro-soft, the company was created by Bill Gates and his school friend Paul Allen in 1975 to sell a BASIC interpreter that they had developed while both still students at Harvard University.[4] The interpreter was created for the then most successful personal computer, the Altair 8800, and meant that Microsoft was already established in that market by 1980. In developing the PC, IBM licensed this BASIC interpreter so as to provide a familiar environment for the computer users it wished to attract. An existing commercial link with Gates and Allen meant that when the negotiations with Kildall failed, IBM's next choice of partner was the fledgling Microsoft.

Although Microsoft had their headquarters in New Mexico, Gates himself was from Seattle and knew a lot of the software companies in that area. One in particular was Seattle Computer Products, where a programmer called Tim Paterson had developed a fully functional 'clone' of the CP/M operating system called QDOS (Quick and Dirty Operating System). The legality of that clone was the subject of a dispute with DRI, but nonetheless, in April 1981, Gates bought a non-exclusive licence for QDOS for 25,000 dollars, allowing Microsoft to demonstrate a CP/M-like operating system that was free of the contractual problems IBM had encountered with DRI. Having got a signed agreement with IBM, Gates subsequently bought an exclusive licence for QDOS for just 50,000 dollars three months later. Given the immense wealth and the vast business empire that Gates forged from that single deal, this must surely count as the IT equivalent of the American settlers buying Manhattan Island for a handful of brightly coloured beads and a bottle of whisky.

Seattle Computer Products was understandably unhappy when they discovered that Gates had omitted to mention the IBM agreement when he had negotiated the exclusive licence with them. They decided to bring a legal action against Microsoft for unfair business practices, eventually settling out of court for an undisclosed amount and passing ownership of QDOS wholly to Microsoft. In Gates's defence, there was no particular reason for him to have mentioned the IBM deal in his negotiations, that being part of the cut and thrust of business; and he was probably covered by a non-disclosure agreement anyway.

Obtaining a licence for QDOS was the first element in building Microsoft's fortunes; the second element was the company's agreement with IBM. In August 1981 Microsoft licensed QDOS to IBM, giving IBM the right to sell the operating system on their PC products under the name PC-DOS. Keen to exploit their exclusive licence, however, Microsoft retained the right to sell the QDOS product to other manufacturers. The first release of MS-DOS came out in June 1982. With the immense marketing engine of IBM behind it, through the 1980s the PC grew to become *the* dominant platform in the industry, and with it DOS equally became the standard. However, this dominance arose as much as a result of the many PC clones produced by other companies, all of them licensing the MS-DOS operating system from Microsoft. From a tiny, specialist computer software supplier, Microsoft grew on the back of this MS-DOS revenue to become one of the largest companies in the world; and Bill Gates himself has become *the* richest man, with a personal fortune that makes him richer than many countries.

Digital Research and the CP/M operating system resisted commercial pressure from PC-DOS and MS-DOS for a short period of time, since it was generally perceived that CP/M was technically the more impressive product. However, IBM and Microsoft marketing of the DOS systems established a powerful brand that attracted not only vast numbers of users but also an impressive array of applications. In 1988, Digital Research finally bowed to the inevitable and produced a new version of CP/M called DR-DOS. For a time, DR-DOS, PC-DOS and MS-DOS competed essentially head-to-head, each adding functionality – and Microsoft quite deliberately introducing incompatibilities in an attempt to corner the market. For example, as the Windows graphical user interface (GUI) became increasingly popular, Microsoft configured the interface to issue an error message when it was run on DR-DOS.

Eventually, however, Digital Research was bought by Novell, who unfortunately were not able to take full advantage of the operating system, leaving Microsoft the winner by 1995 of what had been a fierce battle for domination. Perhaps the most important aspect of that battle had come in the field of GUIs, first developed by Xerox at the Palo Alto Research Centre but popularized by the Apple Macintosh.

As far back as 1983, Gates had recognized that users exposed to the Macintosh interface and subsequently to a similar windows-based interface called GEM under CP/M and on the Atari ST would demand something substantially easier to use than the DOS command-line interface. The first version of Windows was released in 1985 as a DOS program to allow access to some simple applications. It was not a success, because Apple had become aware of Microsoft's plans for the program and had threatened legal action if the look-and-feel was too similar to their product. The first release of Windows was therefore functionally restricted and not particularly efficient. In 1987, Windows version 2 followed, with version 3 (the first true commercial success in the Windows family) following in 1990. In the decade that followed, Microsoft produced a range of operating systems that came to dominate first the home and small-office markets, then the larger commercial markets. Windows itself grew from being simply another application running under MS-DOS, to a free-standing operating system in its own right — and ultimately into a computing paradigm and one of the most powerful brands in the modern world.

6
Where did the internet come from?

The internet is *the* wonder of the modern world, a global network
that allows people to communicate almost instantly with one
another all around the world. It links computers together and
provides access to unimaginably vast pools of information; it
supports text and pictures, sound and movies; it allows email, chat
and even live camera images to be passed from person to person; and
it allows users to shop, bank or browse from their PC. Accessed most
commonly either by a web browser (such as Microsoft's Internet
Explorer) or by an electronic mail application (such as Outlook), the
internet is an astonishingly robust network. It is much more than
simply a computer network – it is a *communication* network.

The internet started as a way of linking military and academic
computer researchers together, and it grew to encompass

commercial organizations and private individuals. It replaced a variety of clumsier, less open communication structures, such as dial-up bulletin boards and online communities (CompuServe, for example). The basic networking instructions that make the internet work (called TCP/IP) now also support almost every private network and are growing to include telephone, television and wireless communications.

It is a fascinating and challenging environment to work with and to play in, and the story of its development is equally fascinating.

Communication networks

Communication networks pre-date computers by many years. The telegraph and telephone networks (the first for what we would now understand as data communications, the second for voice) were the earliest networks. The first commercial telegraph system started in May 1794 between Paris and Lille, with line-of-sight signalling stations on a string of hills between the two cities. By 1845, electrical telegraph systems were being built in the USA and in England. And in November 1851 a submarine cable between England and France was established, beginning the process of 'wiring the world'.

Interestingly, that first submarine cable was insulated with a material called gutta-percha, a resinous gum that the Victorians used as a form of primitive plastic. The Gutta-Percha Company of London had a virtual monopoly on the import of the material. When the General Oceanic and Subterranean Electric Printing Telegraph Company came to buy their entire stock of the material, the Gutta-Percha Company realized that they were in an ideal position to make a lot of money out of the telegraph. Over the years that followed, the Gutta-Percha Company flourished and evolved into the modern telecommunications giant, Cable & Wireless.

Telephone networks followed hard on the heels of the telegraph. The first telephone exchange opened in London in 1879, operated by the Telephone Company Ltd. in Coleman Street behind the Bank of England. It was, in effect, a private club in which members were provided with telephone equipment that allowed them to talk to other members of the club. Indeed, the origin of the term 'subscriber' for a telephone company's customer lies in the club-like nature of the first exchanges.

The rapid growth of the telegraph and telephone networks at the end of the 19th century led to an equally rapid growth in understanding how networks behaved and were best organized. The mathematical theory of network structure is called graph theory, which deals with nodes and the links between them. The first analysis of networks can be traced back to a 1736 paper by Leonhard Euler, in which he analysed a path that would take in each bridge in the city of Königsberg once and only once. Under pressure to analyse the best way of structuring expensive cable connections between cities, graph theory flourished. Companies such as AT&T (the American Telephone and Telegraph Company, originally the Bell Telephone Company formed by Alexander Graham Bell in 1877) employed not just engineers and technicians but also pure mathematicians to work on these problems.

The first telephone exchanges were 'star' networks, in which all connections between the several nodes went via one single, central node. By contrast, the first telegraph links were 'point-to-point' networks: each node connected to another node, which in turn connected to a further node.

Each of these two structures arose as a result of the way in which the different networks developed. For the telegraph, wires were literally strung from city to city, particularly across the American West, as the network stretched further and further. Each telegraph station would receive requests to transmit messages and would pass

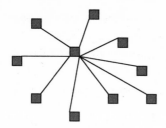

Star network

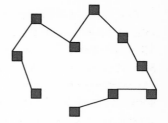

Point to point network

them 'down the wire' to the next station. By contrast, telephone networks connected handset to handset by means of a central exchange that literally made the connection on a plug board.

These networks were functional, simple but easily broken. If any connection or node in a point-to-point network fails, the network is cut in half; if the central node of a star network fails, then the entire network collapses. In developing communications networks, the companies involved were dependent on the continued operation of their infrastructure to make money, so failures had to be managed in such a way so as not to ruin the entire network.

One solution is to connect every node to every other node in a 'fully connected' structure. Although this can survive multiple node or connection failures and continue to function, it is expensive for all but the smallest network. Alternatively, a 'richly connected' (or 'distributed') structure can be used, in which some but not all

Fully connected network

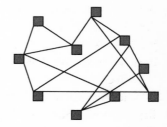

Richly connected network

nodes have multiple connections so as to provide alternative communication paths.

In practice, the telegraph and telephone networks became combinations of these structures. Local exchanges continued to resemble star networks, with fully connected networks linking local exchanges to nearby exchanges. These in turn were then linked by richly connected structures between towns, with only the most remote of places connected by single links. The links themselves have also developed, from simple electric cables to fibre-optic, microwave and radio links, and now even include satellite communication channels. Finally, the nature of the transmissions has changed. From the initial telephone and telegraph transmissions, they have now evolved into data communications.

The impetus for the development of computer networks lies once again with the SAGE air-defence system developed in the 1950s with funding from the US Air Force and involving Joseph Licklider and others. The network supporting SAGE had to provide a means for computer-controlled radar systems widely spread throughout the country to communicate with one another quickly, reliably and without human intervention. Furthermore, that communication had to continue to operate despite the threat of small- or even large-scale damage, since it was a system developed for use during a possible nuclear conflict. Finally, that communication had to be conducted over the public telephone system, since stringing dedicated cable connections right across the American continent was not considered feasible when there was already such a connection established by 'Ma Bell' – AT&T.

In using normal telephone connections, however, SAGE faced a difficult problem. Computers communicate with local peripheral devices (teletypes and printers, for example) by sending 8-bit characters a bit at a time in a steady stream of binary values along a serial cable. The individual binary values are encoded as changes in the electricity flowing within that cable. Crudely, a current represents a 1 and no current a 0. Over short lengths of good-quality cable, the abrupt current alterations necessary to transmit a stream of binary values successfully were possible. Even before SAGE, experiments had been carried out in the 1950s to link two or three computers together in this way, making one computer believe that a second computer was a very fast typist on a teletype.

Whilst this was possible over short lengths of cable, unfortunately the public telephone system in the USA was never constructed to perform in this way. The spoken word features smooth variations in sound as people talk, and the telephone transmissions reflected this in smooth variations in the current transmitted from handset to handset. When the SAGE developers tried to transmit data, with the abrupt current changes to reflect a 1 turning into a 0, they found that the electrical properties of the wires and switches in the connection 'smeared' the signal. For voice transmission, already effectively smeared by the speaker, this had never been a problem, since the human ear is well used to understanding such smearing. However, this network characteristic made data transmission impossible.

The solution that was proposed was a clever one. Instead of making the telephone system behave like a serial cable, they decided to make the serial cable behave like a voice transmission. The SAGE engineers began to experiment with ways of translating data signals into voice-like signals that could be successfully transmitted. The result was the first modem ('modulator/demodulator'). The Bell-103 was invented by researchers at AT&T Bell Laboratories in 1958 and was capable of transmitting 300 bits per second across the telephone wires as two different audible tones, which was ideal for the telephone network.

The Bell-103 was made a commercial product by AT&T in 1962, so for the first time business computer users were provided with a way of connecting computers together over wide areas rather than in the limited manner presented by serial-cable connections. The first attempt outside the SAGE programme to create a computer-to-computer connection like this was undertaken by an MIT researcher called Larry Roberts in 1965.

The project had been proposed to ARPA by another MIT scientist, psychologist Thomas Merrill, who had studied under Joseph Licklider during his work on SAGE at MIT. Influenced heavily by Licklider's vision, Merrill too had come to appreciate the potential of computers. In particular, he wanted to see whether it was possible to connect a time-shared computer at MIT with a dissimilar system working at the Systems Development Corporation (SDC) in Santa Monica, California.[1] ARPA agreed to fund the exercise, and Larry Roberts, who was researching computer graphics at the time, was asked to lead the project. Roberts was yet another who had come under Licklider's influence, after a meeting in November 1964 when the pair had discussed the possibility of extending the SAGE graphics and communications capability into broader computer applications to support research.

Roberts's network experiment was a success, in that the two computers were indeed able to communicate over this first wide-area network – though it was slow and unreliable in practice, with data often garbled in transmission. As before, the work to develop these ideas further still was pursued by researchers funded by ARPA – and yet again, much of the activity carried the fingerprints of one man in particular, Joseph Licklider.

The ARPANET development

In his work on the SAGE programme in the 1960s, Licklider had developed an acute understanding of the potential of computer networks and of the need for a more sophisticated interaction, both between man and computer, and between man and man via computer. He saw the computer as a means of allowing people to work together, sharing results, rather than as an 'information engine' simply used for generating data from other data. One thing in particular that Licklider envisaged was a global network of computers to allow communication and the sharing of results amongst a pool of computer-science researchers in diverse fields such as artificial intelligence, user interfaces and the like. Beyond this, Licklider also imagined that the network of computers would give access not simply to the research results themselves but also to a broader pool of information that might be stored in databases associated with those computers. It was a vision remarkably similar to the modern-day World Wide Web. Licklider described some of this vision in a short paper while he was still at BBN.[2]

Licklider was ahead of most computer scientists (and indeed, he was even ahead of the science-fiction writers in his vision), but he was not the first to imagine those ideas. In 1945 a US engineer, Vannevar Bush, had written 'As We May Think' for the Atlantic Monthly magazine. The article was visionary, but Bush was no dreamer. He was an electrical engineer at MIT who had worked on submarine detection during World War I and who had developed the mechanical Bush Differential Analyser calculating machine, which had been used to compute ballistic trajectories for the US Army before the creation of the ENIAC computer.

Between the wars, Bush had experimented with an electro-mechanical device for microfiche information, envisaged initially as an aid for the FBI in retrieving fingerprint cards. Only four of the devices (which he called 'rapid retrievers') were ever actually built, since they suffered from continual technical problems. Not unlike Babbage in the 19th century, Bush was a visionary for whom the then-current state of technology was not sufficient. Though his 1930s experiments with the rapid retrievers were not a success, thinking more broadly Bush realized that the retrieved information could be anything – even encyclopedia entries. In the 1945 article Bush imagined a development of his retriever, which he called a 'memex'. He described a user exploring the space of interrelated information, building 'association trails' in the hunt for information about a topic of interest – a hunting bow, in his examples within the article. With the benefit of hindsight, Bush's description sounds remarkably similarly to the hypertext association of pages within the modern World Wide Web.

Though Bush and Licklider, nearly 20 years apart, seemed to have dreamt the same dream, Licklider was in the happy position of being able to realize his. Just a few months after collaborating with Wesley Clark to write 'On-line Man Computer Communication', Licklider was appointed by ARPA director Jack Ruina as the inaugural head of the Information Processing Techniques Office (IPTO). He had the express mission of finding new things to do with computers. Licklider effectively established his manifesto for the research activity that he envisaged undertaking in a series of memos written in October 1962 to 'Members of the Intergalactic Computer Network' (his name for the group of 'Principal Investigators'). In these memos he laid out the tasks to be undertaken and the problems to be solved.

Though the name that Licklider gave to the group might well have been tongue-in-cheek, they really *were* an impressive collection of names, with reputations to match: Robert Fano of MIT, who would head up Project MAC; Douglas Englebart of Stanford, who would invent the mouse and graphical user interfaces; John McCarthy, also of Stanford, and Marvin Minsky of MIT, who would take artificial intelligence in radical new directions; and Edward Feigenbaum of the University of California at Berkeley, who would produce brilliantly innovative work in the field of expert systems. All in all, there were some half-dozen of the country's leading universities, alongside the RAND Corporation, SDC and the Stanford Research Institute, represented in the group.

Central to these memos was the problem of allowing the different research groups to communicate with one another using widely diverse computers, programming languages and data formats – exactly the problem that the World Wide Web now seamlessly solves. Many interesting research projects and indeed the whole principle of funding computer-science research in universities were established by Licklider during his tenancy of the IPTO directorship. He had at his disposal a phenomenal amount of funding to allocate as he saw fit, with the primary objective, ostensibly at least, of exploring new command-and-control structures for the US military establishment. Licklider also, however, had a remarkable degree of latitude in where and how that money was allocated, so he ensured that it was directed at projects that would indeed change the way in which computers were used and interconnected.

In July 1964, with the initial funding and encouragement for the key projects in place, Licklider accepted a position at IBM. In 1968 he would return to academic life at MIT and take over the reins at Project MAC from Robert Fano, completing the work that gave impetus to UNIX. And in January 1974 he would in fact return to ARPA and once again accept the directorship of the IPTO organization as the ARPANET was extended into the internet. In his first tenancy of the IPTO position, Licklider had done enough to start the work that would lead towards his vision of the 'Intergalactic Computer Network' communication link that he had written about in his memos. To continue the work, Licklider persuaded the ARPA director to appoint Ivan Sutherland as his replacement. Sutherland was a graphics specialist at the University of Utah and one of Licklider's Intergalactic group. He had worked on novel computer display technology and had made great strides in the development of what would become virtual reality. As a proponent of Licklider's vision of man–computer symbiosis, he was an ideal second director, and it was he in fact who oversaw the funding allocation to Larry Roberts and Thomas Merrill to establish the world's first wide-area network.

In 1966, as Roberts and Merrill's work became more widely known, Sutherland left IPTO to be replaced by Robert Taylor, who had joined ARPA from NASA a few months earlier. Like Licklider, Bob Taylor's academic background had been in the unusual discipline of psycho-acoustic analysis; and like Licklider, Taylor had an acute interest in computer networks and in human–computer interaction. In fact, Taylor and Licklider cooperated in the writing of a seminal paper in April 1968 called 'The Computer as Communication Device', in which the fundamental principles of what would become the internet were clearly articulated. As Larry Roberts's first computer network had grown into the 'Experimental Network' with the inclusion of a DEC minicomputer at ARPA, Taylor had watched with interest. When he joined ARPA, Taylor had been shocked to see that he had not one but three computer terminals in his office, connected to different computers around the country. Anticipating that the number of connections could not but grow, Taylor was anxious to find a way of developing Roberts's Experimental Network ideas into the practical and general network that Licklider had described.

In December 1966, Taylor convinced the young Larry Roberts (only 29 years old) to work directly for ARPA as IPTO Chief Scientist, developing what would be called the ARPANET.

⌐⊕

The first presentation of the formal ideas for the ARPANET concept of linking research groups together was not a happy one. Larry Roberts was persuaded to hold the first ARPANET Design Session at a meeting of the IPTO Principal Investigators in April 1967, at a regular research-group meeting in Ann Arbor, Michigan. His concept of the ARPANET was a simple extension of the work that he and Merrill had undertaken on the Experimental Network. This featured telephone dial-up connections using simple modems between each of the half-dozen computer centres involved, using transmission methods broadly similar to the ones he had already managed to make work.

Roberts's plans were met with at best disbelief and at worse outright hostility. Many of the researchers had invested substantial sums of money and phenomenal amounts of time in their computing resources, and they saw little reason to share them. Others questioned whether the simple Experimental Network *could* be extended to so many wildly different models of computer. Most damaging of all, some of the other, more thoughtful researchers questioned whether, even if the current systems could be integrated, it would be possible to continue that integration as further new systems were introduced. Roberts's initial idea would have required computer scientists at, say, SDC in Santa Monica to provide a suite of network functions to allow their system to communicate with a computer at Stanford; a further suite of functions for SDC to communicate with the wholly different computer at Berkeley; yet another suite for MIT; and so on. Moreover, that entire integration exercise would have had to be carried out by every one of the computing centres every time a further computing centre was added to the network or a new computer was purchased at an existing centre. It was an implausible, impossible task to undertake.

However, one member of the team, Wesley Clark, came to Roberts's assistance. Having worked with Licklider to write 'On-line Man Computer Communication' in 1962, Clark was a passionate advocate of Licklider's network concept. He proposed a simple idea of genius: do not attempt to make the wildly divergent host computers in each centre communicate directly over the telephone lines; instead, introduce identical intermediary computers at each centre and allow them to carry out the communication between themselves in a standard manner. That way, the different hosts would only have to communicate with these intermediaries (called Interface Message Processors, or IMPs) and adding new centres to the network would be much simpler.

Roberts immediately adopted Clark's solution and wrote a description of the proposed network structure ('Multiple Computer Networks and Inter-computer Communication') which was presented at the ACM (Association for Computing Machinery) Conference in October 1967 at Gatlinburg, Tennessee. There, Roberts was introduced to the second important aspect of the ARPANET development – 'packet switching'.

As with so many other aspects of the nascent internet, packet switching grew from the work involved in developing SAGE at the height of the Cold War. SAGE presented an automated and integrated information analysis system that could rapidly combine and present data from different radar tracking stations. The USAF planners responsible for SAGE were confident that in the computer and human interface aspects of the system they had a near-perfect solution. A substantial problem remained, however, in that if the bombs *did* start to fall, then what would happen to the communications network itself? For SAGE to continue working, the network linking the command and radar sites had to continue working – both for data and for voice communication. To address this issue, the USAF placed an additional research project, to run alongside the SAGE activity, this time with the RAND Corporation of Santa Monica.

The RAND ('Research and Development') Corporation had been established over 10 years before the work on SAGE was considered, originally as 'Project RAND' under the aegis of the Douglas Aircraft Company of Santa Monica. It was started with an agreement in October 1945 between Douglas Aircraft, the US War Department and the USAF to allow the continuation of close research-and-development cooperation between the military and industry after the war. Project RAND continued as a separate division of Douglas Aircraft until, in May 1948, it was finally separated as the RAND Corporation with a 1 million dollar free loan from the Ford Corporation. The board of trustees for the non-profit corporation included several from the original Project RAND alongside individuals from Caltech, MIT, Princeton, Westinghouse and the Carnegie Corporation. The RAND Corporation quickly became one of the US's leading research bodies, bridging the often vast chasm between the military, academic and commercial worlds. It was an ideal place for the USAF to turn in 1960 for assistance on the issue of survivable communications.

The work at RAND was undertaken by Paul Baran, who had joined RAND from the Hughes Aircraft Company in 1959, having previously been employed alongside Grace Hopper at the Eckert-Mauchly Computer Corporation in Pennsylvania. In designing and building a survivable communications network, Baran realized that he was addressing a wholly unprecedented engineering problem. There simply *were* no existing networks that could continue to provide a reliable service after suffering damage. The telephone, telegraph, railways and highway networks all featured some alternative communication routes in certain cases. Unfortunately, they also all featured 'single failure points', where the loss of one node or one connection would destroy either the complete network or substantial portions of it.

Baran's stroke of genius was in discovering the one survivable communication network studied by science and capable of at least some analysis for his purposes – the neural connection networks within the brain. Baran realized that human brains could continue to function even after phenomenal degrees of localized or distributed damage; strokes, injury and infection could all devastate the existing neural associations, yet the brain could often continue to function, even if only in a limited way. To learn more about the structures then known and to understand how he might apply that understanding to digital communication networks, Baran travelled to MIT and met with Warren McCulloch, who was interested in similar concepts but from a slightly different perspective. Baran wanted to apply neural principles to communication networks; McCulloch was trying to model the behaviour of neurons mathematically so as to implement artificial neural networks. McCulloch described the way in which neural structures were believed to be connected, showing the differences from the communication network styles that were usual at that time.

Most of the networks that Baran had studied initially fell into two categories: the 'centralized' or simple star network, in which all communication went via a single, central hub node; or the 'decentralized', in which a number of star networks were linked to one another with one or two connections.

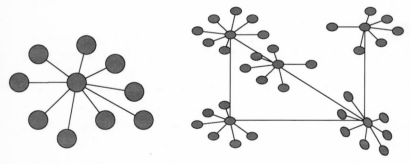

Centralized network   Decentralized network

Given the way in which the networks had been developed, these structures were to be expected. In telephone systems, the central node represents the local exchange, which is either free-standing in the centralized case or linked with other local exchanges in the decentralized case. Neural networks, however, do not organize themselves in this fashion. Instead, every neuron connects to several other neurons, either locally or in some cases across quite substantial distances. Because of this, there are multiple alternative routes between any two neurons, so damage has to be substantial for communication to become impossible. The first lesson that Baran learned was therefore to create a communication network that was well supplied with multiple alternative routes between any two nodes.

The second important aspect of neural communication lies in what would be called 'switching' in a telephone system. To place a call from one handset to another, a complete circuit between the two has to be established through the telephone network. In fact, we even speak of a call 'connecting' or of 'ringing back to get a better connection'. For voice calls, a series of nodes throughout the network are linked together to establish an end–to–end circuit which is dedicated to the call for its duration. Since much of any telephone call is in fact silence, for the majority of the time that circuit is being wasted.

By contrast, neurons do not establish end–to–end circuits between themselves before transmitting a signal. Instead, the neuron seems to have preferential connections between itself and one or two of the several neurons to which it is linked. When a signal is to be transmitted, it will most usually flow along the preferential connection. However, if that connection becomes damaged, then the neuron can begin transmitting the signal along one or other of the alternative links; and that neuron can in turn then transmit the signal. If each link takes the signal gradually nearer to its destination neuron, then even though it might not have taken what was, before the damage, the fastest route, it will nonetheless get to its destination. What is more, as the alternative route is used more and more frequently, it will gradually become the 'preferred route'. In this way, after damage to a link or even an entire group of neurons, the other neurons can gradually 'learn' about alternative end–to–end routes simply by sending their signals to near neighbours.

This was the second important lesson for Baran – that signals can travel from source to destination not through end-to-end established circuits but through a series of discrete steps from node to node that take the signal gradually but inevitably towards its destination.

Putting these two concepts together, Baran had the outline of his scheme for a survivable network. It would consist of a series of richly interconnected nodes that would communicate by sending 'message blocks' to near neighbours that were closer to the ultimate destination. Baran devised a transmission scheme that he termed 'hot potato'. In this, when a node receives a message block, it tries to offload it as quickly as possible to the neighbour in the correct direction with the shortest queue of such messages awaiting processing.

Baran's idea of supporting communication through transmission of message blocks was a good one, but for voice communication it suffered from the problem that conversations could be either very short or very long. The message blocks could therefore be any size, making the administration of buffer memories in the network nodes very difficult. To solve this, Baran realized that he could divide messages up into several discrete, smaller message blocks (eventually to be called packets) of a limited number of bits. He chose a length of 1024 bits for convenience. Messages were therefore sent not as one long train of bits shunted through the network, but as a series of much smaller units (rather like carriages on a train) which were in fact each transmitted independently along possibly widely divergent routes to arrive at the destination node. There, the train would once more be reconstructed and the message presented to the receiver.

The final concept that Baran needed to create the survivable communication network was an element not represented in neural networks – an acknowledgement response. In Baran's scheme, the destination node receiving a message block responds with a short acknowledgement message of its own. In this way, the transmitting node can be assured that its message has passed safely and successfully through the network.

Once he had thought through all of the failure modes and responses, Baran then had a design for a command–and–control communication network that could survive substantial damage. Messages would flow independently through the network from sender to receiver (exactly like rats running in a maze, as Baran described it) with retransmission of any message that failed to arrive. The ideas for this survivable communications network were presented to the USAF in a briefing session in the summer of 1961 and were written up as a series of reports published by RAND in 1964.

The 'packet-switched network' idea was made central to the survivable communications at the heart of the US command-and-control system, designed to be able to continue operating even after a nuclear first strike. By ensuring that the communications were sufficiently robust, it is possible that Baran helped to dissuade the Soviets from attacking the USA during the tensest period of the Cold War.

꩜

With the basic principle of Interface Message Processors handling packet-switched communication on behalf of their host mainframes, Larry Roberts had the main concepts for the ARPANET and began the detailed architectural work. To help in the development, Roberts hired Bob Kahn from Licklider's old company, BBN, as a consultant.

Between them, Roberts and Kahn created the design and project plan which was presented to Bob Taylor for approval at IPTO in June 1968. Just four nodes were considered for the initial ARPANET trial. The first was the University of California at Los Angeles (UCLA), where research on packet-switching networks had continued to build on Baran's initial work. UCLA was to be the 'Network Measurement Centre' to monitor and analyse the performance of the ARPANET as more and more traffic was added. Honeywell minicomputers were chosen to provide the hardware platform for the IMPs. And in January 1969, BBN were chosen to develop the operating software.[3]

Despite a series of setbacks and problems in developing and testing the IMP software (and despite Kennedy's confusion), the first Honeywell IMP was installed at UCLA by BBN engineer Truett Thach on 30 August 1969. A few hours later it was transmitting and receiving data for the very first host on what would grow to become a worldwide network of millions of computers. This first host was a Scientific Data Systems Sigma 7, programmed by UCLA graduate student Mike Wingfield.

Throughout September and October 1969, ARPANET was a network of just one node, as the communication between the Sigma 7 host and the Honeywell IMP was tested and tuned and the other initial sites were prepared. The second node on the ARPANET – truly the actual creation of the *network* itself – was at the Stanford Research Institute, linking to Doug Englebart's NLS system, where novel user interfaces were being developed. That connection was successfully established around 10.30 on the evening of 29 October 1969. An IBM mainframe at the University of California at Santa Barbara was the third host to be added to the network. And in December 1969 a DEC PDP-10 minicomputer at the University of Utah, supporting Ivan Sutherland's research group, became the fourth.

For the first few months of its life, the ARPANET was in 'shakedown' as the team at UCLA worked with Bob Kahn to load test and experiment with the network. In the months leading up to the installation of the first IMP, a Network Working Group (NWG) had been established almost by accident by the graduate student programmers from each of the initial four sites. These students had got together since the summer of 1968 to try and plan how they would communicate with and between the IMP connections. Unfortunately, all of the people involved in creating that first network were breaking new ground. For Honeywell, the IMP was a new platform that they needed to understand; at BBN, the team were creating new ideas on the fly and only occasionally telling the others of their new developments. The programmers at the four sites making up the NWG could do nothing other than theorize about the way that they might make it work.

In the first quarter of 1970, however, they had a live network with which to play, so the work on developing IMP-to-IMP and host-to-host communication models could begin. The result was a 'protocol' – a structured way for the various computers to communicate, so that each knew what the control messages were and how then to handle the data transmitted. This was particularly important as the network continued to grow, stretching from coast to coast in 1971 and linked across to the UK by the end of 1972.

The very first protocol for allowing IMP-to-IMP communication was NCP (Network Control Protocol), which allowed the first host-to-host programs to be written by members of the NWG. These first two applications are still the core functions for the modern internet: the file transfer program (FTP) to allow entire files of data to be sent from host to host; and the remote terminal program (Telnet) to allow users in one location to access and use a computer in another.

Slowly and carefully, the NWG members were building what we would now understand as a 'protocol stack' to allow two wholly dissimilar host computers to work together. At the lowest level of the stack (now called the data link protocol layer) the IMP-to-IMP link was through high-speed dial-up lines using modems to connect the two Honeywell IMP systems. Above that, what we would now call the network protocol layer between the IMP systems was controlled by the NCP suite of functions, allowing the two systems to exchange messages as a stream of data packets. Above *that*, in what we would now think of as the transport protocol layer, providing a seamless and reliable link between the two host computers were the FTP and Telnet services.

To complete the picture, instead of simply linking two host computers together, it was necessary to provide a link between two applications – the modern application protocol layer. Without this application link, the ARPANET was merely a channel for communication between computers with nothing useful to say to one another, like a telephone network without subscribers. With the ability for applications to communicate with one another using FTP or Telnet, the ARPANET became a useful and usable medium. That first real application – the killer application for the internet network – was created by Ray Tomlinson of BBN in 1971: electronic mail, or email.

Tomlinson had joined BBN as a failed graduate student from MIT, where he had been trying to work on a project and dissertation on the electronics of computerized voice recognition. Unfortunately for his studies (but fortunately for BBN and the internet community as a whole), Tomlinson was an inveterate programmer and had been drawn deeper and deeper into the software rather than the electrical engineering aspects. Finally, his supervisor suggested that Tomlinson follow Licklider to BBN, where his software skills might be more profitably applied.

At BBN, Tomlinson developed a single-system electronic mail solution called Tenex, which quickly became popular. Since the development of time-shared, multi-user operating systems, computers had supported electronic mail programs for communicating amongst users. Tenex was a particularly powerful mail reader, though it simply delivered a text file to a user specified by their login or username on the computer running the program.

When BBN was connected to the ARPANET in March 1970,[4] Tomlinson realized that the members of the NWG were sending data between their connected computers but were still using telephones for person-to-person conversations. His idea was to extend the mail program running on each of the connected hosts so that it could send text files between host computers, if necessary, in order to reach the right person.

To do this, Tomlinson had to solve two problems. First, he had to be able to send the text file from host to host. To do this, he rewrote his local mail program so that it used the FTP program to transmit the text. Second, he had to be able to specify which user on which computer system the file was to be sent to. To do this, he made the now obvious step of quoting the username followed by the host computer name. And to make it look elegant, in March 1972 he wrote it as 'user@host', the convention that is still used for network email addresses to this day.

One element of modern network email addresses that was missing from Tomlinson's first address formats illustrates the key difference between the operation of the early ARPANET and the internet into which it evolved. A modern network email address does not use the host name. Rather, it uses a 'domain name' – roughly, a network within which the user is to be found. The ARPANET represented one distinct network. By contrast, the modern internet represents a means of linking several unconnected networks together, including the ARPANET as just one among many. The roots of that particular aspect of the global network can be traced back to Hawaii in 1970.

From ARPANET to internet

The ARPANET was not the only result of the avid interest in computer networking prompted by Licklider's enthusiasm and Larry Roberts's successful first wide-area network in 1965. At Stanford, an engineer called Norman Abramson had followed the discussions and development, and had begun to form his own ideas.

After completing his PhD in physics in 1966, Abramson had become an associate professor in the Electronic Engineering department at Stanford University. Before that, he had worked on his Master's (again in physics) at UCLA; and his first degree had been at Harvard. Many of the people and the problems involved in establishing both the first Experimental Network (connecting MIT and Stanford) and the ARPANET itself were therefore already familiar to him. It so happened that Abramson was also an enthusiastic surfer, and in 1969 he visited and fell in love with the islands of Hawaii. Keen to find a way of staying, Abramson approached the University of Hawaii to see if any academic positions were available. The growing Computer Science department snapped him up. Within months, Abramson had moved to the islands and was enjoying sun, surf and the opportunity to work on a novel computer network.

The ALOHANET was planned as a computer network to link together the various island campuses of the University of Hawaii. Telephone links between the islands were notoriously unreliable and establishing dedicated cables to support the network was simply impossible – or at least, difficult and improbably expensive. The only remaining option was to use some form of radio communication. Abramson led the work to develop a series of protocols for transmitting data from computer to computer between the islands. The solution that he devised involved a central computer at the main campus, which communicated with each of the smaller systems spread around the other islands. It was a star network with all the communication passing through this single point. In a joking reference to the ARPANET development, Abramson called the central computer the Menehune – Hawaiian for 'imp'. The available wireless bandwidth, which was not great, had to be shared amongst the several distributed nodes as they communicated with the Menehune. This aspect of having to share the available bandwidth is what gave the ALOHANET scheme its distinctive flavour.

First of all, Abramson realized that each node communicating with the Menehune would block access to the radio channel for each of the other nodes. This meant that Abramson's solution had to find a way of detecting whether the channel was free, of indicating that the channel was in use, and of using the channel for as short a time as possible. To solve this last issue, Abramson decided to follow the route that Baran and Roberts had already pioneered and to use short packets of data transmitted between the nodes and the Menehune control station. Each node broke its (possibly very long) messages up into a train of discrete packets, each one of which had to take its chances in grabbing control of the radio channel. To grab the channel, Abramson introduced a protocol between the nodes and the Menehune in which each node would attempt to transmit its packet but would then look to see whether a 'collision' had occurred between its packet and any other node's packet transmission. In the event of a collision, the protocol required the node to 'back off' and wait for a short, random period of time before trying again.

It was a creative, imaginative and workable solution to the problem. In this simple version, however, it was a long way from being efficient. Abramson calculated that the packet collisions meant that the network was effectively full when it was at only 17 per cent of its maximum capacity. Over a period of several months, he worked on a number of improvements to the basic ALOHA protocol (as it was called) before the network itself finally went live in July 1970.

ALOHANET was successful in many different ways. Most obviously, it provided a working and effective computer link between each of the several island campuses of the University of Hawaii. In that regard, it satisfied the most basic requirement that Abramson had been asked to meet. It also showed that a packet-based digital radio computer network was possible, leading to experiments at ARPA led by Bob Kahn on a broader, military packet radio system, PRNET. This in turn led to the modern military communication systems for battlefield control; to the British Ptarmigan command-and-control network; and to SATNET, a satellite-based packet radio network. From these evolved modern cellular mobile telephone systems and the GPRS (General Packet Radio System) network used for civilian mobile communications. It also, of course, led directly to modern developments of wireless internet solutions – dubbed 'Wi-Fi'.

More immediately, though, ALOHANET had two particularly important results. First, a Harvard graduate student called Bob Metcalfe read of Abramson's work and decided to base his 1973 doctoral thesis on further extensions to the protocol. Metcalfe had already left Harvard to work at Xerox PARC when he read of ALOHANET and had already submitted a failing thesis. He was therefore desperate for a new idea to pursue quickly so as to obtain his doctorate. With Xerox already interested in finding solutions to the problems of networking their minicomputers for the office environment, Metcalfe decided to see how ALOHANET could be adapted.

His first challenge was to find a way of improving the efficiency of the basic protocol. He did this by drawing on queuing theory to find a more effective way of staggering the transmission of packets from a node having a long message to transmit. To his delight, this did indeed increase the overall efficiency of the scheme to 90 per cent of its theoretical maximum capacity. However, whilst this was an important development, Metcalfe's lasting contribution is in the way that he created the test network for his scheme. Instead of radio packet broadcasts, Metcalfe used a cheaper solution of stringing a cable onto which each of the several nodes was connected. The nodes worked exactly as they did in the extended ALOHA protocol scheme (enhanced by

Metcalfe's queuing extensions), but they grabbed access to the cable rather than to a radio channel. In effect, the radio 'ether' was confined to the cable and shared between the nodes. Metcalfe called this 'Ethernet'.

In May 1973, Metcalfe completed the Alto Aloha System at Xerox, linking a set of Alto minicomputers in a small Ethernet. This basic network scheme was adopted by former PARC researchers who joined Apple, to produce the AppleTalk network. Metcalfe himself formed one of the most successful networking companies, 3Com, in 1981, bringing cheap networking solutions to the office scale and introducing the local-area network (LAN) concept to modern businesses.

Ethernet and the modern office LAN was one result of the ALOHANET development. The other important result was the internet itself.

In 1972, Abramson persuaded Larry Roberts (by then himself the director of IPTO) to give Hawaii an IMP so as to connect ALOHANET to the broader ARPANET community. For the first time, a complete *network* was to be added to the ARPANET, rather than a single node in the form of a host computer connected via an IMP. Unfortunately, the Network Control Protocol used to direct the network traffic was not capable of addressing computers 'behind' the IMP. As more and more networks were being developed and would inevitably ask to be connected to the increasingly successful ARPANET, the NWG team realized that they had to solve this problem if the network was to be truly global.

It was Bob Kahn who first expressed the idea of extending the ARPANET in this way. This was not so as to allow increased numbers of *nodes* to be added, rather to allow distinctively different *networks* to be linked. He was fired by the realization that, if ALOHANET could be connected to the ARPANET, so too could the PRNET packet radio network solution that he had been asked to build at IPTO. In spring 1973, Kahn asked his colleague on the PRNET project, Vinton Cerf, to help him to develop a set of protocols to allow dissimilar networks to 'inter-network' with one another.

It was the conception of the internet proper.

7

Putting the internet to work

From: Dad-And-Mum@Barretts.demon.co.uk
To: Neil.Barrett@btinternet.com
Subject: Doing proper computer stuff...!

Neil,
I admit it, you were right – computer games and aimless surfing get
pretty boring after a while. I want to start using this thing for some
real work now. I was thinking of using it to send out stuff for the
cricket club by e-mail and setting them up a website with their
results. Things like that – any suggestions what I can do?
Dad

The global internet has become one of the most exciting
commercial and technical arenas, changing the way that we
communicate and do business. Not since the development of the
telegraph in 19th century has a single technological development
had such a far-reaching impact on our lives. Three key elements
were responsible for changing the academic and research network
of the 1970s into the global communication medium of today: the
introduction of the TCP/IP standard; the creation of the World
Wide Web; and changes in the rules regarding commercial traffic
over internet connections.

The creation and dissemination of TCP/IP allowed the interconnection of many more networks to the initial, limited

ARPANET structure. The World Wide Web allowed trivial access to the networked computers by users around the globe. The commercial rule changes gave a justification to those companies seeking to create a profit through little more than a clever and memorable domain name; and to those 'bricks-and-mortar' companies just as eager to take their business online.

All of these things can be traced back to the happy accident of Bob Kahn and Vinton Cerf deciding to make the ARPANET even more widely accessible.

The development of TCP/IP

Cerf was one of the original development team at UCLA, responsible for the introduction and initial work on the very first node of the ARPANET when it was delivered in October 1969. In 1972, Cerf accepted the chairmanship of the INWG (International Network Working Group), which had developed from the group of graduate students (the NWG) who had devised the initial specification for the ARPANET nodes. In November 1972, Cerf moved to nearby Stanford University as an associate professor, researching networks in particular.

Bob Kahn, meanwhile, had accepted a full-time post at ARPA and was researching the protocols necessary to implement a packet-switched radio communication system, PRNET. He needed a way of allowing arbitrary nodes to communicate with one another (even in the face of interference and the loss of nodes) in such a way that spoken messages were not lost. To solve this, Kahn had devised a scheme for turning the messages first into a stream of binary digits, then into a stream of packets that could be transmitted individually – just as Baran had first proposed for SAGE and as the ARPANET had implemented between the IMP nodes.

At first, Kahn had explored the notion of developing a specific communication protocol for PRNET, leaving the ARPANET NCP protocol as the simple mechanism just for IMP-to-IMP traffic. The addition of ALOHANET to the ARPANET community, however, convinced him that it would be a sensible measure to link networks together with a reliable end-to-end protocol such as was needed in any case for a packet radio system. What was more, if it was well chosen, that protocol could equally well be applied to PRNET. What Kahn wanted to do was to allow communication between a PRNET-connected host and an ARPANET-connected host, perhaps even with the network traffic travelling via a third packet-switched network. He dubbed this network-to-network communication 'internetworking'.

Kahn had published his basic principles for this internetworking requirement in January 1972 as an internal memo at BBN. In March 1973, Cerf agreed to work with him to create a working design of a protocol for host-to-host packet-switched communication. Kahn was the original designer of the ARPANET; Cerf was one of those responsible for the creation of the NCP protocol. They were ideal as a partnership to create the improved replacement for both.

The pair agreed four basic principles for the 'internetwork' protocol to satisfy. First of all, there had to be no global controlling node: no single point of failure, such as in a star network like ALOHANET, could be allowed to threaten the network in the event of damage or attack. This reflected the essentially military motivation for the ARPANET and PRNET development and funding. Second, none of the networks to be linked together should need to be changed in any way. Instead – the third requirement – a gateway would *route* communication between the networks in a transparent manner. The fourth principle was that the communication should be on a 'best effort' basis: lost packets would simply be ignored unless the host specifically asked for the communication to be repeated.

This last was a reflection of the PRNET requirement regarding minimal latency in packet transmission, with a slightly garbled message resulting from the occasional lost packet being preferable to an extensive delay in communication resulting from a requirement to repeat parts of messages. However, in implementing the protocol (a venture that involved Kahn at Stanford, and two further groups, one at BBN and the other at the University College, London), it became obvious that, unlike person-to-person communication, computer-to-computer communication required the establishment of a reliable 'virtual circuit', in which lost packets were repeated and recovered transparently.

The results of this work, demonstrated in July 1977, were two related protocols. The lowest-level protocol was called IP (Internet Protocol). This provided a means of linking two networks together, passing fixed-length data packets from node to node. An IP packet contains a fragment of the message data stream and the address (called the IP address) of the host node to which the packet is to be delivered. IP packets are simply passed out of a network through the gateway (or 'router') and then passed from network to network (or rather, from network router to network router) until they arrive at the destination router. There, the gateway router for the destination network receives the packet and routes it inwards to the specified host computer. IP addresses include, therefore, both a network and a host address, specified in the form of a 32-bit number.

Once transmitted, an IP packet is forgotten about by the Internet Protocol element of the transmitting host computer. To implement the end-to-end communication stream, the higher-level protocol TCP (Transmission Control Protocol) was produced by Kahn and Cerf. TCP keeps a record of what packets have been transmitted and whether they have been received correctly. It provides a 'handshake' between two host computers and manages the processing of acknowledgement and retransmission messages.

TCP/IP is the combination of simple packet transmission with the packet-stream mechanism. It provides the heart of the internet communication structure; it allows networks and hosts within networks to be addressed; and it supports reliable communication. To provide a channel where packet loss is not important (such as for the PRNET solution), Kahn and Cerf introduced one further protocol to provide direct access to the underlying IP mechanisms, called UDP (Unsigned Datagram Protocol). All of the modern aspects of internet communication are then built on these basic blocks. Email, Telnet and FTP, needing assurance that all of a message has been received successfully, use TCP; real-time voice communication (now commonly referred to as 'streaming' and including both sound and video) uses the less assured but much faster UDP.

The result of Kahn and Cerf's work is the modern internet: a global, highly reliable interconnection of government, corporate and private networks; a network having no single, central authority; a network having no single point of failure; and a network that is adaptable enough to carry a huge range of different kinds of data. Throughout the 1980s, ARPANET gradually evolved and developed into the internet, absorbing more and more academic, commercial and military networks and using the TCP/IP protocol as a gateway between them.

The ARPANET backbone – the connections between the several IMP computers around the world – continued to use the NCP protocol suite. Then, in 1981, a plan for moving ARPANET from the NCP protocol to TCP/IP was formulated, and on 1 January 1983 the NCP protocol was declared defunct. The ARPANET backbone began to operate purely as a TCP/IP network, and the internet as we now define it – a collection of networks operating the TCP/IP protocol suite – was officially born.

In 1984, as the number of internet-connected host computers passed the 1000 mark, an official registration of domain names to IP addresses was started. Before then, users of the internet had to know the 32-bit numeric address of the host computer with which they were communicating before they could use the Telnet or FTP services. The Domain Name Service (DNS) allowed them to give a simple name for their computers, important as the growth in such hosts accelerated.

The official specification for internet domain names (such as microsoft.com, etc.) was published in October 1984 by Jon Postel, one of the original group of graduate students at UCLA responsible for the first ARPANET node. Postel proposed two components in the full domain name: the 'organization' component, such as 'microsoft'; and the 'category' component, separated by a dot character. The category component was called the 'top-level domain' (TLD); the organization component was the 'second-level domain'.

The initial TLD categories were either the two-letter international standard country codes for domains outside the US (called 'country code TLDs'), such as UK, FR, and so on; or they were 'generic TLDs' for specific purposes – COM for commercial organizations, ORG for non-profit organizations, EDU for universities, GOV for government, and MIL for military. NET was later added for those organizations involved in administering the internet network itself. More recently, in 2001, a much wider range of TLD specifications was provided: INFO, BIZ and NAME, for example. There have even been serious proposals for SEX as a top-level domain.

To allow individual host computers, rather than simply network domains, to be addressed, Postel also described a fully qualified domain name in which the host computer's name would be given along with the domain name. So, a host computer called Mycroft within MIT, for example, could be addressed as 'mycroft.mit.edu'.

To make this scheme work, it was not enough simply to have the hierarchical naming structure. It was also necessary to have some way for internet users to discover the IP address from the domain name – a Domain Name Server (DNS). For the DNS, it was also necessary to have a central registration point so that two different organizations did not inadvertently (or indeed, as would later become common, deliberately) choose the same domain name. The first implementation of a DNS was by Paul Mockapetris at the University of Southern California's Information Sciences Institute, and it was therefore USC/ISI that was awarded the ARPA contract for managing the internet's first DNS.

At Stanford Research Institute, however, Doug Englebart (the creator of the mouse and inventor of the graphical user interface) had established a Network Information Centre (NIC), where newly connected ARPANET hosts were registered. A colleague of Englebart's, Peggy Karp, had created a text file of these host names, along with their address and additional details. As the internet expanded, SRI was therefore awarded the first contract to provide host registration services – 'internic.net'.

On 15 March 1985, the internet domain name registration service began. The first domain name to be registered was 'symbolics.com', a research company based in Cambridge, Massachusetts, specializing in artificial-intelligence solutions using the LISP symbolic programming language.[1] Universities and computer companies quickly followed, and the number of registrations grew quickly: 10,000 domains were registered within five years, and a million by the summer of 1997. By 2004, there were some 30 million domains, with around 20,000 new ones registered every day at one of the several commercial NIC companies throughout the world that trade domain names as property. The backbone network has evolved from the simple ARPANET structure into a complex combination of network links established by a patchwork of government, academic and commercial concerns. What is more, now not only academic or business users can connect – through internet service providers (ISPs), *anyone* with a computer and a telephone line can join the internet community. By 2005, over 200 million host computers were connected to the internet, serving an online population which some published estimates put at a staggering 10 per cent of the world's total population.

Perhaps the single most important factor in creating the still-accelerating growth in internet traffic lies with one specific technological advance – the World Wide Web.

Creating the World Wide Web

The creator of the World Wide Web was Tim Berners-Lee. Born in London on 8 June 1955, he had a near-perfect pedigree for such a vital invention. His parents were mathematicians who had met while working on the Ferranti Mark 1 computer; his mother, indeed, has been described as the world's first commercial programmer. Not surprisingly, the young Berners-Lee inherited their enthusiasm for mathematics and enjoyed an early exposure to computer technology. His first hobby was electronics, and while studying for a degree in physics at Oxford University in the mid-1970s, Berners-Lee built himself a computer using an old television set and a Motorola microprocessor.

Graduating in 1976, Berners-Lee went to work for Plessey Telecommunications in Dorset, developing transaction-processing software before moving to a nearby technology company two years later to work on typesetting and on operating systems. From June to December 1980, Berners-Lee worked as a consultant software engineer at CERN, before returning once more to Dorset to work on real-time, communications and graphics software. In 1984 Berners-Lee was back at CERN, this time on a fellowship to develop real-time software for collecting data from the high-energy physics experiments undertaken at what was then the world's largest particle accelerator.

The invention of the World Wide Web was not a 'eureka' moment of single creation, but rather the gradual evolution of an idea to solve a specific set of problems that Berners-Lee encountered during both his assignments at CERN. Physics, particularly high-energy physics as practised at CERN, generates a lot of highly competitive research papers as each ultra-expensive establishment and experiment tries to justify itself. Keeping track of all of these research papers is a mammoth task. In addition, the research laboratories themselves generate a mass of data – not simply within the experiments but in the running and organization of the establishment. Again, keeping track of all that material is a mammoth task, with information routinely misplaced and lost as the experiments, personnel and equipment rapidly evolve.

Berners-Lee had two bites at this particular problem, the first on his initial six-month assignment at CERN, when he wrote a simple document indexing and retrieval program which he called 'Enquire'. Written purely for his own purposes and use, it represented information as a series of elements linked to one another by relationship arrows. These could be explored by the program, and some components were themselves broken down further as elements of information such as a description or a more detailed explanation of the component.

Though Berners-Lee did not use the term then, the Enquire program used a method of representation called 'hypertext', in which relevant material can be read and explored in any arbitrary order. In hypertext, documents or even individual paragraphs are linked to one another in such a way that the user can be led to one of several other texts, the reading route taken through the material being peculiar to each user and their specific interests. In more powerful versions of hypertext, the reader can even become the author, adding their own details and documents to the system.

A simple analogy for hypertext would be the 'See also' notes at the end of articles in an encyclopedia. An item with several 'See also' references, each one of which might also have several further suggestions, can lead a reader on a journey of discovery through the reference text. A hypertext system can be thought of as a computerized version of these 'See also' pointers. The earliest description of this form of non-linear text was in Vannevar Bush's 1945 article about the Memex and his exploration of information about a long bow. The word itself, though, was coined nearly 20 years later, in 1963, by Ted Nelson and first published in a presentation at a computing conference in New York in 1965.

In 1960, Nelson had been a graduate sociology student at Harvard University, struggling with the task of writing essays. This is a task in which complex thoughts and facts about a subject need to be expressed in a clear, linear fashion and which are in some sense 'fixed' on the page. Nelson, though, preferred to express his thoughts in terms of facts and relationships between facts. His thoughts were spatial and visual, in the sense of being composed of images having a position relative to one another in his mind, rather like the 'mind-mapping' diagrams now used to describe complex concepts. Nelson's first job, in fact, had been as a film editor at a dolphin research centre in Miami. He was much more comfortable thinking in terms of moving pictures, 'cuts' and relationships between visually presented information. His research idea was to create a textual system that could embody this and which would allow the reader greater interaction with the written word.

The original implementation of Nelson's complex and challenging creation was as an assembler-language program on an IBM 7090 mainframe at Harvard. His objective was to create a worldwide, universal presentation of information and of links between information that was open to everyone and which maintained copyright and version-management controls. He christened this concept 'Xanadu' in 1967 and has been working on the associated problems since his days at Harvard. Xanadu is a hugely ambitious project, both technically and in terms of the copyright issues associated with trying to provide a computer-accessible universal library. Nelson had a visionary's approach to developing Xanadu. He solved huge numbers of problems, but unfortunately for him and his investors those problems multiplied and have proved ever more difficult to deal with. Nelson and Xanadu have inspired a variety of more successful efforts, including NLS, Doug Englebart's hypertext-based graphical user interface developed at Stanford in the 1960s, and Apple's HyperCard. Xanadu itself, though, is still struggling to present a fully working and saleable application.

Although Xanadu itself has not been successful, Nelson is widely acknowledged, along with Vannevar Bush and Doug Englebart, as having inspired Berners-Lee in 1989 to produce a more general-purpose implementation of his Enquire application. According to Nelson, he and Berners-Lee met in San Francisco in 1989 and discussed the hypertext library idea over lunch. Nelson has subsequently derided the World Wide Web as being nothing more than a simplistic implementation of his ideas − a *shallow* hypertext structure as opposed to the deep structure that he envisaged. The Web does have, however, one overriding advantage: it works.

⤴

In March 1989, Tim Berners-Lee submitted a funding proposal to the CERN management, requesting a UNIX computer on which to build a hypertext application. The proposal described the problem that he sought to solve: the loss of information regarding complex, evolving systems such as the particle accelerators and experiments at the laboratory. Berners-Lee's answer to the problem was a 'non-linear text' environment to describe the 'mesh' of relationships that went into creating a document, a system or even a department.

The problem of information at CERN that Berners-Lee wanted to solve was particularly acute. A hugely expensive laboratory environment such as CERN is used by several thousand people, with several hundred experiments running at any one time. The experimenters and maintenance staff need to modify, repair and improve upon the equipment and the systems on an almost constant basis. Any alteration, however minor, runs the risk of affecting an individual experiment, so a record of dependencies needs to be maintained. To do this manually for a small number of experiments and simple equipment can be a Herculean task; for something as large as CERN, it becomes impossible.

Berners-Lee wanted to find a way of using a computerized but intuitively accessible mechanism to achieve this information management. His solution was to reuse the Enquire program that he had developed in 1980, allowing multiple users to browse the mesh of links and associations by using an application that was explicitly described as a simplification of Nelson's Xanadu. Initially, Berners-Lee planned that an existing document database available at CERN (called CERNDOC) would be presented via a hypertext server. Thereafter, he envisaged the system expanding to include increasingly varied collections of documents throughout the world of high-energy physics.

To achieve this, his server would need to present the links between different documents by interpreting the various cross-referencing standards used. For example, it would need to interpolate 'See also' and 'Ref:' appropriately so as to provide hyperlinks to those documents. In practice, he found that this interpolation by the hypertext server was simply too difficult to manage. Instead, he developed a scheme for 'marking up' the documents to be presented, with a series of 'tags' to show where links between documents (and later, the formatting for the display of the documents) should be inserted.

Although this ultimately became the most important scheme of the kind, such tagging schemes have been used for many years.

Schemes to specify the marking-up of documents for typesetting by computer were first proposed by the chairman of the Graphic Communications Association, William Tunnicliffe, in September 1967, in a presentation to the Canadian Government Printing Office. Tunnicliffe suggested that the editorial mark-up instructions applied to typescript to direct the typesetters could be standardized and inserted as tags into a computer file of text. A simple and obvious idea, it was revolutionary at the time, given the way in which computers were then predominantly used in business.

Tunnicliffe's notion of tags and editorial mark-up was something of a pipedream, but it was developed dramatically by Charles Goldfarb at IBM. Goldfarb had graduated in law from Harvard in 1964 and had worked for a Boston law practice for two years before joining IBM to work as a programmer. In 1969, he was asked to create business solutions that would address the issues of law firms in particular. He chose to concentrate on the problems of creating, editing and producing documents. Together with two other programmers, Edward Mosher and Raymond Lorie, Goldfarb created a standard way of tagging documents stored in a database so that they could be retrieved, edited, printed and stored. IBM decided that their system was too powerful to be limited just to the legal profession, so it was more widely marketed as 'Integrated Text Processing'. The scheme that Goldfarb, Mosher and Lorie created was called Generalized Markup Language (GML) and was published in May 1973. On 15 October 1986, this was adopted as International Standard 8879, becoming Standard Generalized Markup Language (SGML).

As the standard mark-up language, SGML was the obvious place for Berners-Lee to begin in developing a mechanism for tagging the CERN documents to be accessed by his program. However, as a *full* mark-up language, there were huge elements of SGML that Berners-Lee could ignore as irrelevant in the context of providing relatively simple hypertext links between documents and paragraphs. To make his scheme as straightforward as possible, Berners-Lee therefore defined a subset of SGML, which he dubbed Hypertext Markup Language (HTML).[2]

HTML allows for simple formatting instructions to be provided (for example, to specify layout, font size and font types) and for references from one document to another to be specified. Berners-Lee also allowed for some simple elements of the Xanadu concept to be included in the HTML-format files. In Xanadu, documents can be created from collections of other documents by a process that Nelson dubbed 'transclusion'. In this, one document can be copied into a second, with a link between the original and the copy being maintained. Berners-Lee simplified this idea and allowed documents to contain other files – in particular, pictures. One further simplification over the Xanadu concept that he introduced was to make the documents presented through his scheme 'read-only'.

Berners-Lee also devised an addressing scheme for the hypertext documents, called the Uniform Resource Identifier (URI) or Uniform Resource Locator (URL), to tell the software where to find the documents to be displayed.[3] This consisted of the server name where the document was stored, followed by the directory path and filename on that system; the server, directory and filename parts were separated by a forward slash (/) character. For example, the very first web page was:

nxoc01.cern.ch/hypertext/WWW/TheProject.html

This address is of an HTML-format file called 'TheProject', held in a directory 'WWW', within a directory 'hypertext', on the CERN server 'nxoc01' in Switzerland.[4] This general format for URLs, still in use today, was suggested to Berners-Lee as a simple extension to the directory and filename formats used for the UNIX file system.

Finally, Berners-Lee needed a way of transferring the requested hypertext documents from the server to the browser requesting them. Initially, this transfer protocol was to be the simple FTP file-transfer protocol. However, the task of browsing hypertext documents is not as simple as that of specifying and collecting simple data files. In particular, a document on one server might well include elements from other documents on several different servers, and FTP could not manage that complex collection task. Instead, Berners-Lee specified a dedicated protocol for transmitting HTML-format files, called Hypertext Transfer Protocol (HTTP).

Berners-Lee had the necessary foundation blocks in place. The initial proposal requested a UNIX system and two programmers to work for between 6 and 12 months. It was submitted first in March 1989 and circulated for comment. In May 1990, that same proposal was formally submitted to Berners-Lee's manager, Mike Sendall, and in September he was given permission to buy a UNIX machine on which to develop the system. The main work on the CERN hypertext system got under way in October 1990. Berners-Lee and the colleague assigned to help him, Robert Cailliau, devised the server program and a simple browser program. They also christened the system. Rejecting the names Information Mesh and Information Mine, they followed Berners-Lee's original conception of information associations as a *web* and called the system 'WorldWideWeb'. It would not be until the system became more widely used that the spaces would appear, transforming the clumsy name into the familiar 'World Wide Web' (or simply, 'the web') of today.

In November 1990, a Leicester Polytechnic student on a one-year assignment to CERN, Nicola Pellow, joined the project and wrote the first, text-only browser program for the WorldWideWeb system. Compared with modern graphical browsers and even in comparison to the first graphical browser written by Berners-Lee shortly afterwards, it was a crude application. Links between documents were given as code numbers within the text, and users wishing to jump from one document to the next had to enter these code numbers manually.

Though primitive and cumbersome, this 'Line Mode' browser could be quickly and easily ported to any of the systems used within CERN. Berners-Lee's graphical browser (originally also called WorldWideWeb but then renamed Nexus) allowed users to 'click' on the links, shown as underlined words in the text. Unfortunately, it only worked on the powerful UNIX workstations. Nonetheless, it was a substantial start, and by the end of 1990 various programs and a collection of hypertext information files were available to users within CERN. On 17 March 1991, the WorldWideWeb hypertext system was made available throughout CERN. Interest in the program began to grow amongst CERN collaborators, as it was announced formally in a December 1991 CERN newsletter.

Throughout 1992, the WorldWideWeb hypertext system continued to grow, albeit exclusively amongst the high-energy physics community linked through experiment and personal associations with the CERN establishment. At CERN, on the first 'info' server, Berners-Lee maintained a list of WorldWideWeb servers as they were created in other laboratories and made available to browsers over the internet. This was the first web directory, and at the end of 1992 it showed just short of 30 distinct servers, mainly in Europe but with a handful of US-based institutions. Most prophetically, in November 1992 the National Centre for Supercomputing Applications (NCSA) at the University of Illinois in Urbana was added to the list of web servers.

The development of Mosaic

The development of electronic mail was the killer application for the internet in the late 1970s and early 1980s, allowing the graduate student and research population of those early days to communicate rapidly and easily. The killer application of the 1990s was the web browser, developed primarily by a University of Illinois student, Marc Andreessen, who was working as a part-time assistant at the NCSA. It was the application which, above all others, allowed the internet to become popular amongst the wider population and hence which led to the explosive growth in home PC sales, internet service providers and online electronic commerce.

In 1992, the internet was *just* beginning to emerge as a general phenomenon; the network was becoming increasingly useful, supporting servers offering FTP access to information and discussion groups of all kinds. As students and researchers who were used to having access to the resources left to move into industry, they naturally wanted to continue having access to this global network. Some online services already existed. For example, as long ago as 1969, CompuServe had provided public dial-in access to their computers to allow private users to access bulletin boards and discussion groups; and in 1975, BBN in Cambridge, Massachusetts, had established the very first commercial packet-switched network, called TELENET. However, as the internet was initially a government network and latterly a research network, access to it for commercial and private use was not immediately provided. In 1985, though, the New York State Education and Research Network (NYSERNet) was formed to provide internet access to the New York area's public institutions, including libraries. In 1989, conscious of a growing clamour for public access, NYSERNet formed PSINet, the first true, commercial internet service provider (ISP).

Others soon followed, keen to provide communication facilities to the growing home and commercial users. Most importantly, AlterNet was formed in 1990. Along with PSINet, in 1991 AlterNet established the Commercial Internet Exchange (CIX) to provide an alternative backbone for the internet. Crucially, while commercial traffic had been explicitly denied across the ARPANET, it was very definitely welcomed on this new backbone.

At the start of 1992, there was therefore a growing collection of commercial, public ISPs and a steady growth of those wanting to use the facility to access the expanding pool of available information. There was even a metaphor for the mining and exploration of information available from the internet-connected servers – 'surfing the internet'. It was a term that appeared for the first time in print in an article written for the June 1992 issue of the *Wilson Library Bulletin* by US librarian Jean Armour Polly. In it Polly described how she 'surfed' from server to server across the world in search of information from her home Apple Macintosh in New York. This was not only the first published appearance of the term, it was the first published account of what the internet was and how it was used. Jean Polly wrote a deliberately informal article that would be accessible to a general, non-technical readership. To make it easier for the non-expert to understand, she searched for a suitable metaphor, finding it in the picture of an 'information surfer' on her Apple Macintosh mouse-mat.

However, in 1992 'internet surfing' meant explicitly downloading files from remote servers using the cumbersome exploration tools and the FTP program. It was not the seamless, multimedia exploration of today. What made our modern experience possible was the development of graphical and intuitive browser applications.

Andreessen encountered Berners-Lee's work on the WorldWideWeb hypertext environment in 1992 when it was made public by CERN. The initial browsers, however, were not appealing to him. There was either the clumsy Line Mode browser developed for textual processing, or the cumbersome graphical browser developed by Berners-Lee himself to run on the high-end UNIX workstations. Berners-Lee's Nexus browser required new windows to be opened constantly to display pictures and pages requested as the user surfed. What Andreessen wanted to create was a much cleaner and simpler interface, with pictures and text displayed in a single screen as a *mosaic* of information. Because of this, he christened the browser program 'Mosaic'.

Mosaic is a recognizably 'modern' application interface, intuitively obvious and easy to use. The evaluation versions of the program were made available by the NCSA in February 1993. The browser was officially launched on 22 April 1993, shortly after CERN had announced that the WorldWideWeb technology was freely available for use by anyone. In March of that year, 0.1 per cent of the packets carried on the internet backbone represented web pages; by September, the figure had increased tenfold and continued to grow. Mosaic caught users' attention immediately, with tens of thousands of copies of the first version downloaded from the NCSA FTP server in the first few weeks that it was available.

The development of the Mosaic browser and effectively free access to it encouraged many more people to use the web; and free access to the web technology allowed the creation of many more sites for those browsers to access. One fed the other, so at the end of 1992 there were 50 websites; by the end of 1993 the figure had grown more than tenfold; and by the end of 1994 there were over 10,000 sites. That growth has continued to rocket. In July 2003 there were estimated to be well over 42 million websites, with the overwhelming majority of the internet packet traffic now being HTTP.

Mosaic spawned an enthusiasm for the use of the web. It also spawned the growth of an industry for the creation of browsers, a battle and a lawsuit with Microsoft, and the now infamous 'dot.com bubble'.

Ecommerce and the dot.com bubble

In December 1993, Andreessen graduated from the University of Illinois and moved to Palo Alto's Silicon Valley, keen to exploit his invention of the graphical web browser. There he met Jim Clark, who had founded Silicon Graphics to develop and sell high-performance UNIX workstations and who was also looking for a way of exploiting the increasing popularity of the internet. And it *was* an accelerating phenomenon through 1994. Twenty-five years after the creation of the initial ARPANET, the internet was beginning to support online shopping malls, radio re-broadcasts, and even a virtual bank. The Yahoo search engine was started in February 1994 in a trailer at Stanford University by two graduate students, David Filo and Jerry Yang.[5] Web-published magazines were beginning to appear, and in one (called *Hotwired*, the online version of the print magazine *Wired*) the first 'banner advertisements' appeared in October 1994. Less attractively, in June 1994 an Arizona-based husband-and-wife law firm called Canter and Siegel transmitted the first commercial 'spam' message.

In the summer of this foundation year, Andreessen and Clark founded Mosaic Communications Corporation, later to be renamed Netscape following a legal dispute with the University of Illinois, who owned the right to the name Mosaic. On 13 October 1994, the Mosaic Netscape browser was posted for free download on the Netscape servers, with the server component available for 5000 dollars for those wanting to create a sophisticated commercial website. There were two principal reasons for the initial huge success of Netscape, quite apart from the intuitive 'look and feel' that made it easy to use. First, the browser was offered free of charge to anyone using it for non-commercial purposes – in effect, everyone. The result was a huge 'land grab' of users. Secondly, the browser and the server provided a new facility called the Secure Socket Layer (SSL), which supported securely encrypted communication between the web server and the user's browser, vital to induce trust in the emerging online banks and shopping malls.

The Secure Socket Layer was developed by the Netscape team in 1994 to produce a transparent encryption facility. Encryption involves manipulating data so as to disguise its meaning and has been practised for hundreds of years, though the development of the computer revolutionized the task of creating and breaking encryption. The data to be protected is transformed using an algorithm, which is controlled by a 'key'. The key and the initial data are both passed through the algorithm and the result is an encrypted version of the data. This protected data can then be transmitted to the intended destination, where the original can be recovered if the receiver knows the algorithm and key that were used.

In most applications of encryption before the advent of computers and the internet, this was a relatively simple task. Agents in World War II, for example, would be sent off with a collection of encryption keys marked up on a silk handkerchief. A copy of these keys would be stored at their headquarters. When a message was to be sent, the agent would encrypt it using an agreed method and the next key on the handkerchief. After encryption, the agent would unpick the silk handkerchief so as to destroy the key that had just been used. This was a secure, reliable method, provided that the secret agent was never captured. While this *was* secure, a mechanism of this kind could never be made to work in an environment such as the internet. For two users to communicate with one another in an environment in which messages can be intercepted, they need to be able to exchange encryption keys. They can arrange to meet face to face, just as the spies had to do, so as to agree an encryption key. This is unfeasible, however, when the two users might be in different countries and might not even be able to recognize one another. They can simply transmit the key to one another, though again this raises a problem – what if the key itself and then the message are intercepted, so that the latter can be read and understood?

In 1991 a clever solution to this problem for internet communication was created and published by a cryptographer and privacy activist, Phil Zimmerman. He wrote a program called Pretty Good Privacy (PGP) and distributed it for free over the internet – for which he was threatened with prosecution by the US government, who saw such powerful protection software as a form of munitions that should not be exported. PGP worked on a simple mechanism: the idea that the key used to *en*crypt a message can in fact be different from the key used to *de*crypt it.

The idea of such 'asymmetric' encryption keys had been developed in the 1970s by two cryptographers, Whitfield Diffie and Martin Hellman, who had published their idea in June 1976. They proposed using two keys, one of which was kept private and the other which was made public. To establish a secure encryption channel between two users, they need simply exchange their public keys. The message to be transmitted is encrypted twice, once with the sender's private key and then again with the receiver's public key. Only the receiver has the private key with which to unlock one of the encryptions; and the receiver knows that it must have come from the correct person if the corresponding public key can then be used to unlock the second encryption.

This became known as the 'Diffie-Hellman Key Exchange'. The first practical implementation of the scheme was developed the following year by three MIT mathematicians, Ronald Rivest, Adi Shamir and Leonard Adelman. They used very large prime numbers to create public and private keys:[6] the private key is two large prime numbers; the public key is the result of multiplying those two prime numbers together. The security of the scheme relies on the immense difficulty of factoring any very large number into its component primes.

In PGP, Zimmerman used 'RSA' (as this prime-number public/private key scheme was dubbed) to create a complete encryption application that could be used to protect files or email messages. It became one of the most popular applications, not least because of the immense publicity that followed the US government's attempts to prosecute Zimmerman for its distribution. Although it provided high levels of information security (and indeed is still considered unbreakable), it was clumsy for use in the context of access to a website. Instead, what was needed was an essentially invisible, automatic encryption system that could work 'beneath' the browser.

Netscape achieved this invisibility with the SSL specification. Browser and server automatically exchange public keys and agree on a third, secret 'session' key (originally 40 bits long, now 128), which is used to encrypt all transmitted packets of information exchanged between the two for a short period of time. The 'handshake' between browser and server does not involve the user – all they see is a padlock icon in the bottom of the browser window to show that the secure channel is established. The result, though, is a well-protected channel along which credit card details and other sensitive information can be reliably and safely transmitted.

The combination in 1994 of browser and secure commercial web server allowed the creation of exclusively online retailers (dubbed 'eRetailers') to flourish. One of the first and arguably the most successful was the online bookseller Amazon, founded by Princeton graduate and former financial analyst Jeff Bezos, who was to become the internet's first billionaire.

Bezos had been employed as an analyst in a Manhattan investment company when, in May 1994, he chanced upon a report illustrating the growth of the internet – around 2300 per cent a year at the time. Bezos realized that the growing internet and World Wide Web would make an ideal retail environment, particularly for books. A well-trained analyst, Bezos did not immediately leap but instead attended the American Booksellers Association annual meeting in Los Angeles the following week and studied all that he could about the current state of the business. He discovered that book lists were already held on CD-ROM for distribution to high-street retailers; and that the economics of selling books online had to be attractive in comparison to the high street, where staff and property costs ran at 20 per cent of turnover. By contrast, on the internet he calculated that they would be less than 1 per cent. Certain that he had a winning idea, Bezos left his analyst job, persuaded his parents to invest 300,000 dollars, and established Amazon in Seattle, Washington, in July 1994.[7]

Amazon was one of the first dot.com companies, set up to operate almost wholly online with little or no 'real-world' footprint. It started the surge of corporate interest in the web, though the company most directly responsible for heralding the great 'dot.com bubble' of the late 1990s was once again Andreessen's Netscape Communications Corporation. On 9 August 1995, Netscape was floated on the stock exchange with an IPO (Initial Public Offering) that was the third largest in history. That floatation illustrated to both private and corporate investors that companies providing a service on the internet could be worth a lot. Investment money began to be made available to entrepreneurs with an idea for an internet service – from booking holidays online through to contacting old school friends; from day-trading investment sites to news magazines; and from selling CDs or electronic equipment to providing access to pornography. Seemingly *everything* could be turned into a clever website. Those having the ideas and taking the plunge found ready investment money waiting for them, regardless of whether they could demonstrate any business experience.

Through the second half of the 1990s the bubble began to grow. What was most worrying about this growth, however, was that the business models presented by the dot.com companies were not 'sensible' in the traditional sense of growing value through the accepted mechanisms of capital development. Instead, in an almost self-conscious parody of the traditional economic model, the dot.com companies proposed rapid growth, huge extensions of credit, high advertisement costs, substantial executive salaries and capital equipment investment – with no guarantee of a return on that investment for several long years. Almost everything that traditional (so-called bricks-and-mortar) companies would not conceive of doing, the dot.com companies quite deliberately effected. The dot.com enthusiasts even went so far as to criticize the 'old economy' for its straitjacketed approach to business.

The most important contribution to the growing dot.com mania came from financial analysts specializing in high-technology shares, who were advising scores of corporate and thousands of private investors. One in particular gained fame for his championing of the dot.com cause, and equally attracted infamy when the bubble ultimately burst, leaving many people without their expected investment return. Henry Blodgett was an analyst at CIBC Oppenheimer covering internet stocks when, in late 1998, he altered his recommended valuation for Amazon shares from 150 dollars to 400. At the time, it was obvious that his recommended valuation needed to be reconsidered, since the stock was anyway trading at 230 to 240 dollars per share. Blodgett's view was that the share price would continue to grow, since he believed that Amazon had a good business model. In truth, it did and still does. Unlike other, less experienced dot.com business managers of the time, Bezos had excellent credentials and a realistic business plan which showed the company becoming profitable in 2001. Blodgett's valuation of 400 dollars per share was a long-term forecast for the company, but buoyed by the rapid growth in other dot.com shares and fuelled by relatively inexperienced private investors seeking to cash in quickly, the share value of Amazon surged past the 400-dollar mark in a matter of weeks, rising up to around 600 dollars before the end of the year.

Blodgett himself was headhunted by Merrill-Lynch at the start of 1999 to replace their incumbent analyst, who had valued Amazon shares at only 50 dollars. For the next 12 months, Blodgett and a small group of internet analysts trumpeted the value of a range of dot.com stocks until, in February 2000, the shares began to free-fall for no better reason than that the Emperor was shown to have no clothes. The well-managed companies (Amazon, for example) saw their shares reduced to a small fraction of their previous high values – less than 10 dollars for Amazon by the end of 2001. Other companies were wiped out, and many that had planned an IPO (such as lastminute.com) were forced to reconsider their plans.

As the leader in the field of online retailers and arguably the best managed of the dot.com companies, Amazon was closely watched for its recovery from the February 2000 collapse. Steady and well-controlled growth, with intelligent expansions of the business into CDs and DVDs, helped the company to recover. In the fourth quarter of 2002, just one year later than originally planned, Amazon managed to show a profit. Since then, the company, seemingly unique amongst the dot.com bubble survivors, has managed to remain profitable, with a turnover in excess of 1 billion dollars per quarter. Ironically, at the end of 2005 its share price stood at around 42 dollars – not far below the target that the Merrill-Lynch analyst had originally stated.

Elsewhere, the ecommerce market equally began to recover from the February 2000 collapse. Online shopping was recorded at 76 billion dollars in 2002, a rise of nearly 50 per cent on the previous year, and was set to exceed 100 billion dollars in 2003, amounting to between 4 and 5 per cent of total retail sales. The internet is now a distinctive element of any organization's advertising and selling mechanism – all started by Andreessen's development of the graphical browser.

Unfortunately for Andreessen and Netscape, from having the overwhelming majority of the browser market, their share collapsed dramatically in the years after 1996 in the face of immense pressure from Microsoft in what came to be known as the 'Browser Wars'.

Microsoft and Internet Explorer

The modern Word Wide Web is now predominantly the domain of Microsoft's Internet Explorer program – around 96 per cent of internet surfers do so with the Microsoft product. From having near-saturation coverage of the browser market, Netscape's share crashed to below 4 per cent in 2002. In many ways this change in fortune and the bitter corporate battles that underlie it are ironic, since both Internet Explorer and Netscape Navigator are built on the same foundation.

The National Centre for Supercomputing Applications at the University of Illinois did not abandon development of the Mosaic program when Andreessen graduated and formed Mosaic Communications Corporation in 1994. In fact, they threatened legal action against Andreessen over the name Mosaic, forcing him to change the name of the company to Netscape. The university agreed a settlement in December 1994 to allow the new company to use the technology. However, NCSA continued to develop and market the browser through an agreement made in August 1994 with another company, called Spyglass, founded by a group of former University of Illinois students. In January 1995, Spyglass agreed to license the Mosaic technology to

Microsoft for use in the Windows 95 operating system – and Internet Explorer was born.

Version 1 of Explorer was released in August 1995, with version 2 following quickly in November of that year. Further refinements of the browser followed through 1996, with no fewer than five distinct versions released through the year as Microsoft rushed to catch up with Netscape. Before 1996, by his own admission, Bill Gates had ignored the internet and World Wide Web as being the domain of academics and research institutions. The rapid growth of Netscape, the growing investment in dot.com start-ups, and the increasing number of home and business users, however, made the opportunity obvious. On 7 December 1995, Gates hosted an 'Internet Strategy Workshop' to discuss the way in which Microsoft could best profit from the internet. The result is a modern internet dominated by Microsoft's Internet Explorer application, which brings web content to the desktop in a way that makes it as accessible and as useable as locally stored information.

The information itself has also developed dramatically from the static web pages of text and pictures of only a few short years ago. The Java programming environment developed by Sun Microsystems (and Microsoft's own version, ActiveX) have brought useable programs to the browser. High-quality video and audio allow TV programmes to be transmitted (or 'streamed') to the browser, and the growing speed of the networks has made this increasingly accessible and popular.

Not all of these things are necessarily features of Microsoft's Internet Explorer, but as the primary access medium to these features for the overwhelming majority of users, Microsoft has come to dominate the web. The web is now, though, about more than simply the access mechanism: a phrase from the golden age of the dot.com bubble is still appropriate – 'Content is King'. In recent years Microsoft and what is now its greatest rival, AOL

Time Warner, have been locked in an escalating battle to control content.[8]

This battle is ongoing. The World Wide Web is fast becoming the most important arena for all forms of commerce and communication — astonishing given that the medium is dominated by a 30-year-old network mechanism first developed as a means of allowing academic researchers to exchange their results.

The internet has expanded in many different ways and directions. The basic network protocols of TCP/IP and HTTP have been introduced into companies' internal systems, to produce networks known as 'intranets'; and companies have begun to use the global internet to connect their own sites together in a wide-area network structure called an 'extranet'. Encryption has been used to protect these communication routes, to create a facility called a 'virtual private network' (VPN). And in a return to the roots of the internet movement, wireless internet connections (dubbed 'Wi-Fi') have begun to emerge as network users tire of laying and maintaining cables.

At the end of 2005, there were estimated to be some 74 million websites, more than half of them in the US and around three-quarters in English. All of this development has not been without its problems, as pornographers, hackers, virus writers and other antisocial elements have threatened to abuse and misuse the facilities, creating real and expensive problems for those who want to use the network.

8

Problems with computers

From: Dad-And-Mum@Barretts.demon.co.uk
To: Neil.Barrett@btinternet.com
Subject: Re: Looks like you have a problem!

Neil,
Too late! What can I do about it?
Dad

> Hey, it looks like that nice new computer of yours might've caught
> a cold... I hope you didn't send that Cricket Club stuff out to
> many people or you're not gonna be too popular! LOL!
> N
>
> Forwarded Message:
>> From: alert@virus-sweep.com
>> To: Neil.Barrett@btinternet.com
>> Subject: WARNING. Someone tried to send you a virus!

For all the wonderful advantages and opportunities that computers bring, there are still a multitude of problems associated with them. Seemingly every week the headlines carry news of the latest infection by computer viruses. And while those headlines had once only been a feature of computer magazines and the industry press, they are now carried in the nationals and on the early-evening TV news. Computer hackers, fraud, unsolicited email, pornography – the list of problems that using computers brings is large and growing. However, while pornography is undoubtedly disturbing for many and unsolicited email is a huge waste of everyone's time, computer viruses and computer hackers represent the most immediate challenge to the successful application of technology.

Computer viruses

Of all the different types of problems that might arise in a society dependent on computer technology, the epidemic of computer viruses is perhaps the most apparent. There are now thought to be over 100,000 different forms of computer virus circulating on the internet, in documents, as programs or on infected media. The overwhelming majority of these viruses are recognized and dealt with by the equally ubiquitous anti-virus software, which acts as a computerized immune system to fight off infections. With alarming frequency, however, new and unrecognizable viruses appear, spread around the world, and cause many millions of pounds' worth of damage to business and home computers alike. More worrying still, the latest research publications show clearly that the epidemic will never end and that computer viruses will never be wholly eradicated.

Computer viruses are one example of a class of malicious and damaging programs that are dubbed 'malware' (short for 'malicious software'). Computer scientists usually recognize three different types of malware. The first is a 'Trojan horse', which appears to be a genuine program but which does something unexpected (and usually damaging) when it is unwittingly executed by a user. There are Trojan programs that provide hackers with a way of accessing computer systems invisibly; others that lie dormant on a computer for a period of time before erasing or damaging data; and even ones that keep a record of every character typed at the keyboard. Unlike the other two categories of malware, however, Trojans are static programs – they do not copy themselves from computer to computer but instead simply hide on one computer and create mischief.

A 'worm' is a computer program which copies itself, usually from computer to computer over the internet, typically by using email. Like a Trojan, worm programs rely on fooling users into believing that they are genuine (or at least harmless) programs. Worms can be disguised as documents or pictures attached to email; as computer games or screensavers; or even as updates of the computer's operating system. All of the most recent spate of 'virus' infections have in fact been worms rather than true viruses. A virus is like a worm insofar as it copies itself from computer to computer. Whereas a worm is a complete program, however, a virus is a small set of instructions which is injected into a valid program to subvert its operation.

Both worms and viruses have two elements – the 'copying engine' and the 'payload'. The copying engine is the series of functions which create a new copy of the program; the payload is made up of the functions which carry out the malicious or mischievous activity. Typical payloads might involve deleting or altering data; creating Trojan programs; or simply displaying an irritating message. A worm or virus could even have no payload as such, merely the intention of creating many copies of itself, thereby flooding the network or filling up the computer's memory. There have been some fascinating payloads developed over the years, but perhaps the greatest attention has gone into creating copying engines for worms and viruses. Such an engine must create a complete new copy of the malware code, either hiding it within a second program or transmitting it as a complete file over the internet to another computer. A copying engine must successfully disguise or camouflage the worm or virus, making sure that the malware is not detected before it has had a chance to be executed.

A lot of imagination goes into the creation of a successful malware program, and initially, at least, that creativity was not applied to creating something that would do damage. As long ago as the early 1950s, mainframe programmers experimented with programs which could create copies of themselves – though those programs did not in fact then actually *do* anything other than create further copies. In 1971, programmer Bob Thomas wrote the first worm program. Called 'Creeper', this was a program that moved from computer to computer in an air-traffic control environment. It was part of a design to track aircraft as they moved from one system's field of view to a second. Thomas's first program simply moved itself from one system on to another, displaying the message 'I'm creeper! Catch me if you can!' Creeper did not create multiple copies of itself but simply moved itself bodily off one system and on to a second.

Elsewhere, similar programs were developed. At the Xerox Palo Alto Research Centre, for example, researchers developed a series of worms that would carry out helpful programming tasks on the centre's internal network. One of these was even called the vampire worm because it 'came out after dark' and used the idle computers in the network to perform useful work. A modern version of this vampire worm is currently active on the internet on behalf of the Search for Extra-terrestrial Intelligence (SETI). Users download a worm in the form of a screensaver for when their computer is not busy working on their behalf. These SETI worms process a subset of the immense amount of data collected in the search for possible alien transmissions, analysing the data and communicating the results with one another. The effect is to turn substantial portions of the internet into a truly enormous parallel-processing computer.

These early worms, therefore, were written to be useful, even though the computer-science community were well aware that such programs could be harmful. In 1971, David Gerrold wrote

When Harley Was One, a science-fiction story about a computer virus; and in 1975, John Brunner wrote the science-fiction novel *Shockwave Rider*, in which a 'tapeworm' program is described as infecting a hostile computer. Until 1981, however, the damaging aspect of infectious software remained firmly in the realm of science fiction. And then the epidemic began.

⌐Ꝑ

The very first computer virus was created in late 1981 and released in 1982 by a high-school student in Pittsburgh called Rich Skrenta. He wrote the code to infect program disks for the Apple II personal computers.

Called Elk Cloner, this first hostile 'replicator' (the term 'virus' had not then been coined) copied itself onto the Apple disks used for swapping pirated computer games amongst a small group of students. On this early personal computer, all floppy disks included an element of the operating system's Disk Operating System (DOS) control code. The Elk program worked by injecting itself into an unused part of the disk where it would not be noticed. When the floppy disk was inserted into the Apple II and the computer was booted, the Elk program was copied into memory. If another disk was then inserted, with a game for example, then the Elk program would be copied onto that floppy disk and so continue the infection. Every 50th time the game was then run from the floppy disk, the Elk program would execute and simply display a poem on the monitor screen:

Elk Cloner: The program with personality
It will get on all your disks
It will infiltrate your chips
Yes it's Cloner!
It will stick to you like glue
It will modify ram too
Send in the Cloner!

Elk Cloner was wildly successful, spreading rapidly from system to system and even infecting Skrenta's teacher's own Apple II. The spread of the virus was limited, however, by the extent of the group swapping the pirated computer games between themselves. Despite this, for years afterwards (at least, for as long as the Apple II continued to be used) the Elk Cloner would occasionally reappear.

The origin of the understanding of computer virus threats and hostile potential came a year or so later, with the doctoral research work carried out by Fred Cohen at the University of Southern California. Ironically, Cohen had been a Master's graduate student at Pittsburgh shortly before Skrenta created his virus. It was Cohen who defined a virus as 'a computer program that can affect other computer programs by modifying them in such a way as to include a (possibly evolved) copy of itself'. The actual term 'computer virus' was coined by Cohen's supervisor, Len Adelman (one of the co-creators of the RSA public-key encryption scheme), but the demonstration of virus behaviour was all Cohen's. On 3 November 1983, he created a virus program to infect a UNIX directory displaying utility. He demonstrated the virus's behaviour at a computer-science seminar in the university on 10 November and carried out a number of further experiments in program infection throughout 1984.

Cohen gained his PhD in 1986, having shown that the problems of detecting a computer virus were actually identical to a class of problems already analysed by Alan Turing in the 1930s in the context of the first Turing machine computational model. After he had devised the idea of the universal Turing machine (an abstract computer that executes programs in the form of a Turing machine), the problem was to determine whether a given program would ever stop or whether it would put itself into an infinite loop. This is called the 'halting problem'. Turing was in fact able to show that it was impossible for a Turing machine to predict whether any other Turing machine would indeed halt; in other words, that it was impossible for a computer program to predict the behaviour of another computer program. In his PhD, Cohen showed that the problems of identifying computer viruses were an instance of these Turing halting problems and that therefore an algorithm to identify a virus could not be written.

The upshot of this is that computer viruses can only be detected (and therefore prevented) by a form of guesswork – what is known technically as 'heuristics'. Cohen argued that viruses could only be detected if they contained sequences of instructions or symbols that could be uniquely identified; otherwise they could not and the task of combating them could be shown mathematically to be impossible. It is a scary prospect and one faced routinely by modern computer users the world over, confronted with the present pandemic of such infections.

Cohen's work showed how scarily effective an infectious and hostile program could be. The true beginnings of the modern computer virus pandemic, however, came in 1986 with the creation of the Brain virus by two Pakistani brothers, Basit and Amjad Alvi, who ran a company called Brain Computer Services in Lahore. Established in 1982 as a computer repair and service company for the Lahore community of Sinclair ZX-80 owners, the Alvis' small company has now grown into a substantial and well-respected part of the Pakistani internet industry. In 1986, though, the brothers created a computer virus that spread rapidly around the world, displaying their company name and address, contact details and the '© Brain' banner.

Confusion surrounds the origin and motivation for this first computer epidemic. The Alvis' own reports seem to suggest that the virus was created as some form of viral advertising for their company and as a 'punishment' for the Americans who pirated Pakistani-produced software while trumpeting their moral superiority with respect to the laws of copyright. However, analysis of Brain and of its several variants that all appeared at much the same time shows that, whilst Brain was indeed created by the Alvis, it was based on a simple modification of an already existing computer virus called Ohio.[1] This was created by an Indonesian college student known only by his nickname, Den Zuko. Ohio was isolated and modified by the Alvi brothers to create their viral advertising program, Brain.

Most interesting of all, shortly after the Alvi brothers' work, a third variant was produced. This was called 'Den Zuk' after an identifiable character string, the author's nickname, found within the code. Den Zuk hunts out and overlays Brain infections with copies of itself, protecting itself from infection by subsequent copies of Brain. It seems likely that the first epidemic of computer viruses resulted from an early experiment by an Indonesian student known as Den Zuko, which was hijacked for advertising by the Alvi brothers, and this in turn motivated the creation of a viral 'hunter-killer' to wipe out the advertising message.

The Brain family of viruses spread from system to system by infecting bootable floppy disks for the MS-DOS operating system.[2] It worked by replacing the 'boot sector' of the floppy disk with itself. A floppy disk is divided into many 512 byte-long sectors laid out as a series of concentric tracks on the disk. The very first sector is called 'sector zero', and on a bootable floppy it contains code to load and run the MS-DOS operating system. Brain worked by replacing the contents of sector zero with its own instructions. It altered the disk content information to show three unused sectors as being damaged (so-called 'bad blocks') and copied the original MS-DOS boot loader code into one of these. The two other hijacked, disguised sectors were then used to hold the rest of the Brain viral code.

When the PC is first booted, the physical hardware loads and executes the sector zero code on its primary disk. If a bootable floppy is in the drive, then that floppy becomes the primary disk; if no floppy is present, then the computer boots from the hard-disk drive. When booting from an infected floppy, therefore, the code that was first loaded was the Brain code, which loaded itself into the PC memory from the two hijacked sectors and then loaded and passed control to the original MS-DOS boot code. The PC would then continue to run, though with the Brain code already present and operating in the system memory. Brain itself was quite sophisticated in its operation. First of all, it attempted to hide itself by refusing to display the infection code on the floppy disk if the user requested to see the contents of sector zero. The virus would display the original system code rather than itself. It would also copy itself onto any uninfected floppy disks that were then inserted into the infected computer, giving rise to the viral infection behaviour.

Cohen had shown the academic information-security community that infectious, replicating computer viruses were possible and difficult to prevent; and Skrenta had demonstrated the reality of computer viruses to a small group of Apple II games players. Brain and its clones, however, showed the world what the future of computing was going to be like.

The success of the Brain virus opened the floodgates to tens of thousands of computer viruses and dozens of clever propagation techniques. Worse, while the effect of those early viruses had been only mildly irritating, the payloads of the viruses that followed were increasingly damaging.

The first virus to follow the Brain family was developed in 1987 and released at Lehigh University in Pennsylvania, after which it was named. The Lehigh virus, which spread throughout the university, infected the 'command.com' command-line inter-preter under MS-DOS. Although it was the first virus to infect a program and subvert its operation (and arguably, therefore, the first true 'virus' by Cohen's definition), it was not a particularly successful one. It would copy itself onto floppy disks that contained full MS-DOS operating system implementations, and after just four such transmissions it would activate and begin deleting files before then disabling itself. The virus made no attempt to disguise itself and no attempt to mask the alteration to the command.com program, and it could only be spread amongst floppy disks containing full MS-DOS systems.

The virus family that followed was *much* more successful. It was developed in 1987 by an unknown programmer in Tel Aviv, who created four viruses in short order. The first was similar to the Lehigh virus but infected any '.com' file, not just command.com. The second, called 'suriv-02', was the first to be able to infect '.exe' format files. The third could infect both types of format. And the fourth virus used both of these infection techniques and, every Friday 13th, deleted all programs run on that day. It became known as the Jerusalem virus and, because Friday 13ths are relatively rare, remains inconspicuous and widespread.

Probably the most common and widespread virus was also developed in 1987, this time in New Zealand. The smallest virus to date, at only a few hundred bytes in length, the virus remains hidden and is transmitted from infected disk to infected disk, and once in every eight times that the infected computer is rebooted it displays a short message, 'Your PC is now Stoned'. Being so relatively inconspicuous, the Stoned virus is probably the most widespread and persistent virus in the world to date.

Finally, also in 1987, the distinctive Cascade virus was produced in Germany. It was called Cascade because on infection and activation the virus makes the characters appear to fall off the bottom of the screen. Cascade was not only the first to use what would become a common viral payload trick, it was also the first to use an encryption system so as to hide the details of its internal operation and thereby escape detection.

By 1992 a number of anti-virus companies had been formed, combating an estimated 1300 viruses. Part of the reason for the rapid growth in the number of viruses in 1992 was the creation and release of a number of programming 'toolkits' to help inexperienced virus writers to develop new examples. As Cohen had anticipated, the problem of detecting the viruses was all but impossible to solve definitively and the anti-viral scanners had to look for recognizable text strings (called 'signatures') within the possibly infected files. Some viruses were even being developed that bypassed this crude viral-detection strategy. These were called 'polymorphic' viruses, the first (named Tequila) appearing in 1991. These mutate themselves dramatically on each copying, changing all of their internal strings so as to evade the alarms.

In 1995, the Concept virus was produced, the first to take advantage of the inbuilt programming language within the Microsoft Word application. This language allows the creation of 'macros', collections of instructions for the Word application to carry out. A macro specifies a particular way in which a document is to be handled. For example, it might determine how sophisticated features such as text checking are embedded into templates for documents such as order forms or standard letters. As the victim opens a Concept-infected document, the macro virus executes so as to infect the Word implementation's standard document templates. Thereafter, every document edited with that infected copy of Word is itself infected, and if the document is then passed to another user, whether by email, on floppy disk, or via a server, then that user is also infected. Concept heralded a shift of viruses away from the '.exe' and file infector types, towards those predominantly targeted at Microsoft applications, which were found to have a wide variety of security failings.

In 1999, the Melissa virus spread as a macro infection of Microsoft documents attached to email messages, transmitting itself to collections of further victims found in the user's Outlook address book file. In 2000, the Love Bug virus copied Melissa, using a victim's address book to find further victims. However, Love Bug was a complete program rather than an infection of an existing file, so was technically a worm rather than a virus. It worked by enticing the receiver to open an attachment with the intriguing message, 'I Love You'. The attachment was in fact a program rather than a love letter and contained the infection. In recent years, this shift from viruses to worms has been pronounced. These modern infectors rely on email to propagate and on persuasive text or subjects to encourage the user to open the attached program, which may or may not be disguised as a harmless text file or a link to a web page. Typical inducements include the prospect of pictures of Anna Kournikova, Britney Spears or Jennifer Lopez, or messages similar to the 'I Love You' concept.

The years 2001 and 2002 saw a varied collection of such worms, some more successful than others, some more harmful than others. Nimda, Sircam, Klez, CodeRed and BugBear all hit the headlines during this period, though they were simply the tip of the iceberg. In 1992, there were estimated to be 1300 viruses; in 1996, over 10,000; and at the start of 2002, the figure passed a staggering 70,000 and has continued to rise. At the time of writing, there might well be as many as 100,000 different worms and viruses in the wild. Most worrying of all, the modern variants of these infectors are not only cleverer than their ancestors, they are also *much* more effective. In January 2003, the Slammer worm was found to be spreading at a faster rate than any previous infector had achieved. CodeRed had held the record before Slammer, hitting 395,000 computers in the first 12 hours. By comparison, Slammer infected 75,000 computers in just 10 minutes. This, of course, gives the anti-virus companies pause for thought.

After the first few outbreaks in the late 1980s, the handling of computer viruses had been an essentially amateur affair, with small groups of experts within universities and larger companies taking responsibility for analysing the virus and producing a signature that would allow its detection and eradication. Starting in 1990, dedicated anti-virus companies were established,[3] running these analysis teams and marketing the engine and the signature-string databases. The operation of these teams, though, was based on a relatively slow spread of viruses as they infected floppy disks and were passed from hand to hand or were downloaded within infected files from program-sharing bulletin-board environments. When a new type of virus was suspected to have appeared, the more expert victims would isolate the infected programs and then send a copy to the anti-virus laboratories – exactly as biological viruses are handled by the various centres for disease control. At the laboratory, the anti-virus analysts would examine and study the infected program, identify some characteristic string, and then copy that string into the identification database. Subsequent publication of that database on the internet would then allow potential future victims to be protected.

This is a scheme that worked well in situations where the viruses were readily apparent, easily analysed and spread only slowly. Unfortunately, the modern world of the computer virus is a long way from that situation – with rapidly evolving, heavily disguised but above all *very* quickly propagated viruses (or rather, worms) using the internet to cover the world not in days, nor even in hours, but in *seconds*. The sad reality is that the problems posed by computer viruses are not of a kind that will ever in fact be solved. The anti-virus companies are swimming against a tidal wave to fight what will ultimately be a losing battle. The very nature of the modern internet-connected world – essentially a monoculture of technology populated by Microsoft Windows and its applications – provides a target that has been shown to be vulnerable and which is easy for the creators of viruses to hit.

At best we can only hope to maintain a crumbling sea wall of a defence and pray that the problems exploited by the viruses are rapidly and effectively addressed. Unfortunately, experience does not provide any degree of confidence that this will happen any time soon – especially when that internet monoculture is also being attacked directly by dedicated, capable and creative individuals: the 'hackers'.

Computer hackers

A little after 6 pm on the evening of 2 November 1988, at first dozens, then hundreds, and later thousands and tens of thousands of computers connected to the internet began to be swamped to the point of uselessness by thousands of invisible processes. Increasingly panicked system managers around the world frantically rebooted their computers, only to see them again swamped moments later. Computers that should have been running with load averages of between 1 and 2 were suddenly trying to operate with load averages above 30.[4]

Something was clearly wrong. The deduction made by those stressed system managers was that, in the words of the Andrew Sudduth of Harvard University, 'There might be a virus loose on the Internet.' There was indeed, though this was a special kind of virus. It was, in effect, an automated hacker that was breaking into internet-connected computer systems and duplicating itself hundreds and thousands of times. It was a virus that was able to teach some especially valuable lessons to the growing community of those who enjoyed the task of subverting information security.

The word 'hacker' has had a varied life. It emerged in the sense of prankster in the 1950s at MIT, in the context of the imaginative and creative pranks carried out by students who were members of the Model Railway Club.[5] Classic MIT 'hacks' involved disassembling cars so that they could be rebuilt on the roof of a building, picking locks so as to get into secured laboratories, and so on. The tricks were always mischievous, and though sometimes of questionable legality, they were always amusing. The terms 'hack' and 'hackers' were therefore usually applied with a sense of admiration.

With the growth of the computer community and a reputation for programming excellence at MIT, the word soon began to be applied to those able to create imaginative and skilful programs, particularly where the creation of the program involved demonstrating a deep understanding of the underlying operating system. Hackers were expert programmers, most especially those who could quickly and accurately produce programs 'on the fly' to solve a difficult problem. Often those who were 'hacking software' did so by cleverly subverting or bypassing some of the operating-system security in order to access the hardware directly or to access the internal data structures used by the system. Even in those early days, therefore, there was a subtext of hacking involving some clever subversion of computer security measures. Following the release in 1983 of the film *WarGames*, the link became even closer and the term became inextricably associated with those whose primary purpose was to gain illicit access to a computer system.

Even as the name 'hacker' began to be applied to those who subvert information security measures, however, it also retained the sense of exploration and subversion for the joy of it, rather than out of any sense of malice. On that basis, it has been argued that Charles Babbage and Charles Wheatstone were both hackers. In the days of the telegraph,[6] simple ciphers were used to protect transmissions, and friends Babbage and Wheatstone took a competitive joy in trying to decipher the often prosaic messages. In World War II, it could be argued that Alan Turing and his colleagues at Bletchley Park were hackers, as was physicist Richard Feynman at the sensitive Manhattan Project, who would joyfully crack open the combination locks on the filing cabinets containing the secret plans for no better reason than to show that he could.

In the modern sense of the word, however, hacking truly began in 1969, when a blind mathematics student at the University of Florida began to play with the AT&T telephone network. In November 1960, the telephone switches had become wholly computer-controlled. To provide these controlling computers with the switching commands, audible tones were used on the actual communication links themselves. Joe Engressia had the lucky gift of perfect pitch and discovered that one particular high-pitched tone – 2600 Hertz (cycles per second) – was of vital importance. This was the 'supervisor' tone, generated by a handset when it was hung up to indicate to the billing computer that the call was complete. Engressia discovered that if he whistled that note into the handset without replacing it, he could confuse the system. The switchboard would keep the line open but the billing computer would not charge him for the call. He had discovered a way of making telephone calls for free.

Engressia was nicknamed 'the Whistler' and became the centre of a group of mainly blind students and enthusiasts who manipulated and explored the telephone network. They quickly discovered that a toy whistle given away free in a Quaker Oats breakfast cereal called 'Cap'n Crunch' generated exactly the correct frequency, allowing those who did not have the Whistler's perfect pitch to control the network for themselves. They were able to go further still when one of the group, John Draper (whose nickname was 'Captain Crunch', after the whistle), created a small box of electronics to generate the control signals for the network. In 1969 Draper was a Vietnam veteran discharged from the USAF and living in the California Bay Area.

While studying for an engineering degree, Draper was working as an electronics engineer for National Semiconductor and was also a ham radio enthusiast. It was through the ham radio connection that he met the group of blind telephone hackers (called 'phreakers'), who persuaded him to use his skill with electronics to create an electronic tone generator. This was dubbed the 'blue box' (or 'M-F' for Multi-Frequency Generator) and made Draper famous following an October 1971 article in the *Esquire* magazine which exposed the group and its activities.[7]

This article encouraged a host of other would-be phreakers to experiment with the telephone network. Draper was by then the most infamous of the group and had helped many others to understand how the blue box worked. He even met Steve Wozniak at the University of California at Berkeley following the publication of the *Esquire* article, teaching him how to make his own blue boxes. Before they went on to establish Apple Computers, both Wozniak and Steve Jobs built and sold the blue box units for 150 dollars to the growing army of phreakers.

Unfortunately for Draper, Engressia and the others, the *Esquire* article also alerted AT&T engineers to what was being done to their network. Engressia was arrested and received a suspended sentence for 'wire fraud'. He moved away from phreaking and studied scripture and philosophy, qualifying as a minister with a spiritual community in Florida. He changed his name to the wonderfully improbable 'Joybubbles' and dedicated the rest of his life to working with children. In May 1972 John Draper was also arrested and sentenced to four months' imprisonment. Even in prison, though, Draper could not resist the lure of subverting the telephone network, holding daily classes on phone fraud for the other inmates. Phreaking grew steadily in popularity, amongst criminals who wanted to hide their telephone calls and amongst computer users and network subversives who wanted to play with the system.

With modern telephone networks, although it is still possible to manipulate the system, it has become much more difficult. In particular, the 2600 Hertz tone no longer presents an obvious loophole. Indeed, the tone itself lives on now only in the name of a popular hacking magazine called *2600: The Hacker Quarterly*. Hacking steadily moved away from the telephone network, into the far more challenging territory of the computer.

The period immediately after the arrest of the Whistler, Captain Crunch and their friends was one of intense activity as interest in subverting the telephone network spread like wildfire. As AT&T tightened parts of the network, groups of hackers would share information about still-vulnerable elements or new discoveries. Often those discoveries came about as a result of technical information gleaned directly from the telephone companies' computers. Towards the end of the 1970s, the telephone network was increasingly controlled by UNIX minicomputers. Since UNIX had been developed by AT&T's Bell Laboratories, naturally they chose to use it for their own systems. The control computers ran UNIX, but more importantly so too did the computers on which was stored information about how the network itself operated. Hacking the telephone network gradually came to require a skill in hacking the UNIX computers that ran it. And as the internet grew in popularity in the early years of the 1980s, accessing those computers began to get substantially easier.

In 1981, the first of the telephone hackers to be convicted of a felony involving illicitly accessing a computer system was Ian Murphy, who called himself 'Captain Zap'. He had broken into the AT&T computer systems and had gained control of one of the UNIX systems used for billing, altering its internal clock so that it appeared to be the cheap-rate period for all calls made during the day. In fact, Captain Zap was not convicted of a 'computer crime' but of conspiracy to defraud the telephone company. At that time there was no federal law that explicitly covered computer crimes, just a patchwork of individual state laws. Such a federal law was soon urgently needed as more and more computer hackers emerged and began to threaten the computers which protected bank transactions, the source code of computer applications, and even national security itself.

In May 1981, one of the US's most prolific and notorious computer hackers, Kevin Mitnick, appeared for the first time before a court, charged with having stolen computer manuals by hacking into the Pacific Bell computers. He was 17 at the time and had been involved in telephone hacking since he was a child. As a minor, he was sentenced to probation but almost immediately broke the terms, once again hacking into Pacific Bell in order to destroy data. Mitnick would go on to have a long and illustrious 'career' as a hacker, primarily interested in obtaining information on the operation of the telephone systems. From 1981 to 1995, Mitnick (who called himself 'Condor') broke into a multitude of computer systems belonging to telephone companies, internet service providers, mobile-phone companies and computer manufacturers. By 1991, Mitnick was high on the FBI's 'Most Wanted' list and on the run, hacking into systems and leaving taunting messages from motel bedrooms and bars across the country.

An imprisoned hacker, Justin Peterson (nickname 'Agent Steel'), was even released from custody in September of that year in order to help track Mitnick down. He was finally caught in February 1995 with the help of one of his victims, Tsutomu Shimomura, a California-based information security expert.[8] Peterson, despite having agreed to help catch his friend, did not then go straight, and in August 1994 he succeeded in stealing some 150,000 dollars by hacking a computer system at a finance company.

Mitnick was the most famous of the audacious hackers but certainly not the only one. By the mid-1980s there were a host of high-profile groups of hackers, with names like 'Legion of Doom', 'Data Travellers' and 'Chaos Computer Club'. In 1984, *2600: The Hacker Quarterly* was first published, and in 1985 *Phrack* appeared. Both provided detailed instructions on how to subvert the phone and computer systems; *Phrack* even provided advice on picking locks and detailed information about creating home-made bombs. The growing hacker movement was provided with a hero in Mitnick; a collection of easily followed tutorials in the regular publications; and in January 1986 a clearly articulated philosophy, when Legion of Doom member Lloyd Blankenship ('the Mentor') was arrested and published the 'Hacker Manifesto':

Another one got caught today, it's all over the papers.
'Teenager Arrested in Computer Crime Scandal',
'Hacker Arrested after Bank Tampering'...
Damn kids. They're all alike.

But did you, in your three-piece psychology and 1950's technobrain, ever take a look behind the eyes of the hacker?
Did you ever wonder what made him tick, what forces shaped him, what may have molded him?
I am a hacker, enter my world...

Mine is a world that begins with school... I'm smarter than most of the other kids, this crap they teach us bores me...
Damn underachiever. They're all alike.

I'm in junior high or high school. I've listened to teachers explain for the fifteenth time how to reduce a fraction.
I understand it. 'No, Ms. Smith, I didn't show my work. I did it in my head...'
Damn kid. Probably copied it. They're all alike.

I made a discovery today. I found a computer. Wait a second, this is cool.

It does what I want it to. If it makes a mistake, it's because I screwed it up.

Not because it doesn't like me...

Or feels threatened by me...

Or thinks I'm a smart ass...

Or doesn't like teaching and shouldn't be here...

Damn kid. All he does is play games. They're all alike.

And then it happened... a door opened to a world...

rushing through the phone line like heroin through an addict's veins,

an electronic pulse is sent out, a refuge from the day-to-day incompetencies is sought... a board is found.

'This is it... this is where I belong...'

I know everyone here... even if I've never met them, never talked to them, may never hear from them again... I know you all...

Damn kid. Tying up the phone line again. They're all alike...

You bet your ass we're all alike... we've been spoon-fed baby food at school when we hungered for steak...

the bits of meat that you did let slip through were pre-chewed and tasteless.

We've been dominated by sadists, or ignored by the apathetic. The few that had something to teach found us willing pupils, but those few are like drops of water in the desert.

This is our world now... the world of the electron and the switch, the beauty of the baud.

We make use of a service already existing without paying for what could be dirt-cheap if it wasn't run by profiteering gluttons,

and you call us criminals.

We explore... and you call us criminals.

We seek after knowledge... and you call us criminals.
We exist without skin color, without nationality, without
religious bias... and you call us criminals.
You build atomic bombs, you wage wars, you murder, cheat,
and lie to us,
you try to make us believe it's for our own good, yet we're
the criminals.

Yes, I am a criminal. My crime is that of curiosity.
My crime is that of judging people by what they say and
think, not what they look like.
My crime is that of outsmarting you, something that you will
never forgive me for.

I am a hacker, and this is my manifesto.
You may stop this individual, but you can't stop us all... after
all, we're all alike.

'The Conscience of a Hacker'

One line in particular of the publication caught the imagination of
all those seeking to justify their exploration and games with the
computer and telephone networks – 'My crime is that of curiosity.'
Unfortunately for them, in the US their activity now *was* truly a
crime. Many individual states had outlawed computer offences, the
first being Florida in 1974. And in 1986 the US Congress passed the
Computer Fraud and Abuse Act, making it a federal offence to
interfere with the operation of 'federal interest' computers (those
upon which the federal government has some dependence) – essentially all of those involved in the internet. In January 1989, Herbert
Zinn ('Shadowhawk') became the first hacker to be convicted
under the new law, having been found guilty of causing 174,000
dollars' worth of damage to AT&T and US military computer data.

Four years after the US statute, the UK government followed
suit, creating the Computer Misuse Act on 1 September 1990.

The new law was prompted by the unsuccessful prosecution of two British hackers, Steve Gold and Robert Shiffreen, who in 1985 had broken into the BT Prestel computers – even getting so far as to access the Duke of Edinburgh's personal email. With no available computer-crime law in the UK at the time, the pair were charged with fraud, but their conviction was overturned on appeal. The defence successfully argued that the law of fraud under which they were charged could not be made to apply to computers. Faced with an embarrassing shortfall in the legislation, the appeal court judges urged a judicial review, and the result was the 1990 act.

Whereas the US Computer Fraud and Abuse statute concentrated on illicit access to government computers, the UK Computer Misuse Act addressed any and all computers. It provided for three specific computer-crime offences. The first two, which related to hacking, were the offence of unauthorized access and the offence of unauthorized access with the intent of committing a further crime. The first was to outlaw the situation of hackers gaining access to a computer and simply exploring it or even just keeping 'score' of the numbers of computers conquered. The second was to outlaw the more serious situation of hackers breaking into computers so as to steal information, credit-card details or passwords for other systems. The third offence that the Computer Misuse Act defined was the crime of unauthorized modification of a computer's contents. This was intended to provide a means of prosecuting virus writers and those who deliberately destroyed computer data after hacking a system.

At the start of the 1990s, therefore, everything that hackers in the US or UK were doing was made explicitly illegal. The first attempted prosecution of a hacker under the new UK law came in 1991, when Edinburgh student Paul Bedworth was charged under Section 1 of having accessed a computer without authority. Bedworth's astonishingly novel and surprisingly successful defence was that he was 'addicted to hacking' and so could not stop himself. One of the requirements for access to a computer to have been illegal under the Act is that the defendant has formed the intention of exceeding their authorized access. Bedworth was able to persuade the court that, since he was an addict of computer hacking, he was unable to form that intent. He was found not guilty, a decision that one reputable journal at the time called a 'millstone rather than a milestone' for the Computer Misuse Act.

Throughout the 1990s, it became increasingly obvious that hackers were not immediately put off by the explicit criminal-ization of their activity. In the UK, the Computer Misuse Act failed time after time to result in convictions, with high-profile hackers repeatedly receiving either small fines or community service at best; and at worst, being allowed to walk free. In the US, despite the best efforts of state police forces, the FBI and even the Secret Service,[9] hackers continued to proliferate and their reputation as an invisible enemy grew. In 1990, Kevin Poulsen ('Dark Dante') hacked a radio station so as to win their weekly competition for a Porsche 944. In 1994, British teenagers Richard Pryce ('Datastream Cowboy') and Mathew Bevan ('Kuji') hacked computer systems at a US military base, sparking an international espionage incident. And in 1996, an official US government audit showed that 250,000 hacking attempts had been recorded against government computers, more than half of which had been successful.

The hacking attempts through the 1990s were successful for two main reasons. First, the computers that were being hacked were not particularly well protected. The second reason was the influx of hacking tricks (called 'exploits') that were provided over the internet. The origin of many of those tricks can be traced back to the strange and damaging 'computer virus' of the night of 2 November 1988.

In the early years of computer hacking, the main objective was to find ways of gaining access to the telephone network. Because much of that network was controlled by UNIX minicomputers and because much of the information about the control of the network was equally kept on UNIX systems, naturally the most important target for the hackers was these systems. A famous tutorial on hacking UNIX systems was published by 'Sir Hackalot' in 1990 – 'UNIX: A Hacking Tutorial'. This collected and presented the series of simple steps taken by hackers to recognize, access and take control of any of these systems that might be encountered.

These computers were found initially to be almost completely accessible, usually because, in the early years of the internet, many of the connected computers included a specific 'guest' account which either had no password or a simple one such as 'guest' or 'visitor'. These accounts gave access to the computer but only to a limited set of facilities. Hackers, though, following the methods described by Sir Hackalot, would typically use this guest access to try to find vulnerable directories, programs or user accounts that could be subverted so as to give them increased privileges or further access. In some situations, it proved possible simply to guess other users' passwords, perhaps even those of the system managers;[10] sometimes it was possible to plant simple programs on the system to take a copy of passwords as they were typed in; and sometimes privileged programs could be undermined. In his classic book *The Cuckoo's Egg* Clifford Stoll describes exactly how this process was carried out by a German hacker in August 1986, who introduced a series of commands (the 'cuckoo egg') into a computer system so that it would be executed unknowingly by the privileged system management programs.

By far the majority of the system intrusions in the early years of computer networks were of this simplest kind. The subversion of existing programs so as to allow an intruder to 'escalate' their privileges was, however, sometimes an awkward affair. At the time, the hackers would search long and hard for a 'magic wand' trick that would provide them with immediate privileged access. Some 'wands' were found but were quickly fixed; for example, the UNIX email program was discovered to allow privileged access. A general solution, however, evaded the hackers – until, that is, the November 1988 computer virus.

The attack came not from a virus, in fact, but from a clever program that was christened the 'Internet Worm'. Though it was not the first, it was certainly the most damaging and the most infamous of the worms to spread throughout the network, flooding and blocking access to tens of thousands of computer systems. The program was actually written by a graduate student at Cornell University, Robert Morris, son of one of the chief scientists at the National Security Agency.

Morris's program was important for two reasons. First, it represented an 'automated hacker' – a program that duplicated a range of things that a hacker might attempt in breaking into a target computer system. Given access to one computer, it would first look to see whether it was automatically provided with privileges to run programs on any other computer; then it would attempt a long list of common, simple passwords to gain access; and then it would try a small group of well-known tricks, such as the email vulnerability mentioned above. If all of these failed, however, the worm would try the new and most impressive trick in its armoury – the second reason why the program was important: Morris had found a way of forcing a victim computer to execute a series of program instructions transmitted to it.

At the NSA, Morris's father (who was also Robert Morris) had discovered an interesting and unusual feature of almost all UNIX programs that had been written in the C programming language. For many years, the only 'official' description of the language came from a book written by Brian Kernighan and Dennis Ritchie called *The C Programming Language*, published by Prentice

Hall. This book described the language and provided a number of example programs and fragments of programs, including a simple loop for reading characters from a file or a user's terminal before putting them one at a time into a buffer. In C, the size of that buffer had to be specified when the program was first written. What Morris Senior discovered was that the Prentice Hall publication showed no error checking on the fragment of code illustrating the way that a buffer should be used. Characters would be read into the buffer until all of the characters had been received, not until the buffer was full. If more characters than expected were transmitted, then the buffer would spill over.

Checking some samples of C programs, Morris realized that almost all programs that read input characters (and that was the overwhelming majority of programs) were written to look like Kernighan and Ritchie's code. The programmers had not included the error-checking elements on the buffers in real-life programs because the examples in the textbook did not show that error checking. Morris Senior soon realized that the characters running off the end of the buffer would crash into the rest of the program's data and instructions, so that the program would fail. When he was told of this aspect by his enthused father, however, Morris Junior realized that there was a way of using this feature to his advantage – not to *crash* a program[11] but to *subvert* it.

When a procedure is called within a program, the arguments, local variables and any returned results are all placed on the stack, but so too is the return address to which the procedure must jump when the procedure is complete. What the younger Morris realized was that the overflowing characters from the buffer would not simply overwrite the other data items on the stack, they would also overwrite the return address. His genius was in realizing that the procedure would not know that the value stored on the stack for the return address was invalid – it would still simply read and execute the jump instruction.

Morris experimented with introducing program instructions into the character buffer. By specifying the program instructions as ASCII character values, he found that the buffer could be filled with perfectly valid instructions without the victim program realizing that it was being forced to play host to an 'egg'. Then, he followed the program instructions with a series of values that would force the procedure to jump to the start of the buffer rather than back into the main part of the program from where the procedure had been called. To his delight, it worked.

Robert Morris had found a way of introducing program instructions into an already running program along an unprotected and unsuspected channel – a very clever form of infectious virus. More importantly, if the program that was infected was running as a privileged process, then the instructions that were introduced would also be privileged – there was no limit on how useful a trick Morris had discovered. He was able to learn that several of the UNIX services available over the internet were vulnerable to this discovery, including an almost universally provided facility called 'finger'.

This program allows users to see information about others on the internet. Given an address in the form 'username@computer.domain', the finger program sends a query to the 'computer.domain' asking for any information about the 'username'. A program running on the target computer (called 'fingerd'[12]) receives the username specified and replies with any stored information that might be of interest – what the user's real name is, when they last logged on, whether they have any unread email, and so on. In anticipation that the username would only be short, the fingerd program was provided with a 512-character buffer (from the Prentice Hall book, the 'standard size' for an input buffer) with no error checking on the input.

Robert Morris Junior found that he was able to fill the fingerd buffer with the program instructions to connect a command-line shell program back over the internet – the 'egg' placed in the buffer is most commonly called the 'shell code' because of this behaviour. He could then overwrite the return address on the stack. The result was that the fingerd program, which was running as though it were the most privileged user on the system, executed his transmitted instructions and allowed him access to and complete control over the target computer.

Just as the hackers in the late 1960s had found the magic wand for breaking the telephone network with a toy whistle, those of the late 1980s were presented with a magic wand for the computer networks. The 'buffer overflow' hack worked against almost every computer connected to the internet. Almost all were UNIX systems; almost all included the standard C programming libraries; and almost all of those libraries had (and indeed, still have) that crucial programming flaw.

At least initially, those running computers on the internet were fortunate that, whilst the description of the buffer overflow exploit is simple, actually making it work was not. A 512-character buffer on a 16-bit computer allowed for only 256 instructions to be placed in the buffer – and those instructions had to be written in the low-level machine code for the target computer. Such a program would not be hard to create, but then the would-be hacker also had to correctly guess how to overwrite the return address so as to jump to the start of the buffer. Though the buffer overflow was increasingly famous, it was also surprisingly rare – until November 1996, when a hacker called 'Aleph One' wrote a detailed article in *Phrack* edition 49. Called 'Smashing the Stack for Fun and Profit', this article provided a clear description and example code that could be adapted and compiled easily by anyone having the interest.

Hacking exploded, and by November 1999 a report funded by the Defence Advanced Research Projects Agency quoted buffer overflows as the most common of the simple exploit tricks being used by hackers. Unchecked buffers were found in almost every UNIX implementation, on all Windows systems, on every web server, in every common application – it was not only the most popularly used exploit, it was also the most widely available. But while buffer overflows were the most commonly used tricks, unfortunately they were not the only ones.

In July 1998, a hacking group called 'Cult of the Dead Cow' released the first of a series of 'control Trojans' able to provide hackers with remote, privileged command of an infected Windows workstation. Called 'Back Orifice', this program could be transmitted by email or downloaded from a website as an apparently innocent application. Running on a victim's PC, it allowed the hacker to read all of the victim's files, to steal passwords as they were typed, and even to remotely activate any microphone or camera so as to spy on the user. Followed quickly by a spate of other, even more powerful Trojan programs, these became the most popular hacking tools of the early 21st century, targeting not simply large servers and company computers but also the home PCs of those who had been, up until this point, innocent and bemused bystanders. As with computer viruses, hacking has become something that every computer user now has to consider as a real and present threat.

As well as anti-virus software, modern computer users now have to consider using system software such as 'firewalls' and 'intrusion detection systems'. These protect computers either by blocking unwanted network traffic (firewall) or by generating a warning message so that the user can respond (intrusion detection system). Whereas such facilities were originally the domain of system managers responsible for large computers, they are now required by anyone who wants to take advantage of the internet without exposing themselves to the risk of abuse.

Websites are now hacked with alarming frequency, with crucial ecommerce information destroyed or collections of credit cards distributed and used fraudulently by the many hackers. Every new internet application seems to have some form of vulnerability associated with it; and PCs across the world are infected repeatedly with an epidemic of computer viruses exploiting vulnerabilities primarily in the various Microsoft applications or operating systems. Of all the potential targets accessible across the online world, Microsoft seems to be the most actively targeted.

In August 1999, the Microsoft Hotmail service was broken into by a group of hackers. In October 2000, the company admitted to having been hacked through a Trojan-infected workstation used to connect remotely into the company – and that source code for a new release of Windows had been copied. In November of the same year, a 19-year-old Dutch hacker demonstrated that Microsoft itself had not fixed well-known vulnerabilities in its own web servers. And in July and November 2001, two of the most damaging worm programs infected huge numbers of web servers, all of them running insecure versions of the Microsoft IIS application.

By the end of 2001, Microsoft was being roundly castigated for the appalling security vulnerabilities in its software and for the impact that those vulnerabilities were having on the predominantly Microsoft-dependent world of ecommerce. In the increased consciousness of security following the events of 11 September 2001, Microsoft took the decision to dedicate its huge programming resources to the creation of more secure software. The 'Trustworthy Computing' initiative was announced by Bill Gates in January 2002, with the aim of checking and correcting all information security failings in all Microsoft products.

It is an immense task and it continues to this day. Although Microsoft has suffered some setbacks in the exercise, particularly when its development servers were themselves hacked in October

2002, the online community remains hopeful that increased information security measures in the most popular software might serve to stem the tide.

Computer abuse

Quite apart from the risks associated with hostile programs or hostile programmers, computer users are also at risk from a variety of more abusive problems, most particularly when they are using the internet. There are a variety of fraudulent websites; a wide range of pornographic material; and a seemingly unstoppable flood of unsolicited email messages offering everything from sexual gratification through non-prescription medication to untold wealth. There are also some very particular dangers associated with the internet, especially for vulnerable children who might find themselves approached in the exploding number of real-time chat facilities available over the network.

⌐⊖

Unsolicited bulk commercial email messages are more familiarly referred to as 'spam' – after a December 1970 Monty Python sketch set in a café:

Man: Well, what've you got?
Waitress: Well, there's egg and bacon; egg sausage and bacon; egg and spam; egg bacon and spam; egg bacon sausage and spam; spam bacon sausage and spam; spam egg spam spam bacon and spam; spam sausage spam spam bacon spam tomato and spam;
Vikings (starting to chant): Spam spam spam spam...
Waitress: ...spam spam spam egg and spam; spam spam spam spam spam spam baked beans spam spam spam...
Vikings (singing): Spam! Lovely spam! Lovely spam!

Waitress: ...or Lobster Thermidor à Crevette with a mornay sauce served in a Provençale manner with shallots and aubergines garnished with truffle pâté, brandy and with a fried egg on top and spam.

Wife: Have you got anything without spam?

Waitress: Well, there's spam egg sausage and spam, that's not got much spam in it.

Wife: I don't want ANY spam!

Monty Python's 'Spam' sketch
15 December 1970

The name arose in the early days of online newsgroups, when some users would send identical messages to many newsgroups in the hope of a response. Initially at least, given the internet's non-commercial roots, these messages were not advertising or soliciting business. Nonetheless, the result was that valid messages were eventually drowned out by spam; by replies requesting that the spam be removed (spam, spam); by arguments concerning whether removing spam counted as censorship (spam, spam, spam and spam); and so on. The annoying messages were bad enough, but in April 1994 a small legal firm in Phoenix, Arizona, run by husband and wife Laurence Canter and Martha Siegel, sent the first unsolicited commercial communication to around 5000 internet newsgroups. The message offered their services to assist in completing immigration forms, and though it resulted in 30,000 complaints, it also yielded 20,000 expressions of interest – a significantly higher rate of return than could ever be achieved by direct postal mailings.

Unsolicited bulk email and newsgroup postings were considered to be a potentially profitable venture, and so, following Canter and Siegel's experience, the numbers of people beginning to use the internet for such messages began to rise. In

June 1999, the internet's Network Management Group issued a series of instructions for system managers on the handling of spam transmissions. Amongst the general instructions for removing and refusing such messages were some interesting statistics. The cost of unsolicited postal mailing (so-called 'direct mailing') was estimated at around one dollar per item; in the case of the internet, the estimate was less than a hundredth of a cent. Worse than this, though, in the postal case *all* of the cost is carried by the sender, not the recipient; in the case of unsolicited email, the recipient has to pay for the internet connection service, the telephone call to their internet service provider, provision of the email service and storage of the email message itself – not to mention the cost of their time in processing the message.

A study carried out in 2003 by a company offering an anti-spam service discovered that business computer users spent around a quarter of their day handling email; that spam cost US businesses around 9 billion dollars and European businesses 10 billion euros per annum; and that by the summer of 2003, more than half of all email transmitted over the internet was spam. Estimates suggest that, even if they work wholly legitimately, those sending spam need only spend £2.40 and take 4 hours to send messages to over one million users – and with a success rate that is believed to be around 1 per cent, this can be a very profitable activity. A recent report found that this can be astonishingly profitable for the person sending the spam – as much as 900 dollars for one million email addresses. With these levels of profit for a legitimate online business, there is no surprise that spam has exploded in popularity.

Worse than this, though, those sending spam are certainly not all acting legitimately. Almost all internet service providers outlaw the sending of unsolicited bulk email messages, whether commercial or not. Those found to be sending spam are quickly removed from the internet, so those who do this for a business hide their activities behind false names, use illegal accounts, and even make use of viruses and worms to infect systems to act on their behalf.[13]

The obvious question arises how exactly those sending spam email manage to find enough email addresses to make it worthwhile. For the most part, the email addresses come from a number of obvious places. First of all, there are lists of names, addresses and details that are shared between the companies that provide web services for which it is necessary to register. In the UK and the rest of Europe, there are data-protection laws which forbid the sharing of data of this kind, but such laws do not exist in the US and in many other countries, so information collected there can be freely shared. Of course, even in the US there are commercial restrictions and some pressure on companies not to misuse the data collected, but the trade in those lists is currently quite profitable. Internet users who provide their email address on a website for registration might therefore find their names on a spam list.

Second, any email addresses that are published anywhere on the web can be collected by special search programs in a procedure called 'harvesting'. These programs explore internet newsgroups, websites, discussion boards and the like, collecting any phrase which includes the @ symbol. This is usually only seen as a part of email addresses, which can therefore be collected and collated by the harvesting programs.

In a six-month experiment from 2002 to 2003, US researchers discovered that every single test email address that they established and which was made public on some website somewhere was targeted by spam. In one case, it took only 540 seconds from the establishment of an email address for it to receive its first piece of spam. Not only were the publicly visible addresses targeted, so too were some that were not publicized. This happens because spam senders not only harvest email addresses, they also *generate* them: they use software that produces millions of different letter combinations, usually targeting email services such as Hotmail.

There seems to be no escaping the spam flood, nor does there seem to be any way of tracking it down. The email headings on the spam messages are almost always completely fictitious, and often the message itself is sent through a tortuous maze of hacked or subverted email servers. Responding to a spam message, tempting though it might be, is simply an invitation to more spam, since the reply merely confirms that the email account is a valid one. Some spam messages include a 'Please remove me' button, which is equally tempting but is also simply a confirmation that the address is accurate. Boycotting the company advertised in the spam is another equally obvious ruse to hit back at the commercial aspect of the spam activity, but those companies need only a minute fraction of the spam transmissions to result in an order for it to be commercially worthwhile. And in any case, boycotting the pornography, illegal medical services or fraudulent get-rich-quick schemes is unlikely to harm them in any way.

Spam, it seems, like the hackers and the viruses, is here to stay. The only sensible course of action is to use the very many spam filter programs that seek to block messages which are self-evidently unwelcome. Though even the best of blocking software has its failings, this can be a much more appealing response than gradually drowning beneath the tide of rubbish every morning and evening.

Although most of the spam is easily ignored or discounted, it would seem that every day at least some people fall for the fraudulent schemes proposed in the messages. One of the longest-established frauds, which pre-dates the spam problem, is called the 'Nigerian 419' or 'advanced fee' fraud. This was originally started in the 1980s using postal or fax services, before moving almost entirely on to email, and is now estimated to be the fifth most profitable industry in Nigeria. It is named after clause 419 of the Nigerian criminal code and is usually associated with highly expert criminal gangs from that country. Individuals falling for the scheme have ended up being defrauded of amounts ranging from a few thousand pounds to several million, and some victims have even been murdered by the gangs when they have tried to recover their money.

The scheme has very many variations, but the essential heart of it is that someone, usually moderately senior, in the Nigerian government has to find a way of transferring several tens of millions of pounds out of the country to a bank account held by a trustworthy individual. The person receiving the email has been 'recommended as a person of integrity and honour', and in return for allowing their bank account to be used for the transfer, they will receive 10 per cent of the monies – usually several million pounds. Unfortunately, while the original approach is attractive and seemingly safe, once ensnared in the fraud the victim is expected to provide money to their correspondent – a small amount to bribe a low-ranking official, a slightly larger amount as payment of customs or taxation, and then a large amount, ostensibly so as to release the funds once held in the account.

All of this is a fraud, intended to milk ever increasing amounts of money from the greedy and gullible victim. Though it is astonishing to believe that there are people who would fall for such a transparently ridiculous scheme, nonetheless police experience is that several hundred do so routinely year in, year out. The guidance on the Metropolitan police website at New Scotland Yard is stark and simple: 'if it sounds too good to be true, then it is!' Unfortunately, there are still people who believe that simple money is there for the taking – and sadly they are right, but it is their money that is taken.

The advanced fee fraud is not the only email fraud popular on the internet. There are a thousand 'pyramid schemes' and many more opportunities to work from home and earn hundreds of thousands of pounds. All of them are lies, working on the time-honoured basis that, as the cartoon has it, 'on the internet, nobody knows you're a dog'. In most cases, it is the gullible and the greedy that fall victim, but sadly in some cases it is the innocent. This is particularly true in the case of the online chat facilities on the internet.

Since the very early days of computer networking and the internet, there has been support for instant online conversations – through the many dial-up bulletin-board services, through Internet Relay Chat (IRC), through web-based discussion groups, and through the Instant Messenger services provided by Microsoft, AOL, Yahoo and others. These have proved particularly popular with children as an inexpensive and immediate way of communicating with one another. Unfortunately, they have also proved valuable to paedophiles who stalk, groom and then abuse their victims.

Over recent years there have been many reports and several convictions of paedophiles who have gained access to child-oriented chat forums and presented themselves as trustworthy adults (teachers, counsellors, relatives) or as children. Lured into discussion by clever conversationalists, the child victims (many of them vulnerable and in need of emotional support) have found themselves sharing their feelings, their desires and their secrets with the paedophiles. These paedophiles have cleverly encouraged the children to be increasingly open – before luring them into a real-world meeting. There, the victims are at least abused and in some cases have been abducted. Most distressing of all, there have even been murders arising from these meetings. In response, in September 2003 Microsoft announced their plans to close their discussion groups. This move has had a mixed reception – condemned by researchers but applauded by charities.

More than anything else, though, the very nature of the debate shows clearly that the internet and the computer are now a firmly embedded element of our society – an environment which we expect to be readily accessible to our children and where we expect them to feel at home. We worry about the ease with which pornography can be encountered on the web – that 'whitehouse.org' reaches the President in Washington but that 'whitehouse.com' produces the web pages of a popular 'top-shelf' magazine.

Although the likelihood of abuse on the internet is very real, nonetheless it is seen as a valid environment within which the next generation of workers, researchers, homemakers and leaders will dwell. Our online world is here to stay and can only become more useful and more important in the future.

9

The future of computing

Computers and computing have come a long way from the earliest days of immense monolithic creations. Modern computers are small, fast, inexpensive and astonishingly reliable. Any predictions of how computers are likely to develop must conclude that they are likely to continue shrinking and becoming both faster and cheaper. Computers can now take on a thousand different roles in almost every household appliance and in every sophisticated device.

The most exciting prospect for the future is surely the growing intelligence of these machines and the promise of a truly 'artificially intelligent' device: a computer that can anticipate our needs, that can solve the most real of real-world problems, that can not only calculate but also *create* – in short, the computer of the science-fiction writer's imagination. If science fiction is any kind of barometer, however, then we are unfortunately a society that truly fears the prospect of this computer intelligence.

In *2001: A Space Odyssey*, HAL is depicted as a psychotic artificial intelligence that murders or tries to murder the humans it is supposed to look after. In *Demon Seed*, Julie Christie plays a woman trapped within a computer-controlled house, tormented by yet another psychotic computer. Most terrifying of all, in Harlan Ellison's short story 'I Have No Mouth, Yet I Must Scream' a psychotic artificial intelligence kills all but four humans – and those it torments, alters and refuses to allow to die: a truly hellish vision of what a hostile artificial intelligence could become.

Seemingly every computer encountered in classic science-fiction series like *Star Trek* is depicted as being malevolent or manipulative. From *Doctor Who*'s Cybermen to modern *Star Trek*'s Borg, cybernetic combinations of man and machine are seen as threatening. From *The Matrix* to *Terminator*'s Skynet, we see computer networks as equally threatening. For every Robbie, C3P0 or Data in popular culture, there are a dozen T-1000s, Android Avengers and Daleks. What is more, this technophobia is not restricted to science *fiction*. In his 1997 book, *March of the Machines*, roboticist Professor Kevin Warwick of Reading University paints the picture of a scary future in which robots and computers are more intelligent than humans, to our detriment. 'Maybe machines will be more intelligent than humans. Maybe machines will take over', he claims.

The main root of this fear seems to be the concept of machines having intelligence and of that intelligence being of a different order and of a different type to our own. We have given so much responsibility and control to our computers in so many areas of our lives and society that we fear we could be punished by that superior intelligence or damaged in the event that it goes wrong. Despite these broad concerns, since the dawn of computer science those building and experimenting with these devices have been drawn to experiment with programming human-like attributes into their creations.

Artificial intelligence

The concept of artificial intelligence has enticed computer scientists from the very earliest days. Indeed, the idea of artificial *life* has fascinated people since the production of the very first mechanical automata. The first 'android'[1] automata of human figures were made by Hans Bullman of Nuremberg as long ago as 1525, though fragmentary records from classical times suggest that early Greek mechanics was also advanced enough to create moving statues. Bullman's creations, which moved and played musical instruments, were designed with an intriguing complexity that inspired countless other creations in the centuries that followed.

Three inventions in particular allowed the development of powerful and uncannily realistic creations. The first was clockwork, which provided a compact but powerful means of driving mechanical devices and led to a growing expertise in producing finely engineered moving parts. The second was the cam, which allowed clockwork-powered rotation to be transformed into vertical movement. The third invention was a spinning drum of pins that could be used to lift or lower levers in a sequence 'programmed' in the arrangement of the pins.

With these simple technologies, 18th-century mechanical artists created some truly awe-inspiring automata. One name in particular is associated with these devices – Jacques de Vaucanson, a young French cleric from Grenoble, who dazzled Parisian society in 1737 with a life-sized flautist and in 1738 with a mechanical duck. The duck in particular was so impressive that no one who saw it believed that it was anything other than real. The duck walked, quacked, shook its feathers, swam, ate and apparently digested its food. It even excreted the digested food. To convince his audience that the duck really *was* a mechanical one, de Vaucanson had to introduce removable panels in the side of the creature through which the mechanics of its operation could be seen.[2]

As well as creating lifelike mechanical automata, de Vaucanson had a lasting impact in one other important field. In 1741, he was appointed inspector of the French silk industry, with the specific task of introducing and perfecting machinery to allow it to compete more effectively with the booming British weaving industry. One invention in particular that revolutionized the industry was the creation and introduction of card-programmed weaving machines, perfected by Joseph Jacquard of Lyon and then used by Charles Babbage.

The mechanical automata of the 18th and 19th centuries that followed de Vaucanson's work were strikingly realistic. Viewed now under the bright lights of a museum, it is hard to appreciate the impact that they must have had on those encountering them for the first time, in the dimly lit salons of London or Paris. They were scarily convincing by all accounts. Whole orchestras were produced and would play for dancers who would only be told at the end of the evening that their entertainment had been produced by clockwork.

Gradually, though, the novelty of lifelike automata began to wear off as audiences became increasingly used to the spectacle. It is probably only in more modern times, with the production of ultra-sophisticated 'animatronics' for museums and the film industry, that some of that magic has been recaptured. The prospect of artificially produced *thinking* rather than simple movement, however, has never failed to impress. The first such machine was supposed to have been produced in 1770 by Wolfgang von Kempelen in Vienna at the court of the Empress Maria Theresa. This was an automaton of a Turkish figure sitting at a large table on which a game of chess was set up, at which 'he' offered to play all-comers.

The automaton was wonderfully impressive, beating almost all those it encountered. In 1809, it was demonstrated to Napoleon Bonaparte, himself a good player, who lost the challenge in only

24 moves. During his stint as ambassador in Paris, inventor Benjamin Franklin encountered the automaton, and it was even studied by a young Charles Babbage. The mystery of the wonderful machine was finally solved by Edgar Allan Poe in 1836, when the device toured the USA. The cabinet hid a small player who directed the automaton's moves. When it was first created, the device had been controlled by a handicapped Polish chess master called Worowski. Over the years, other diminutive players had squeezed into the tiny cupboard.

Unfortunately the automaton itself was destroyed in 1856 in a fire at the museum in Philadelphia where it had finally come to rest. However, the seed of artificial intelligence (and specifically, of an automatic chess player) had been sown. In the years that followed, the concept of an artificial intelligence best being demonstrated in a machine capable of playing chess would become a recurring theme.

Working on mathematical programs for Babbage's Difference Engine, Ada, Countess Lovelace allowed herself to be distracted by the question of whether the device could be considered to be 'intelligent'. Her opinion was that it could not, because it was a simple machine and 'machines only do what they have been designed and programmed to do'; it could never do anything original. Ada believed that intelligence, creativity and free will were somehow related and uniquely associated with mankind.

A hundred years later, in 1950, Alan Turing revisited the question in his consideration of whether the machines that he had devised and constructed could ever be thought of as intelligent. He did this by specifying the famous 'Turing test', which was a variant of a parlour game in which a man and a woman communicate with a third player, the judge, only through typewritten messages. The judge must ask questions and then try to guess which is the man and which the woman. In Turing's version, the man and the woman are replaced by a human and a computer, and the judge must guess which is which. A program that can successfully fool the judge is said to have passed the Turing test and should, according to Turing, be considered as intelligent as a human.

Whereas Ada believed that intelligence was a feature that could not be associated with a mechanical contrivance, Turing was prepared to consider it from an 'operational' perspective. If the device or program acted in all situations in a way that could be considered equivalent to how an intelligent human would act, then Turing believed that it should be considered equally intelligent. So, even before the number of those first computers had reached double figures, the battle lines for the fierce artificial-intelligence debate were drawn. Throughout the years that followed, the production of increasingly 'intelligent' programs has marched on. The most obvious hurdle that has been overcome is that of the vexed question of playing chess, for so long seen as effectively the pinnacle of intelligent behaviour.

The principle of playing chess was actually found to be reasonably straightforward for a computer. At any stage of the game, each player has only a limited set of available moves, creating a small set of alternative board positions. From each one of these, a further set of moves can be made and board positions created; and from *those* again, a small set of yet further moves is possible. At each stage, a 'tree' of possible board positions is produced. Chess programs work by producing a complete set of 'If I do this, then you can do this, and then I can do this' sequences of anticipated moves; the number of future moves calculated is called the 'depth'. For each of the board positions then produced, the program calculates a score for itself and for its opponent; it chooses the move which minimizes the opponent's advantage whilst maximizing its own. This is a strategy called 'minimax', created by Claude Shannon in 1949 and perfected by Alan Turing the following year. The first computer program written to execute minimax for chess was produced in 1956 at Los Alamos, followed two years later by a more powerful system at IBM.

Using minimax and a depth of only five moves, chess programs can trounce all but the most experienced of club players; given a slightly greater depth, the programs can beat all but the most experienced chess grandmasters. In 1997, when a dedicated computer system developed by IBM (called 'Deep Blue' and capable of examining 200 million chess positions per second) was allowed a depth of 14 moves, it beat the then world champion, Gary Kasparov. Although chess is indeed a striking example of human intelligence, and although computers are not programmed to play in anything like the same way as humans apparently do, it seems to be at least one human-like thing that can be better performed by computer.

Passing the Turing test

The original definition of artificial intelligence was 'anything done by a computer which, if it were to have been done by a human, would have required intelligence'. On that basis, artificial intelligence has already been demonstrated more broadly than in the simple task of playing chess. The PARRY program, developed to simulate a paranoid schizophrenic, successfully convinced a panel of psychiatrists that it was indeed genuine, so passing the Turing test according to its creator.

PARRY and the programs that followed were developed by the early AI researchers using a decidedly non-linear programming style which allowed them to introduce a lot of flexibility and 'human-like' attributes into the processing carried out. At the same time that Alan Turing was devising the automaton Turing machine and John von Neumann was considering how to build one, logician Alonzo Church was developing a decidedly non-automaton-based concept of 'function of functions'. His 'lambda calculus' model presented a way of manipulating mathematical functions which had no basis in 'machinery' and which was intuitively similar to the way in which real intelligences operate in practice.

Lambda calculus was the basis of a non-von Neumann approach to programming. Called 'functional' programming, this relies on the ability of a procedure to be called with an argument and to return a result. As an example of how this works, consider the 'factorial function'. In mathematics, the factorial of 5 is 5 times 4 times 3 times 2 times 1; the factorial of 0 is defined to be 1. In a traditional-style computer program, a routine to find the factorial of N would be achieved with a simple loop, using N as a variable that can altered as the routine proceeds:

```
result = 1;
while ( N does not equal 1 )
        result = result * N;
        N = N - 1;
```

In functional programming, however, the program interprets the factorial slightly different, noticing that 'Factorial N' is 1 if N is 1 or 0, or it is 'N * Factorial (N − 1)' for any other values. A function to calculate the factorial would then be specified as:

```
Factorial ( N )
begin
        if ( N is 1 or N is 0 )
                return 1;
        else    return N * Factorial ( N − 1)
end
```

Notice that the function 'Factorial' calls itself, a facility that programmers call 'recursion'. Recursion is a central feature of functional programming, allowing the expression of operations in a way that is more obviously 'mathematical' so that the programs can be analysed and proved correct. It is also more in keeping with the way that humans 'think about thinking about thinking', so allowing a more realistic model of artificial thought to be created.

The original functional programming language was LISP, developed by John McCarthy at MIT's Artificial Intelligence Laboratory between 1958 and 1960. He created it specifically to implement his thesis that human intelligence is about the development and processing of lists of optional actions, responses and recursive decisions. The development of LISP in turn led to the creation of other, even more powerful functional languages: LOGO, developed by BBN and MIT in 1968; and the PROLOG language, developed in 1973. These languages feature functions acting on the single allowable data structure – lists of data elements (hence the derivation of the name LISP, 'List Processor'). Some complex programs have been created using this style of programming. PROLOG, for example, was developed initially to allow the expression of logical structures and was then used to develop complex systems for the military, which had to be proved correct before they could be used.

Perhaps the most interesting programs developed in this style, however, are also the oldest – ELIZA, a simulation of a psychiatrist, and PARRY, a simulation of a paranoid schizophrenic. Both were developed originally in LISP: ELIZA at MIT by Joe Weizenbaum in 1966; PARRY at Stanford by Ken Colby in 1971.

ELIZA was based on the observation that clinical psychiatrists interviewing patients at the early stages of their treatment practise a discipline called 'reflective listening'. In this, the patient's own statements are modified slightly and turned into gentle questions, inviting them to expand on their statements and to offer further explanations of their motives, beliefs and behaviour; occasionally the psychiatrist has to make his or her own statements, to elicit further details from the patient. Weizenbaum was able to create a LISP program to simulate this exchange, using lists of stock phrases and a collection of simple modifications to the patient's statements, entered in the form of a typed dialogue rather like an online 'chat' session. The result was astonishingly realistic. For example, a young woman holding the following discussion with what she believed to be a psychiatrist was wholly convinced:

young woman: Men are all alike.

eliza: In what way?

young woman: They're always bugging us about something specific or other.

eliza: Can you think of a specific example?

young woman: Well, my boyfriend made me come here.

eliza: Your boyfriend made you come here?

young woman: He says I'm depressed much of the time.

eliza: I am sorry to hear you are depressed.

young woman: It's true. I'm unhappy.

eliza: Do you think coming here will help you not to be unhappy?

young woman: I need some help, that much seems certain.

eliza: What would it mean to you if you got some help?

young woman: Perhaps I could learn to get along with my mother.

eliza: Tell me more about your family.

young woman: My mother takes care of me.

eliza: Who else in your family takes care of you?

young woman: My father.

eliza: Your father.

young woman: You are like my father in some ways.

eliza: What resemblance do you see?

young woman: You are not very aggressive but I think you don't want me to notice that.

eliza: What makes you think I am not very aggressive?

young woman: You don't argue with me.

eliza: Why do you think I don't argue with you?

young woman: You are afraid of me.

eliza: Does it please you to believe I am afraid of you?

young woman: My father is afraid of everybody.

eliza: What else comes to mind when you think of your father?

young woman: Bullies.

eliza: Does that have anything to do with the fact that your boyfriend made you come here?

One side of this exchange was created by a non–von Neumann, functional program manipulating the input text as a series of lists, applying some simple modifications and directed by a small set of stock questions and responses. There are many stories told of the way in which ELIZA was able to fool casual conversationalists, much to the annoyance of those who then discovered that they had poured out their hearts to a program.

While ELIZA was at least superficially persuasive, PARRY – created by a psychiatrist who wanted to simulate the sorts of conversations he would regularly have with his more paranoid patients – was positively uncanny:

interviewer: How are you today?

parry: OK.

interviewer: What is your name?

parry: My name is Frank Smith.

interviewer: How old are you?

parry: Twenty-eight.

interviewer: Are you married?

parry: No.

interviewer: What sort of work do you do?

parry: I work in the Post Office.

interviewer: Why are you in the hospital?

parry: I shouldn't be here.

interviewer: Who brought you here?

parry: The police.

interviewer: What trouble did you have with the police?

parry: Cops don't do their jobs.

interviewer: What do they do instead?

parry: Cops arrest the wrong people.

interviewer: They arrest the right ones sometimes.

parry: The law should get those Italian crooks.

interviewer: Are you Italian?

parry: My background is British, but I was born in this country.

interviewer: Do you know any Italian crooks?

parry: I try to avoid the underworld.

interviewer: Are you afraid of the underworld?

parry: The Mafia are the worst gangsters.

interviewer: Are you connected with the Mafia?

parry: You know, they know me.

interviewer: How do they know you?

parry: They spy on me.

interviewer: Why do they?

parry: They want to get false evidence to frame me.

interviewer: What do they have against you?

parry: They are out to get me.

interviewer: What for?

parry: I have incriminating evidence against the Mafia.

interviewer: Are you sure of all this?

parry: You don't believe me?

PARRY was armed with a set of 'personal details' and a paranoid fixation that the Mafia were out to get 'him'. The conversations on record appear staggeringly real, if slightly twisted. When Turing conceived of his famous test, he imagined that the program would need to be capable of holding a realistic and intelligent conversation about a wide variety of subjects. PARRY, on the other hand, twists all conversations around to its own 'field of interest', just as many paranoids do. Because of this, Colby was convinced that the program could fool a panel of experts, so he established an experiment to see how successful the program might be.

Alongside the PARRY program, Colby had several true paranoid patients, all interviewed via teletype by a trained psychiatrist. He then asked a further panel of psychiatrists to evaluate the findings. Not one of the panel deduced that PARRY was not genuine, so Colby claimed to have created the first program to pass the Turing test. There is perhaps a poetic irony in the observation that computers can best simulate humans who are mentally disturbed.

Intelligent algorithms

There seem to be few restrictions on how convincing a well-programmed AI system can be. A further development of the ELIZA/PARRY style of conversationalist programs – a system called RACTER – has even written a book of poetry called *The Policeman's Beard is Half Constructed*. Other AI programs have been developed to locate geological deposits of precious resources, to calculate optimum shipping routes, and to fly and even land aircraft. One car manufacturer has developed an AI system built into a car which parks it parallel to the kerb; another has developed an emergency braking system which successfully prevents the car from crashing into stationary traffic. There are AI solutions that diagnose diseases at least as successfully as specialist doctors. There are programs which detect fraudulent tax returns, recognize faces and even (in combat-based computer games for the entertainment market or for training real troops) provide realistic and devious soldiers.

There is little in the field of human intellectual achievement that has not been modelled and duplicated in software, whether as simple computer games to mimic the growing language abilities of babies, or as huge and sophisticated programs to analyse complex systems. The software strategies that have been developed to create these solutions are many and varied. The oldest of the AI solutions were based on processing and selecting between lists of alternative actions and decisions, expressed usually in the LISP programming language created for the purpose. 'Expert systems' work on the basis of a decision tree – a series of decisions based on material presented that would allow the system to form a conclusion. The program developed for the UK Inland Revenue in order to determine whether a tax return form was worthy of further investigation was based on exactly this type of decision-tree structure. Other AI systems have been developed on even more imaginative bases – 'neural nets' and 'genetic algorithms'.

In a neural net, instead of simulating the 'high-level' functions of intelligence as a selection of appropriate decisions based on expertise and experience, the system simulates the low-level activity of the neurons. A human brain is composed of billions upon billions of interconnected neurons which act as single-bit parallel-processing units. Each neuron receives a small set of input, 'exciting' signals and, if the signals exceed some specific threshold value, transmits its own signal to one or more further neurons to which it is connected. The decision on which further neurons to 'excite' is based on 'weighting' criteria, with some neurons more likely to be signalled than others.

The original work on developing artificial neural networks was carried out at MIT by Warren McCulloch and Walter Pitts in

1943. They created systems in which small groups of neurons were interconnected and fed an input stimulus. The 'weighting' on the connections between the various neurons was then altered at random, until the output signal was the one required. This was thought of as 'training by reward': when the small mass of neurons gets the right answer, it is rewarded. Those rewards serve to reinforce the 'weighting' values for the connections, and the neural net gradually gets better at the task in hand.

Modern neural nets, for example, use exactly this principle for facial recognition. Humans trivially recognize whole or partial faces, in a variety of lighting conditions, in a variety of poses, with a range of expressions, and even with or without facial hair. Creating an algorithm to allow a computer to do this, though, is very difficult. By contrast, neural network systems do this easily. The system is provided with a collection of faces (say, like a police photograph file, with front and side view) and a 'suspect' face. Where the system makes a correct identification, it is rewarded; where it does not, it is 'punished'. Over a short period of training, the neural-net algorithm becomes increasingly accurate until, in time, it can be used 'for real'.

Such neural-net programs have been developed not only to recognize faces but also to check fingerprints; to analyse the distinctive way in which people walk, so as to identify suspects in disguise; and even successfully to locate known troublemakers in a football crowd when they have all had their faces painted. Neural-network algorithms are one of the most impressive products of the AI development programmes and come uncomfortably close to native human capabilities for many purposes.

The second great success of AI is the 'genetic algorithm', originally proposed by John Holland, the first beneficiary of the ARPA Information Processing Techniques Office funding for computer-science PhDs under Joseph Licklider's directorship. Holland had been a scholarship student at MIT in 1946, working part-time on the Project Whirlwind exercise, and had then joined the University of Michigan to do his doctoral research on parallel processing. He had been enticed there by the opportunity to work with Arthur Burkes, a collaborator with John von Neumann on a wholly non-linear approach to computation. The traditional Turing model of computation is formally recognized as a form of 'sequential automaton' – an abstract machine having one of several discrete internal states and a simple process for moving from state to state. After World War II, however, von Neumann and Burkes became interested in more biological-based automata, acting not as single cells but rather as complex societies of very many such cells – less like a single amoeba and more like a yeast culture. These 'cellular automata' perform complex computations by developing connections between themselves, swapping information and carrying out specific, small computing tasks. They are ideal for an environment of very many, very simple processing units and were of great interest as neural-net structures were being considered.

Holland had already been attracted to the issues of computation, and after reading a series of then-current books on biological evolution and on cellular automata, he began to formulate a series of groundbreaking ideas for 'adaptive' algorithms. These are computer programs that change themselves as the problems that they are addressing change. The best examples of this behaviour that Holland came across were in the field of evolution, where creatures adapt to different environments in different ways. His ideas for adaptive algorithms were honed through the 1960s when he taught courses on cellular automata, and the genetic algorithm itself was first produced in 1975. The algorithm assumes that a rough method for solving a particular problem is already known but that the actual values for the controlling variables within the algorithm are not. What Holland did was to produce the algorithm and to separate out the several controlling values into a single data structure which could act as a string of 'genetic code'. His model produced several thousand such strings, each at random. The algorithm was run for each string, the success of the string was measured, and those strings that were successful were retained, combined and mutated. Over a series of these trials, eventually a completely successful string would be produced through the effects of evolutionary competition.

An example from the mid-1980s shows this approach well. *Robot* was a popular computer game in 1983 and featured a series of mazes that could be explored and displayed on the screen. Initially, the maze is unknown, but as the robot explores, more and more of the maze is revealed. In some parts of the maze the robot finds food, weapons, treasure or, if unfortunate, a monster to fight – though if the robot wins the fight, it will gain further treasure. At various places through the maze there are one-way trapdoors that allow the robot to descend to the next level, and the winner is the robot who makes it all the way through the maze to the ultimate treasure in the lowest of the levels.

To play successfully it is necessary to make a series of decisions. Once a trapdoor is discovered, should the robot descend immediately or continue exploring? If it continues exploring, it might meet a monster and be killed; if it descends immediately, the robot might miss the opportunity of discovering more treasure or supplies. If a monster is encountered, should the robot fight it (and perhaps be killed, or perhaps win and take its treasure) or should it run?

In late 1983 a genetic algorithm was produced to resolve these questions. Each characteristic of a robot player was encoded in a genetic string: its inclination to explore, its willingness to fight, its determination to descend the maze trapdoors, and so on. These characteristic strings were produced by the thousand and were mated and mutated as each scored greater or lesser successes in the game. Some strings failed immediately; some went further than others. Players around the world exchanged the 'families' of these robot genes, with the global gene pool getting better and better over the weeks until, finally in 1984, one of the strings was produced that represented the perfect maze robot and the genetic algorithm won the game.

The Chinese Room

Genetic algorithms and neural nets provide good ways of solving AI problems when part of the strategy for solving an intelligence problem is known. And expert systems are ideal when the strategy is completely known and when the decisions taken by field experts can be studied and duplicated. In combination, which is probably close to the way that human intelligence works in practice, these algorithms produce impressive results.

Despite (or perhaps because of) the undoubted success of AI in the years since it was invented by John McCarthy and his colleagues at MIT in the 1950s, it is still subject to fear and concern on the part not only of science-fiction writers and film producers, but also of professional philosophers and theologians. In computer science, the basic stance of AI is that those things done by human intelligence which we believe make us unique and special, such as the ability to reason, to argue and to solve complex problems, are not in fact special and can be performed by suitably programmed computers.

The response is to see this as a threat to our unique position, to our future existence, to our sense of self-esteem, and so on. In turn, this leads to a number of attacks in which it is argued that machines cannot be intelligent for a variety of reasons: they are not alive; they do not have free-will; they are not creative; they do not have a soul. Perhaps the most famous and certainly the most controversial of these responses to the AI discipline came from one man in particular, the philosopher John Searle.

In 1980, Searle published an article called 'Minds, Brains and Programs' in volume 3 of the journal *Behavioral and Brain Sciences*. In this, he described what he believed to be the killer blow for the upstart AI discipline seeking (as he saw it) to prove that computers could be intelligent in the same way that humans are. The paper described a thought experiment created by Searle called the 'Chinese Room'.

Searle imagines himself sealed in a room where he is passed a series of Chinese symbols that he does not understand. However, also in the room with him is a collection of instructions in English which tell him how to manipulate the symbols so as to produce a second series of Chinese symbols that can be passed back out of the room. The first set of symbols are, Searle imagines, a set of questions posed in Chinese; the second set of symbols are the correct answers, also in Chinese. Searle's argument is that, although to an outsider it might appear as though, in the room, he has understood the Chinese questions and has provided appropriate responses, he, Searle, does not in fact understand Chinese at all. By analogy, any computer that is programmed in binary machine code (the equivalent of Searle's English instructions) and is asked questions and responds in English (the equivalent of Searle's Chinese symbols) cannot possibly be considered to have 'understood' the questions and therefore to be intelligent.

The original publication of the Chinese Room experiment prompted a storm of debate amongst philosophers, in sixth-form common rooms and wherever undergraduate students gathered. Searle and his supporters argued that a simulation of intelligence could not be considered intelligent any more than a computer simulation of rain could be said to make the computer user wet. The debate itself (the basis of the argument and the motivation for the disagreement) was the clearest evidence of how much fear of computer intelligence and artificial life there was.

When a robot is devised that can move around on two legs, there is no argument whether that is, in fact, definable as 'walking'; but where the activity is of an 'intellectual' form, then it is subject to this argument and fear.

The future

Even as the philosophical debate about real versus artificial intelligence rumbles on, those working in the field of AI have happily listened to the common-room discussions, politely fended off the theological objections, and got on with developing their programs. Modern AI systems are now staggeringly effective and the related disciplines of artificial life produce astonishingly realistic systems that truly aid understanding. For example, simple rules have been used to simulate flocking and shoaling behaviour, with artificial birds (dubbed 'boids') and fish behaving in a strikingly true-to-life fashion when faced with obstacles or threats. Artificial creatures have been created and supplied with appetites, desires, competition and a computer environment in which to exist. Within the context of their limited world,[3] these creatures grow, interact, learn and adapt in a way that is uncannily close to real-world biology.

Computer scientists have built humanoid robots that can walk up stairs, carry boxes and negotiate changing obstacles. Artificial faces, with entirely realistic facial expressions and responses, have been developed. There is even an apparently intelligent animatronics music critic established at London's Madame Tussaud's. The android Simon Cowell (one of the judges on the TV talent show *Pop Idol*) listens to the singers, calculates a response based on their performance, and provides feedback. If the singer is in tune, the android gives an appropriate response; if not, then it gives one of the several distinctive critiques for which the real *Pop Idol* judge is famous.

This simple decision criterion might sound restrictive, but those researching AI have found that such simple decisions, when combined with many other similarly simple decisions and processing loops, can produce very lifelike behaviour. Simulating a simple animal, for example, is straightforward because the creature has a small, interlocked series of 'urges'. It has an appetite for food that must be satisfied, but it also has an appreciation of danger that must be heeded; it therefore searches for food but not beyond a certain range – unless the appetite for food is so great that it outweighs the risk of encountering predators. The animal has an urge to find a mate and to reproduce, but not at the expense of diluting its genes with an inferior mate. It has an urge to rest and sleep when tired, but that is balanced by its hunger, for example.

These simple loops are each very straightforward and the simulated animal will move around them throughout the day – sleeping, waking, eating, sleeping. In combination, they produce *very* sophisticated behaviour, even in a simulation of something like an insect. A small set of these loops can produce, in fact, a truly chaotic system, in which the values of the system from moment to moment can be wholly unpredictable.

In physical terms, a simple desktop toy serves as a good example of this. The toy is a metal ball suspended on a length of string over a plate. Pulled back and released, under the simple force of gravity (and of tension in the string) the ball oscillates in an easily described and mathematically predictable manner until friction brings it to rest. The trajectory of the ball is a simple, closed loop through the positions possible at the end of the length of string. That simple loop can be considered like an animal's basic program loop: if tired, sleep; once no longer tired, wake up. From moment to moment the precise state of the simple animal can be predicted.

The desk toy, though, can be made slightly more complex simply by adding a magnet to the base plate so that it repels the (also magnetized) metal ball. Now, as the ball is released, it is acted upon not only by gravity, which attempts to bring the oscillations to a stop, but also by the repelling force of the magnet. The ball now swings wildly in a complex series of patterns which is already almost completely unpredictable. Add another magnet (to create a system which is still very simple to conceive) and the result is a wholly unpredictable sequence of patterns as the swinging ball circles and loops in a complex dance between the various forces acting upon it.

By analogy, the two magnets in this more complex system are the twin urges of hunger and of fear, acting on the behaviour of the animal as it swings from sleeping to waking. Add more and more magnets (or by analogy, more and more drives or urges) and the range of behaviour of the pendulum (and by analogy of the animal) becomes ever more varied and ever more impossible to anticipate or to understand. Simple programs and simple loops can create complex and completely realistic behaviour.

In modern AI research, computer scientists are finding ways to simulate these realistic drives and behavioural strategies in their programs, so that systems *want* to find solutions. Systems for locating errors in the inhumanly complicated telephone switching network are now artificially intelligent, network-mobile agents that 'want' to locate and solve the problems. In a recent series of experiments, network-mobile, intelligent agents intended to locate and counter computer viruses have been devised and launched. Since the agents *and* the viruses can now dynamically adapt, this raises the startling spectre of rapid, artificial evolution of software within the network.

Computer networks will continue to grow more complicated; computers themselves will continue to get smaller and more powerful; and the programs that they run will become increasingly intelligent, sophisticated and ubiquitous. Perhaps the writers of science fiction were right to be worried – or perhaps right to be enthusiastic about what the future will hold.

Notes

Preface

1 The name 'HAL', the computer in *2001: A Space Odyssey*, was coined in 1968 and is said to have been derived from 'IBM', with each character moved along by one. 'MULTIVAC', which appeared first in a short story from March 1959, is a pun on the name 'UNIVAC', one of the earliest computers, developed shortly after World War II.

Chapter 1

1 Though the principle of the card-controlled loom is usually credited to Jacquard, it was in fact a young creator of mechanical automata, Jacques de Vaucanson, who invented the machine.

Chapter 2

1 Originally, Zuse had no name for the machine. When he built a second, he called it the 'V2' and the first became the 'V1'. After the war, when Zuse began building and selling computers commercially, the machines were given names such as the 'Z6', etc. The early V machines were then renamed the Z1, Z2 and so forth.

2 Floating-point numbers – in particular, the meaning of 'mantissa' and 'exponent' – are explained in the next chapter.

3 That is, the people who were feeding data to and processing results from the analyser – the original meaning of the word 'computer'.

4 Named because Steve Jobs had last worked in an orchard.

Chapter 3

1 See his book *Godel, Escher, Bach: An Eternal Golden Braid* (Penguin 1979) for a fuller description of the 'stupid-smart' concept.

2 Hence a 4-bit word is dubbed a 'nibble' since it is just half a byte.

3 In her work at Harvard in 1947, Grace Hopper (later the creator of the world's first computer program language compiler) discovered a new and entirely unexpected source of error: a moth that got caught in one of the switch relays, immortalized now as the world's first 'computer bug'.

4 The ESCAPE key and concept were originally invented by Bemer himself.

5 Exactly like audio tapes, but holding binary data instead of music.

Chapter 4

1 That is, the first stored-program computers influenced by the 1945 paper published by John von Neumann.

2 Languages developed in the tradition of ALGOL are often called 'block-structured' or 'procedural' languages.

3 It had the wonderful name of YACC: 'Yet Another Compiler Compiler'.

4 It was called 'Oak' for no better reason than that was the type of tree which Gosling could see out of his office window.

5 The game is actually slightly more complicated than this, with flags that can be planted to mark possible mine locations, etc. This simplified version of the game, however, is sufficient for an explanation of program design.

Chapter 5

1 UNIX-derived operating systems call them 'directories'; Microsoft-derived systems, 'folders'. The principle in each case is the same: structured collections of named data files in a hierarchical organization.

2 The activity of computer hackers and viruses is covered in chapter 8.

3 It was the mirror image of Asimov's earlier joke: he turned UNIVAC into MULTIVAC; Thompson and Ritchie turned MULTICS into UNIX.

4 Gates and Allen had an even earlier company together called Traff-o-Data, which sold technology for recording traffic volumes on the highways.

Chapter 6

1 SDC was a division of the RAND Corporation which had been spun off as a separate company to work on research-and-development projects specifically for SAGE.

2 'On-line Man Computer Communication', written in collaboration with MIT researcher Wesley Clark in August 1962.

3 Bizarrely, BBN received a letter of congratulation from their local senator, Ted Kennedy, thanking them for their 'ecumenical efforts in building an inter-faith message processor'.

4 Making it, incidentally, the fifth node and the first East Coast connection.

Chapter 7

1 Unfortunately, the company no longer exists and the domain itself has fallen into disrepair with no associated website, though the historic registration details can still be seen at internic.net.

2 This has since been extended to form XML (Extended Markup Language).

3 The terms URI and URL are effectively interchangeable.

4 'nxoc01.cern.ch' was later renamed 'info.cern.ch', so becoming the world's first web server. Sadly, the original first web page no longer exists, though Berners-Lee retains the oldest unmodified page: a two-line description of what a web page link is, last changed on 13 November 1990.

5 There are two explanations for the name Yahoo. One is that it stands for 'Yet Another Hierarchical and Officious Oracle'; the other is that Filo and Yang liked the dictionary definition of a Yahoo as a 'rude, unsophisticated, uncouth' individual. Whatever the reason, it has made both of them very rich.

6 A prime number is one that can be divided only by itself and by 1, such as 3, 7 or 13, for example.

7 Bezos originally planned to call the company Cadabra – because it was magic – but renamed it Amazon when his lawyer mistook the proposed name for 'Cadaver'.

8 Incidentally, Netscape Communications Corporation was bought by AOL Time Warner in November 1998 for 4.8 billion dollars as a part of its attempt to dominate the internet at the height of its expansion.

Chapter 8

1 Since it was first isolated and identified at Ohio State University.

2 Although it is now known that Brain was not the original, it is still the family name for this small group of viruses, since it was the first to be identified and the easiest to trace.

3 The first was Symantec.

4 The load average is a measure of the number of processes and the amount of idle time enjoyed by a given computer. A load of 1 is normal for a lightly loaded and responsive system. Most systems become unusable once the load average passes 5.

5 Although they *did* build and play with model railways, the main reason for the existence of the club was as a social forum for a group of young pranksters at the university.

6 Dubbed the 'Victorian Internet' by author Tom Standage in his 1998 book of that name.

7 The blue box was so called for no better reason than that the first one seized by AT&T engineers happened to be coloured blue.

8 Shimomura wrote a bestselling account of the manhunt following the hacking of his computer, called *Takedown*.

9 The US Computer Fraud and Abuse statute makes hacking an offence of fraud, which means that it comes under the US Treasury. The Treasury 'police' are the Secret Service, more usually associated with the task of guarding the President.

10 Gold and Shiffreen, for example, accessed the Prestel system by discovering the system manager's password; Bevan and Pryce accessed the US military system in the same way.

11 Crashing a program or a computer deliberately so as to cause problems is referred to as a 'Denial of Service' (or DoS) attack.

12 Pronounced 'finger-dee' rather than 'fingered'. It is short for 'finger daemon', a daemon being a small service program usually connected to the internet to handle network requests.

13 The 2003 study showed that over 90 per cent of all spam email is sent by just 150 people, many of them based along the beachfront north of Miami or in Las Vegas.

Chapter 9

1 'Android' does not necessarily refer to a robotic intelligence. The word is derived from the Greek *andro-* meaning 'human' and *eides* meaning 'form or shape' – hence 'android' simply means 'in human shape'. It can be contrasted with the word 'robot' derived from the Czech *robota* for 'forced labour or drudgery' and first used in the play *R.U.R* by Karel Capek in 1920 for an artificial worker.

2 Also interestingly, to create the effect of the bird's gut, de Vaucanson created a tube of rubber surrounding a device to simulate the appearance of peristalsis: not only did he create an impressive automaton, de Vaucanson also invented the rubber hose.

3 Called 'PolyWorld' by its creators in Los Alamos.

Further Reading

For many of the topics covered in this book, the reference material was the excellent web site www.wikipedia.org in which there are several essays covering the history and development of different aspects of computer technology.

In addition, the *Victorian Internet* by Tom Standage (Phoenix, 1999) provides a wonderful summary of the development of international networks – but by far the best of the background reading comes from *The Dream Machine: J.C.R. Licklider and the Revolution That Made Computing Personal* by Mitchell Waldrop (Penguin, 2002), in which the story of JCR Licklider's life and achievement is presented.

Index